Quality Improvement Tools & Techniques

Quality Improvement Tools & Techniques

Peter Mears

McGraw-Hill, Inc.

New York   San Francisco   Washington, D.C.   Auckland   Bogotá
Caracas   Lisbon   London   Madrid   Mexico City   Milan
Montreal   New Delhi   San Juan   Singapore
Sydney   Tokyo   Toronto

Library of Congress Cataloging-in-Publication Data

Mears, Peter.
    Quality improvement tools & techniques   /   Peter Mears.
       p.   cm.
    Includes index.
    ISBN 0-07-041229-4 (book with disk : alk. paper)—ISBN
0-07-852726-0 (disk).—ISBN 0-07-041219-7 (book : alk. paper)
    1. Quality control.   I. Title.   II. Title: Quality improvement
tools and techniques.
TS156.M4   1995
658.5'62—dc20   94-34752
                                          CIP

2 3 4 5 6 7 8 9 0   DOC/DOC 9 0 9 8 7 6

ISBN 0-07-041219-7

The sponsoring editor for this book was James H. Bessent, the editing supervisor was Fred Dahl, the designer was Inkwell Publishing Services, and the production supervisor was Donald Schmidt. It was set in Palatino by Inkwell Publishing Services.

Printed and bound by R. R. Donnelley & Sons Company.

Familiar-sounding names of individuals, products, and companies are used in this book so that the examples will be easy to understand. All names are fictitious. No reference is made or implied to any actual person, firm, place, or product.

Contents

Contents

Preface

This book will teach you how to use Quality Improvement (QI) tools and techniques to identify and solve quality problems found in all organizations. These tools provide objectivity and clarity in our work by separating opinions from fact.

This book will remove the "mystique" associated with Quality Improvement tools by using the tools in a graphical, problem-solving approach. This is *not* a high-powered math book: A commonsense approach is taken so that we can use the same quality tools and techniques used by the quality "masters." Each QI tool has a specific application that will guide us in analyzing quality and in explaining our quality analysis to others.

A simple, yet powerful Continuous Quality Improvement (CQI) story approach is explained so that others will understand why the improvements are necessary. By following this fact-based format, personalities are minimized and you will be able to obtain support for your ideas.

Peter Mears

Quality Improvement Tools & Techniques

The Continuous Quality Improvement Story

Have you heard the following sayings?

"I know quality when I see it."

"Like beauty, quality is in the eyes of the beholder."

The problem with improving quality is that the quality of many products and most services is a subjective attribute. It is difficult to identify major factors and to explain them to others. Personality issues inevitably arise, and negative findings are often viewed by the recipient as "Nonsense, you never did like me anyway!" That is, when confronted with a quality problem, the typical reaction is to defend oneself against a personal attack. The problem in need of improvement becomes secondary.

One way to define *quality* and what we want to do with it is to think in terms of telling a Continuous Quality Improvement (CQI) story to others. You do not have to use statistics, nor do you have to worry about complex formulas or medical procedures. However, you must be able to tell your story in a simple, objective manner so that others can understand the problem and take action to improve the situation. The math used in the majority of the Quality Improvement (QI) tools and techniques will not be difficult. However, it will be difficult to define subjective attributes such as opinions and attitudes so that changes in these factors can be monitored and discussed.

This brings us to the real use of statistics: Data tends to be more objective than general statements. For example, suppose products were being shipped late from your firm, and you stated this fact to the shipping manager. You would most likely be rewarded for your frankness by being asked to leave the office.

However, instead of an aggressive confrontation with the shipping manager, suppose a QI team prepared a chart showing the number of late shipments by day. Also suppose that along with the chart, a customer survey was included in which key customers stated that the major problem in dealing with your firm was that shipments were late. Note that neither an individual or, for that matter, a team is "causing" this negative news. It is hard to argue against facts because the "data speaks for itself," thus removing personalities from the discussion.

The CQI story is a structure that a QI team follows to display their work in an objective, standardized fashion.

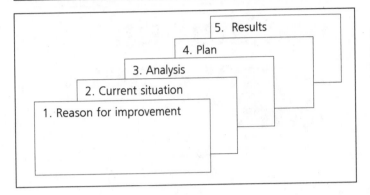

All CQI stories follow the five QI steps shown. Whenever possible, each step should be described in a single page.*

The Friendly Texan Insurance Company

Offices in:
Houston -   4
Galveston - 1
Dallas -   5

Let's use a hypothetical firm to explain how various QI tools and techniques could be applied. Our firm, The Friendly Texan Insurance Company, is based in Houston with 10 agencies in three Texas cities. They specialize in providing a wide range of consumer insurance needs including automobile, homeowner, renters (often called apartment insurance), life, and personal property insurance.

Step 1. Reason for Improvement

1. Reason for Improvement
Problem Statement

The objective of the first step in the CQI story is to identify a *theme* (problem area) and a *problem statement*. The theme must be an important issue that will serve as a focus for the QI team throughout the improvement process. Do not assume others understand the importance of a situation just because it is obvious to you. The reason for the QI project has to be clearly stated and carried through all portions of the CQI story.

*The story approach for reporting quality improvements originated with Dr. Kume. This approach formed the basis of a seven-step quality reporting process used by Florida Power and Light (FPL). The five-step CQI story used in this book is a simplification of FPL's approach.

For example, suppose that Ms. Susan Jackson, Vice President of Administration located in the Houston office, noticed an alarming increase in the number of written customer complaints received. Complaints were counted and it was found that 300 customer complaints were received in 1993.

At this point, she could simply "rationalize" the problem. Since The Friendly Texan, including their branch agencies, has in excess of 100,000 customers, the 300 complaints could be divided by 100,000 to identify the percent of customers who complained. That is, only three-tenths of 1 percent of the customers complained. She could "legitimately" conclude this is an insignificant problem.

However, customers have to spend time to put their thoughts in writing—perhaps many other customers had the same concerns. If underlying causes could be identified and resolved, customer service quality would be improved. I hope she takes the latter option and "digs deeper" to develop an understanding of the complaints. A commitment to continuous quality improvement requires that we understand what is occurring from the consumer's viewpoint.

Suppose she reviewed the office files, counted the complaints received each year since 1988, and charted these yearly totals on a graph. By doing this, she has assembled facts to support an alarming finding: "Customer complaints are increasing."

That is, by finding out more information about a vague problem, she has identified a theme that is worth our time to analyze. We are not going to allow our analysis to get side-tracked onto other insurance issues because our activities will be focused on finding out why "customer complaints are increasing."

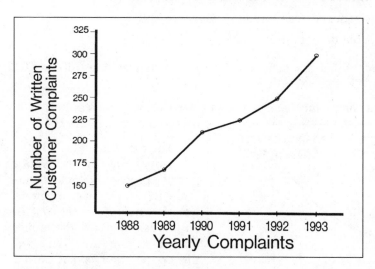

Suppose she constructed a *run chart* (often called a *trend chart*) to show the increase in complaints. (We'll explain how to construct the run chart later.) Step 1 in a CQI story must state an important "negative" problem. After completion of the chart, she should ask: "Is this something of interest to a broad range of insurance professionals?" Of course it is, and because of this, she has intuitively started the first step in a CQI story.

Are You a Total Quality Person?

I treat others fairly.

	Seldom	Sometimes	Always
	☐	☐	☐

Step 1. Reason for Improvement

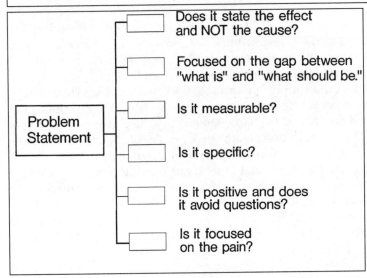

Problem Statement
- Does it state the effect and NOT the cause?
- Focused on the gap between "what is" and "what should be."
- Is it measurable?
- Is it specific?
- Is it positive and does it avoid questions?
- Is it focused on the pain?

However, look closely at the graph. It doesn't have a "zing" to it. What are we really talking about here? Our first step is not complete because a problem statement is needed to further focus the QI activities. A problem statement should focus on the gap between "what is" and "what it should be."

The following checklist will help in developing a problem statement. A good problem statement should:

- State the effect of the problem.

- State the gap—the difference between the performance standard and the current performance level.

- Be specific and use facts—avoid broad categories such as productivity, lack of communication, etc.

- Be measurable—include how often, how much, when, and who.

- Focus on the pain—stress discomfort and annoyance.

- State the problem, but do not imply a solution.

The problem statement that Ms. Jackson developed to finalize Step 1 of the CQI story was:

"Customer complaints have increased from 250 complaints in 1992 to 300 complaints in 1993."

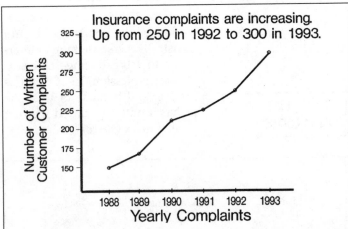

Insurance complaints are increasing. Up from 250 in 1992 to 300 in 1993.

Number of Written Customer Complaints

Yearly Complaints

The completed Step 1 in the CQI story is shown here. Notice how the problem statement reinforces the graph. Since the problem statement does not contain an implied solution, the immediate questions are "Why did this occur?" and "What caused it?"

The graph, along with the problem statement, visually directs the reader to Step 2—the next step in the CQI story.

However, before leaving Step 1, notice that the reason for improvement is a strong quality indicator and that the indicator is from the "customer's" point of view. Tracking the degree of dissatisfaction, rather than satisfaction, over time creates the largest impact on the reader. Hence, we are focusing on the pain so that everyone at Friendly Texan Insurance Company understands the need for improvement.

Typical QI Tools Used in Reason for Improvement	
Trend chart	Show increasing problem
Flow chart	Show complex process and problem area
Control chart	Show out of control condition

Step 2. Current Situation

2. Current Situation
   Component Parts
   Supporting Graphics
   Target Improvement Goals

Step 2, the *current situation*, breaks down the broad theme into its component parts and identifies which component part has the largest impact on the customer. Step 2 is also page 2 in our CQI story. Recent complaints were analyzed and found to involve problems with:

- Claim payment delays.
- Claim payment amounts.
- Insurance rates.
- Insurance coverage.
- A few general complaints labeled as "other."

At this point, we have identified that the major category of complaints deals with problems regarding claim payment delays. Since claim payment delays is the largest complaint category, this category was further subdivided into complaints dealing with:

- Automobile claims.
- Homeowner claims.
- Apartment claims.
- Other claims.

Step 2. Current Situation

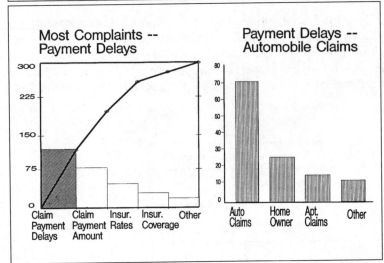

Most Complaints -- Payment Delays

Claim Payment Delays / Claim Payment Amount / Insur. Rates / Insur. Coverage / Other

Payment Delays -- Automobile Claims

Auto Claims / Home Owner / Apt. Claims / Other

Step 2, the current situation, is shown here. A *Pareto diagram* identified that most complaints were concerned with delays in claim payments. A bar chart was used to further subdivide this category. (We will discuss how to create these charts later.)

We now have enough information to develop the following target improvement goal:

Reduce complaints regarding claim payment delays from 70 per year to 30 complaints per year or less.

Note that this is a reasonable target toward our real goal of eliminating all customer complaints of any type. However, many people would consider such a goal unrealistic, and we would have difficulty eliciting their support. Nor would it be realistic to assume we could eliminate all complaints regarding claim payment delays. That is, a target is only a realistic, attainable step towards a goal. In a football game, the *goal* is to win the game. The *target* might be to obtain the next first down. A target should be challenging, but achievable within a year. When establishing a target consider:

1. Needs and expectations of the customer.

2. Performance of similar operations at similar agencies.

3. Your own past performance: Have you accomplished anything like this before?

An insurance firm, like most organizations, is a complex environment with many technical functions. Yet, by organizing our work, we have the attention of vastly different technical groups. This is the power of QI tools: A graphic portrayal of a problem can keep the attention of people with different skills and backgrounds. Organize your work so it immediately makes the point you are trying to get across. Do *not* expect the reader to wade through verbiage in order to be able to understand your point.

Typical QI Tools Used in the Current Situation	
Pareto diagram (This is almost always used.)	Separates the vital few from the trivia many
Run chart (often called a trend chart)	Shows increasing or decreasing problem
Bar chart	Further breakdown of categories
Histogram	Shows dispersion of data

Now It's Your Turn*

Develop problem statements for Problems 1 through 5 in the space provided.

1. *Our commercial suppliers have returned about 15 percent of our order forms for additional processing (correct errors, fill in missing information, incorrect material codes, etc.)*

2. *We need to improve sales by 20 percent.*

3. *We are not meeting our second-day delivery promise to our in-town customers.*

4. *It takes us five days longer to produce our quarterly inventory reports than it did a year ago. Other departments are complaining and we are spending a great deal of time giving them the ending balances they need on a timely basis.*

5. *We need to reduce customer returns by 10 percent.*

Now It's Your Turn*

Answer Problems 6 through 8 in the space provided.

A top manager at Big City Electronics has relayed the following story to a QI team. Although this problem did not occur last year, this is the fourth time this year that a problem similar to this did occur.

A customer read an ad in a local newspaper for a color TV at Big City Electronics for $299. He went to the store and the sales clerk said, "No, there is an error." That set is $375 and it cannot be sold at a lower price.

6. *Develop a possible theme for this CQI story.*

7. *Develop a problem statement.*

8. *How do you think that the analysis of this problem might proceed?*

*The answers to these problems are in the appendix.

Step 3. Analysis

3. Analysis
   Identify and Verify Root Cause
   (Fishbone Diagram)
   Cost/Benefit Analysis

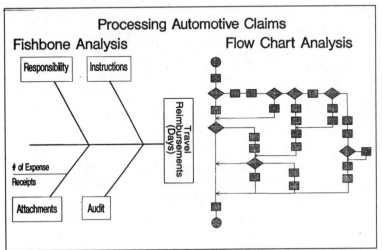

This step focuses attention on identifying the root cause(s) of the problem. That is, the analysis focuses on what is involved in processing automotive payment claims to identify the root cause of the problem. Either a flow chart or a *fishbone diagram* (often called a *cause-and-effect diagram*) is used to visually display general relationships.

Typical QI Tools Used in the Analysis Step	
Flow chart	Shows overview of process involved
Fishbone diagram (This is almost always used.)	Identify and verify root cause of problem
Scatter diagram	Shows possible cause and effect
Cost/benefit analysis	Shows estimated savings and cost impact

A *cost/benefit analysis* may be included in Step 3, particularly if a substantial investment is required in revising computer programs, or in training adjusters in a new method. A simplified cost/benefit approach consists of calculating:

Benefits from new/revised system
- Cost of installing system
  _____
  Savings

Total quality cost =

   Control costs   (prevention costs and costs to remove defects from the process)

+ Failure costs   (costs incurred as a result of defects in the process)

The basic concept is that an increase in prevention costs (such as a quality training program) should result in a larger decrease in failure costs, thus reducing total quality cost. Care should be taken to identify internal and external cost of poor quality for all departments. Hidden costs can often account for 25 percent of profits. In addition, hidden costs due to lost customers and loss of good will have a long-term negative impact.

A good way to get a "handle" on potential quality costs is to construct a spreadsheet of the departments and the category of costs incurred.

Intangible Costs from Poor Quality

✓ Decreased morale
✓ Increased frustration/aggravation
✓ Decreased job satisfaction
✓ Loss of pride and respect
✓ Decreased voluntary compliance
✓ Loss of confidence
✓ Loss of good will

Quality Cost Spreadsheet—Partial Listing of Department/Cost Categories

Departments/ description	Administration	Purchasing	Engineering	Marketing	Production	Shipping	Production control
Customer surveys							
Design support							
Service design qualification							
Field trials							
Supplier reviews							
Supplier ratings							
Internal failure costs							
External failure costs							

Step 4. Action Plan

4. Action Plan
Describe Action to Be Taken
(Who, What, When, Where)

An *action plan* is a detailed outline of how the QI team proposes correcting the root cause of the problem. This is a series of statements that specify the exact action that will have to be taken. The plan should answer: who, what, when, and where. The plan can be used by the QI team to communicate ideas to management and coworkers. In this case, the QI team has met with the key departments that will be involved in reducing the time required to process automotive claims.

A sample action plan is shown that will identify the root cause(s) of the problem. Note that the action plan shown identifies who is to take what action, when it is to be taken, and the current status. (An action plan is often called a *deployment chart*.)

Step 4 - Action Plan

What	When	Who	Status
Barriers to Overcome -			
Train adjusters	2/15	VP- Adams	Started
Standardize forms	4/15	Auditing	Completed
Train sales staff	5/15	Sales Dept.	Unknown
Other Assignments -			
Develop claim tracking program	3/10	MIS Dept.	Not Started

Now It's Your Turn

Develop your own personal action plan to learn more about QI tools.

Personal Action Plan to Learn About QI Tools

What	When	Who	Status

Step 5. Results

5. Results Confirm That Conditions Have Improved

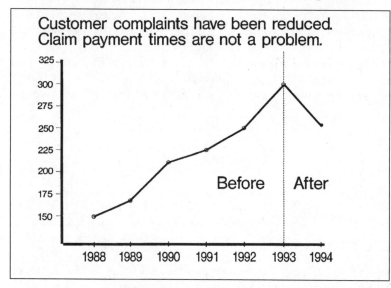

Customer complaints have been reduced. Claim payment times are not a problem.

The objective of Step 5 in the CQI story is to confirm that the problem and its root causes have decreased. This step should identify if the target for improvement has been met. Results are typically displayed in graphic form showing the conditions before and after the change.

Results should be distributed throughout the firm for several reasons. First, success breeds success. It is very satisfying to see that your ideas have been incorporated into a plan to improve service quality. Second, and equally important, others may be having similar problems, and your solutions could encourage them to take action.

Typical QI Tools Used In the Results Step	
Revised trend (run) chart (either a run or Pareto chart) is almost always used)	Shows "before" and "after" change
Pareto diagram	Shows categories "before" and "after" change
Radar chart	Shows changes in perception
Bar chart	Shows changes

Benefits of Using the CQI Story

The CQI story approach to problem solving begins with a general quality theme that defines the problem. Then, a closer evaluation is made regarding the current situation that is occurring in order to identify the specific problem that warrants further investigation. Next, the problem is analyzed to identify the fundamental root cause(s) and an action plan is constructed that will correct the root cause(s) of the problem. Finally, results are demonstrated and distributed. Although it is desirable that all CQI stories follow this standardized approach, we should not be locked into what is irrelevant or unnecessary. For example, if management identifies an area for improvement and appoints a team to look into it, there is no reason to spend any time on Step 1, "Reason for Improvement."

Also, if the CQI story is at the proposal stage, it is doubtful that the QI team would have Step 5, "Results." In fact, no attempt should be made to include a results step until after the project is installed and deployed throughout the organization.

Now It's Your Turn

Review the following minicase and answer the questions.

National Builders' Supply has 12 stores in the United States and provides an extensive array of building supplies to contractors and do-it-yourself homeowners. All stores are reasonably successful except the store located in Louisville, Kentucky.

The Louisville store has poor sales, poor profits, and a high labor turnover. Despite help wanted advertisements, few qualified people apply for jobs at the store. This has resulted in poor consumer services because store personnel are not trained in the products they are selling.

A morale study identified several problems. Interestingly, although there was no question on the survey regarding pay, in the comments section, many employees stated they wanted more money, and several people threatened to quit. However, the pay for a typical sales position is equal to or better than comparable area businesses.

9. *What is a likely theme for this CQI story?*

10. *What is the current situation for this CQI story?*

11. *How might the analysis proceed for this CQI story? What additional information is needed?*

Basic Quality Improvement Tools

There are seven "original" Quality Improvement tools. They are:

1. Flow charts.
2. Check sheets.
3. Histograms.
4. Pareto diagrams.
5. Cause-and-effect diagrams.
6. Scatter diagrams.
7. Control charts.

We will expand this list to include checklists and run charts. These basic QI tools can be found in all quality applications. The tools are designed to be simple so that they can be used and understood by all employees.

Basic Quality Improvement Tools

Tool	Problem-solving step
Flow chart	Understanding the situation
Check sheet Checklist	Finding facts
Pareto diagram Histogram	Identifying problems
Fishbone diagram	Generating ideas
Scatter diagram	Developing solutions
Run chart Control chart	Implementation

Here's an overview of the basic Quality Improvement tools we will be discussing in this section.

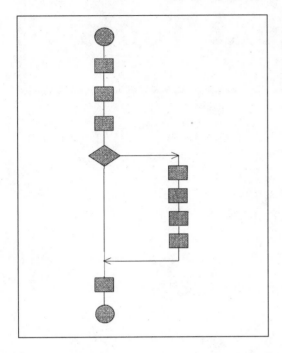

Flow Chart

Description	Purpose	Method
Symbols to show steps in a process.	Visual "feel" for complexity involved.	Layout process steps using standardized symbols.

Check Sheet

Description	Purpose	Method
Form for entering data under predetermined categories.	To collect data.	Design form for clarity and ease of data collection.

Travel Reimbursements 8/1/94–9/1/94

Categories	Sales Dept.	Claims Dept.
Completed pretrip staff voucher	✓✓✓✓	✓
Vouchers approved by department manager	✓✓✓✓✓✓	✓✓
Supporting nvoices attached after trip	✓✓✓✓	✓✓✓
Finance Dept. review	✓✓✓	✓
Payroll Dept. processing	✓✓✓✓✓	

Checklist

Description	Purpose	Method
List of items that are checked off upon completion.	To record progress.	Simple "To Do List" for checking off completion of tasks identified.

Learning to Use QI Tools

Item	Done
Review CQI story	✓
Read about the QI tool	✓
Work the problems	
Develop your own application	
Apply tools	

Pareto Diagram

Description	Purpose	Method
A bar chart with percent arranged so bars touch. Bars are in descending order from the left.	Helps identify what category is most significant.	Frequencies are on left and cumulative percent on right.

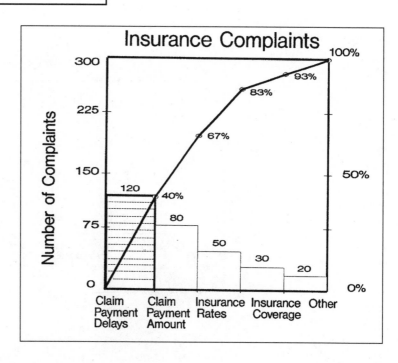

Insurance Complaints

Basic Quality Improvement Tools

Histogram

Description	Purpose	Method
Bar chart showing data set divided into classes (bars) of equal width. Height of bar shows quantity.	Shows patterns in dispersion of continuous data or large discrete data sets.	Draw bars touching to show pattern as a whole (that is of interest) not the individual classes.

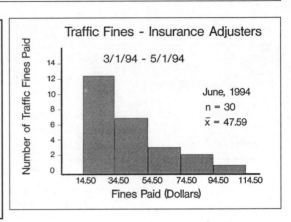

Cause-and-Effect Diagram (Fishbone Diagram)

Description	Purpose	Method
Shows cause and effect relationships.	Aids in identifying root cause.	Fish's head (main activity) on right. Ribs contain major process steps.

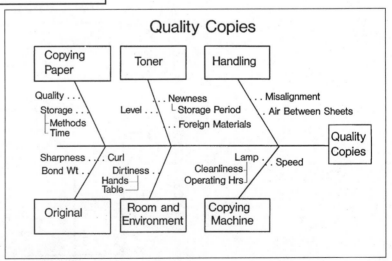

Scatter Diagram

Description	Purpose	Method
Chart where data for x and y variables are entered as dots to see if they form a pattern.	Shows if a casual relationship exists between variables.	Suspected cause should be on x axis and the effect on the y axis.

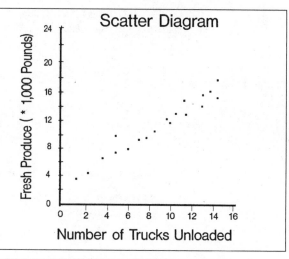

Run Chart—Often Called a Trend or Line Graph

Description	Purpose	Method
A chart with x and y axes. Data values are shown as points connected by lines.	Shows direction (trend) and change over time.	x axis shows time and y axis shows the measurement scale.

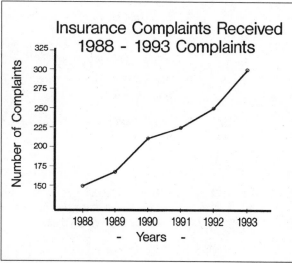

Control Chart

Description	Purpose	Method
A line graph with an average line and control limit lines.	Monitors an ongoing process and detects changes in output.	Separate types of charts for continuous and discrete data.

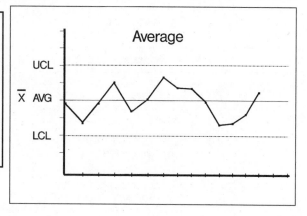

When selecting a QI tool, select the tool that will make your point at a glance. That is, don't get "bogged down" in statistics.

Now It's Your Turn

I'll bet you already know more about QI tools than you give yourself credit for knowing. Select the QI tool(s) that would be appropriate to answer the condition stated. If you are not sure of which one to use, come back to these questions after you have read this section.

1. *Display the reduction in automobile deaths after the speed limit was reduced.**

2. *Display the five major categories of the city's annual budget to determine if each area is "getting its fair share."**

3. *Identify the major customer complaint from a recently completed customer survey.**

4. *Show that customer returns have decreased since we've trained our sales employees.**

5. *Display what our firm has to do to restock a returned item into inventory.**

6. *Display the top three consumer satisfaction scores in a recently completed attitudinal survey.*

7. *Identify what could be the cause of consumer dissatisfaction with the quality of our food.*

Constructing a Flow Chart

Whatever You Choose to Call It
Process Flow Charts
Process Mapping
Flow Charting
Flow Diagrams
Continuous Improvement Through Training

The first problem-solving step is to develop an understanding of the situation. A *flow chart* is a picture that shows the sequence of steps required for a process. A flow chart is a communication device that helps people develop an objective understanding of the process.

*The answers to these problems are in the appendix.

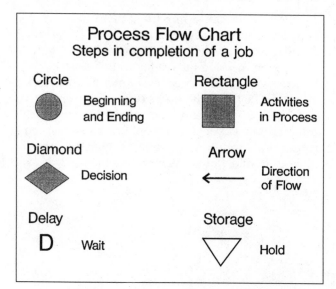

Process Flow Chart
Steps in completion of a job

Circle

Beginning
and Ending

Rectangle

Activities
in Process

Diamond

Decision

Arrow

←

Direction
of Flow

Delay

D Wait

Storage

▽ Hold

Think of a flow chart as a map to be followed in completing a job. Standard flow chart symbols are shown.

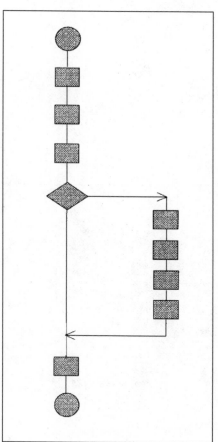

An example of a *process flow chart* is shown. Short flow charts with minimum detail are called *macro charts*.

Before constructing a process flow chart, map the process by:

- Defining customer needs.
- Identifying the methodology.
- Identifying key quality parameters.

Since a process flow chart is constructed *after* a detailed problem statement is developed, the beginning and ending boundaries of the process are usually known.

Constructing a Flow Chart

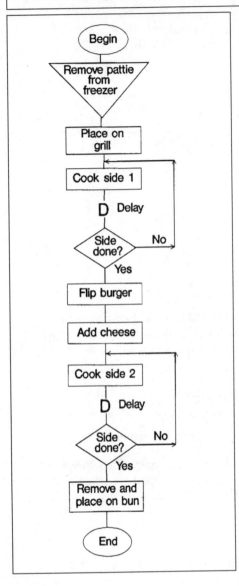

Perhaps the most important point to remember is that you are conveying a picture for a CQI story. Detailed steps are left out of a macro flow chart to avoid overpowering the reader with excessive steps. If "massive" detail is needed to describe a particular step, then that step should be on a separate page.

The simplified flow chart on the left reflects the product flow in cooking a hamburger in a fast-food restaurant. You might want to question the *D* (delays) to find ways of eliminating them.

The *macro flow chart* shown is a "trap." The only thing the flow chart conveys is that the process is rather complex.

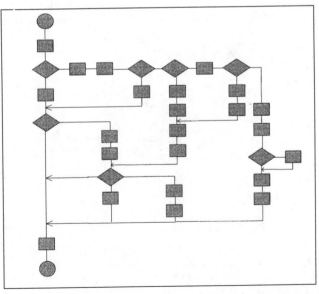

After constructing a flow chart, analyze the chart to see where improvements can be made in the process. Eliminate nonvalue-added activities from the process.

1. Examine each decision symbol.
   Is this check necessary?
   Is this a complete check or do errors go undetected?
   Is this duplication of effort?

2. Examine each activity.
   Is this activity redundant?
   What is the activity's value relative to its cost?
   Eliminate signature cycles.
   Is a storage really needed?
   Would this be needed if we had no failures?

3. Examine each document.
   Is this really necessary?
   Is this data really needed?
   How is this kept up to date?

Let's go back to the problem Friendly Texan Insurance Company was having regarding customer complaints on the lengthy time required for automobile claim payment. Suppose a QI team was formed and a macro level flow chart was developed of the process as shown.

| Police file accident report | → | Friendly Ins. agency paperwork | → | Adjuster reviews damages | → | Adjuster's office prices work | → | Bodyshop accepts estimate | → |
| Repairs made to car | → | Adjuster verifies repairs | → | You accept car | → | Customer drives car without problems | → | Bodyshop paid for work | |

This flow chart prompts several questions. First, what is the probability of the bodyshop getting paid for their work if each group (or person) gets their part of the job right 90 percent of the time?

The answer? Multiply .90 (that the police correctly file the accident report) times .90 (that Friendly Texan Insurance correctly completes the paperwork) times .90 (that adjuster..., etc.) for each of the 10 steps in the process. The flow chart indicates that the process will work correctly only 35 percent of the time (calculated as $.90^{10} = .350$). It will not really make a difference if everyone at Friendly Texan Insurance works harder and makes fewer errors. There are simply too many steps in the system, and the system itself must be simplified.

Friendly Texan Insurance's QI team should carefully analyze this flow chart, not to "nit-pick it" but to find out what steps could be eliminated, and if steps could be combined. Note: This is a classic empowerment application. Why can't the insurance adjusters be empowered to perform more steps? If the customer is willing to accept a "cash" payment to live with the damage, then the process could be vastly speeded up.

Constructing a Flow Chart

Now It's Your Turn

Develop a high-level flow chart of the process required to obtain a dress for sale to the consumer in woman's dress department in a large department store.

Dresses are purchased by the corporate procurement office and are shipped from various vendors to the dress department for retail sale. Jack is the QI team leader; Susan is also on the team. They are questioning Joyce who is Department Manager of the Dress Department.

JACK: What are the boundaries of the process of receiving and stocking dresses?

JOYCE: It starts when the vendor ships the dresses to my department and ends when we move the dresses into our racks on the floor.

SUSAN: Is your inventory on your floor racks or do you have another storage area?

JOYCE: All our inventory is on the floor racks where customers have access to the clothing.

JACK: What occurs after the vendor ships the dresses?

JOYCE: They are received by our Shipping Department who notifies our Dress Department.

JACK: What do you do?

JOYCE: We notify inside transportation to deliver them to us ASAP!

SUSAN: Then what?

JOYCE: We check our purchase list to see if there are any known problems with the supplier or with the order. Suppliers have been known to ship wrong dresses, defective dresses, or even dresses not ordered.

SUSAN: And if there are problems?

JOYCE: We put a tag on the clothing saying "Not for Sale." We then call Central Purchasing and tell them about the problem. In addition, we call Accounts Payable and tell them to hold payment.

JACK: How often does this occur, and how long does it take to resolve problems?

JOYCE: This happens with about 10 percent of our receipts. I give them two weeks to resolve the problem, which they normally do.

SUSAN: And what do you do when it is resolved?

JOYCE: We follow the normal procedure of stocking the item on our racks, filling out Form DD-4 which is sent to Accounts Payable saying all is well, pay the vendor.

JACK: What happens if the issue is not resolved in two weeks?

JOYCE: I bundle everything up, ship it back to the vendor, and notify Accounting and Purchasing not to pay the vendor.

After developing your flow chart, review the diagram. What questions would you like to see answered? How can the process be streamlined?

Constructing a Check Sheet

The fact-finding phase of problem solving typically involves data collection. *Check sheets* are used to assure that data are captured in a systematic manner. All check sheets list the data collection categories. In simplified check sheets, whenever data is collected, a check mark is made in the appropriate category.

Difference Between Data and Information

✓ Data = raw, unorganized facts.

✓ Information = data organized so that it is useful in decision making.

✓ Information is useful data.

✓ Data, by itself, is seldom useful.

When designing a check sheet, keep in mind that the reason we gather data is to make a decision. Data are raw, uncoordinated facts. By themselves, data are not much use. However, when data is grouped in an organized fashion that can be used in decision making, then it becomes useful information. Check sheets should be designed to provide both ease of recording the data, and if possible, an organization of the data so that we can see what is happening at a glance.

Pitfalls in Data Collection

Operational problems	Not following established policies and procedures.
Perception bias	A tendency of the data collector to "see what they want to see."
Incomplete data	Missing data can bias the results due to nonresponses. Or part of the process may have been left out.
Interaction bias	The act of collecting the data may influence the operation under study.
Sampling error	The data should be collected at times that fairly represent the process (i.e., lunch crowds at restaurants).

There are several pitfalls in data collection that you want to avoid. These are summarized as shown. I don't think people would deliberately introduce perceptual bias, it more than likely occurs because of the background of the person collecting the data. He/she may simply see the world through "rose-colored glasses" and not be aware of what you are attempting to capture.

Asking Key Questions of the Process

Before designing the data collection instrument, consider the questions you are asking of the process. It is best to write out the specific questions you are trying to answer before designing the check sheet. The data collection will be more accurate, and it will be easier to obtain the cooperation of the people. Employees have their regular tasks to perform and gathering any type of data is troublesome. They are more apt to cooperate if they believe the QI team knows exactly what they are looking for, and provides them with a well-designed check sheet for capturing such data.

Constructing a Check Sheet

Designing a Data Collection Form	
KISS principle	Keep It Simple Stupid
Reduce possibility of errors	Minimum words; minimum numbers; maximum checks
Self-explanatory	Minimum instructions
Look professional	If it is not professional, you cannot expect people to take care

A check sheet (often called *data sheet*) is constructed by laying out a matrix with boxes large enough to enter data such as check or slash marks. The columns and rows of the matrix are labeled to represent the data categories of interest. Familiarize yourself with the process under examination before designing the form. Then ask fact-finding questions such as the following:

☐ What (what happens)?

☐ Who (who does it, who is responsible)?

☐ Where (what place, what department)?

☐ When (time, day)?

☐ How (how does it happen, how much, how long)?

This is a universal approach that can be applied to any industry. For example, it would be possible to develop a check sheet to monitor the temperature of the grease used in cooking french fries at a Flame Burger, a fast food restaurant.

Flame Burger Fries

Inspector:_____   Date:_____

Notes:

Time of Day	Temperature °F
11:00 - 11:14	
11:15 - 11:29	
11:30 - 11:44	
11:45 - 11:59	
12:00 - 12:14	
12:15 - 12:29	
12:30 - 12:44	

There is no set format for a check sheet other than it should be a simple means of data collection. For example, a check sheet to record part defects might appear as shown.

Defective Item Check Sheet

Product:_____

Inspector:_____

Date: _____

Type of Defect	Check	Subtotal
Cracks	~~++++~~	5
Surface scars	~~++++~~ ||||	9
Wrong part number	|||	3
Poor paint	~~++++~~ ~~++++~~ ||	12
Other defects	||	2
	Grand total:	31

Suppose Friendly Texan Insurance formed a QI team to evaluate how employees were reimbursed for travel expenses. A check sheet to guide the team in conducting their study of the Sales and Claims Departments is shown. The sheet is used to assure that the appropriate documents are studied from each department. Note that the team studied four completed pretrip staff vouchers from Sales, but only one voucher from the Claims Department was studied. Additional vouchers will have to be acquired from the claims department for analysis.

Travel Reimbursements 8/1/94—9/1/94

Categories	Sales Dept.	Claims Dept.
Completed pretrip staff voucher	✓ ✓ ✓	✓
Vouchers approved by Dept. manager	✓ ✓ ✓ ✓ ✓ ✓	✓ ✓
Supporting invoices attached after trip	✓ ✓ ✓ ✓	✓ ✓ ✓
Finance Dept. review	✓ ✓ ✓	✓
Payroll Dept. processing	✓ ✓ ✓ ✓	

Constructing a Check Sheet

On the other hand, suppose the Vice President of Administration at Friendly Texan Insurance wanted to know the days that customers were likely to phone in regarding an automobile accident. Furthermore, let's assume the Vice President has completed a statistic course, and is concerned with the dispersal of the data.

A possible recording form for use by the receptionist answering the phone is shown. The instructions accompanying the form are to place an "X" in the lowest unoccupied box under the appropriate day the customer initially phoned an accident. (Saturday and Sunday's totals are obtained from the messages left on the answering phone.)

The forms would have to be collected weekly. As with any data collection form, the people who record the data on the form should be told why the data is being collected, and they should be asked if there are any questions or comments. Based on the data gathered so far, it appears that a better method might be needed for serving Saturday phone-in. A completed form would provide totals, and give a visual indicator of the "dispersion" of the data.

Accident Recording Form

Su	Mo	Tu	We	Th	Fr	Sa

Accident Recording Form

Su	Mo	Tu	We	Th	Fr	Sa
					X	
	X				X	
	X				X	
	X				X	X
	X				X	X
	X				X	X
X	X				X	X
X	X	X	X		X	X
Su	Mo	Tu	We	Th	Fr	Sa

Now It's Your Turn

1. *The sales manager for "City Slickers and Country Cousins" furniture store wants to find out: How long does it takes to process an order for furniture from the time the customer gives us the order, until it is delivered to the customer? Design a data collection form to solve the sales manager's problem.**

2. *Several employees have complained about the temperature in the sales office of Ajax Printing Company, located in Orlando, Florida. No data is available regarding office temperature. Design a data collection form to solve the office manager's problem.**

3. *Management of "Flame Burger Restaurant" (a local, high-volume, fast-food restaurant chain) feels customers are waiting in line longer than at other successful businesses. A QI team was assembled and met to identify some of their major requirements. The QI team first developed the sketch of process at Flame Burger shown. Then after their first meeting, the QI team members agreed that:*

   - *Peak hours are the critical times.*

   - *There was no information on waiting times.*

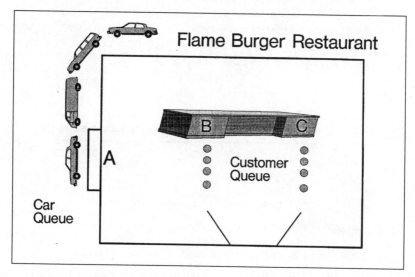

   Design a data collection form. Be prepared to defend your design.

4. *Develop brief numbered, written questions prior to designing the data collection instrument for the conditions shown. Then design the check sheet to capture the necessary data:*

   - *Customer complaints about our restaurant are increasing.*

   - *Repeat customers in our florist shop are decreasing.*

*The answers to these problems are in the appendix.

Facts Versus Inferences

Whenever using data, consideration must be given to facts versus inferences.

Fact: A statement that is known to be true.

Inference: A statement about the unknown, based on what is known.

Sounds simple? Hardly. There are shades of "gray" in even a seemingly obvious "fact" that results in the "fact" being an inference.

Now It's Your Turn*

Carefully read the following paragraph, and then answer the questions. You may refer back to this paragraph when answering the questions, but try to limit yourself to two "backward" references.

> *Pat Johnson, employed by Thompson Engineering, was delivering revised engineering drawings to Ajax Builder's construction site. After leaving the Engineering Department, and while in route to the site, the secretary called, stating that the drawings not be delivered and to return for the Engineering Department's 11:00 a.m. meeting to pick up the latest drawings. Johnson called the Engineering Departmental secretary, who after checking with several people, knew nothing about the 11:00 a.m. meeting.*

Identify If the Statement Is a Fact (F) or an Inference (I)	
Statement	F/I?
1. Pat Johnson works for the Engineering Department.	
2. Mr. Pat Johnson is employed by Thompson Engineering.	
3. Pat Johnson has left the Thompson Engineering building.	
4. Engineering drawings for Ajax Builders have again been changed.	
5. No one in the Engineering Department knew about the 11:00 A.M. meeting.	
6. Pat Johnson has a mobile phone.	
7. Ajax Building's construction is at a site remote from Thompson Engineering.	

*The answer to this problem is in the appendix.

Constructing a Checklist

Learning to Use QI Tools	
Item	Done
Review CQI story.	✓
Read about the QI tool.	✓
Work the problems.	✓
Develop your own application.	
Apply tools.	

A *checklist* is a limited, special form of a check sheet. A checklist is a "to-do" list of items to be accomplished. Checklists are used so that you can check your progress in gathering data. A checklist for learning how to use the QI tools discussed in this book would appear as shown.

When designing a checklist, think about what needs to be accomplished and the order the activities should be completed. Arrange the checklist items in sequential order and check off the items when completed. Remember, a check sheet is more complex than a checklist, in that check sheets are concerned with who, what, when, where, and how to facilitate data collection. Checklists only reflect progress made.

Now It's Your Turn

Develop a checklist of basic QI tools that look like they would be of interest to you. (See the categories printed on the upper left- and right-hand corners of this book.)

QI Tool	Done

Constructing a Pareto Diagram

In our problem-solving steps, flow charts were used to understand the situation, check sheets were used to gather facts, and now the Pareto diagram will be used to identify the problem.

In 1897, an Italian economist, Vilfredo Pareto, presented a formula showing that the distribution of income is uneven. The largest share of world income was held by a small number of people. Then in 1907, a U.S. economist, M.C. Lorenz,

Pareto Diagram

- Separates the vital few from the trivial many:
  Problems
  Symptoms
  Causes
- 80–20 rule: 80 percent of the problems come from 20 percent of the causes.
- Type of frequency chart.
  Bars arranged in descending order form the left.
- Provides order to the activity.
- Visual support for CQI story:
  Keeps project focused.
  Displays cumulative contributions.

expressed a similar theory in a diagram. Later, quality control expert, Dr. J. M. Juran, applied Lorenz's diagram method to classify problems of quality into the "vital few" and "trivial many." Dr. Juran named this method *Pareto Analysis*.

A Pareto diagram is a way of organizing data that visually highlights categories for more detailed study. That is, the diagram shows the major factors that make up the subject being analyzed. It is a type of frequency chart in which the bars are arranged in descending order from left to right. This results in highlighting the major problems as shown.

A Pareto diagram separates the vital few from the trivial many. Careful selection of appropriate categories, ordering data, and constructing the Pareto diagram can vastly improve a CQI story. Note how the diagram shown highlights that the insurance complaints are about delays in claim payment. In fact, 40 percent of all complaints involve claim payment delays, surpassing even insurance rates—a notorious category.

Let's walk through how this Pareto diagram was constructed. The process began when Ms. Jackson closely examined the complaint letters received by Friendly Texan Insurance. Complaints were grouped into the categories shown. The "other" category is a catch-all category consisting of complaints regarding personality problems, contract interpretations and renewal complaints.

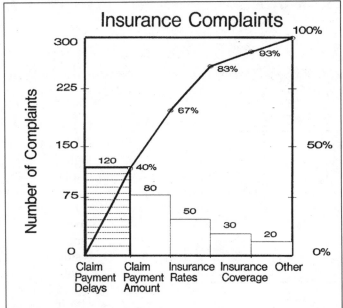

Complaint categories	Number of occurrences
Claim payment delays	120
Claim payment amount	80
Insurance rates	50
Insurance coverage	30
Other	20

The first step in constructing a Pareto diagram is to develop a cumulative percent table as shown. This has to be accomplished before plotting the graph.

Complaint categories	Number of occurrences	Cumulative occurrences	Cumulative percent (%)
Claim payment delays	120	120	40.0
Claim payment amount	80	200	66.7
Insurance rates	50	250	83.4
Insurance coverage	30	280	93.4
Other	20	300	100.0
Totals	300		

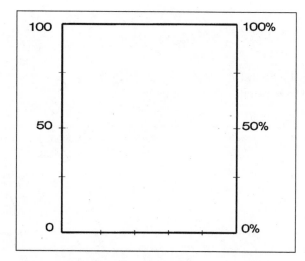

Next, a rough grid has to be created to display the data without too much distortion. The left side of the y axis contains the number of occurrences which range from 0 to 300. The right side of the y axis is the percentages ranging from 0 percent to 100 percent. The midpoint of the occurrences is 150 which corresponds to 50 percent of the total number of complaints in the Pareto diagram.

It takes a little practice to obtain a meaningful scale that permits both the occurrences and the cumulative percentage to be presented nicely on the same graph. An example of this "rough grid" layout is shown.

Constructing a Pareto Diagram

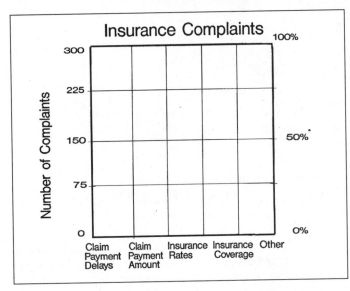

Next, "grid-in" the box to aid in drawing the bars. Label the x and y axes as shown.

Now we have the framework to sketch in our data. Add the appropriate bars, sample sizes percentages, and cumulative percent values. Then connect the cumulative percent values with a line to produce the final Pareto diagram previously shown.

Let's take a few more examples so that you can see the versatility of Pareto diagrams. Assume a check sheet was developed on items that were ordered by a Shop Supervisor from Inventory Control, but were not usable when they arrived in the work center. At the end of sampling 100 inventory problems, the totals were tabulated for each inventory problem category as shown.

Inventory problem categories	Number of occurrences
Broken	10
Wrong part number	50
Wrong paperwork	20
Scratched or dirty	15
Other	5

First, arrange the inventory problem categories in ascending order as shown so that a cumulative frequency table can be constructed.

Inventory problem categories	Number of occurrences
Wrong part number	50
Wrong paperwork	20
Scratched or dirty	15
Broken	10
Other	5

Notice that it is easier to construct the cumulative percent table this time. This is because the supervisor used a sample size of 100, a number which is easy to work with. The cumulative percentages can be quickly calculated, and appear as shown.

Inventory problem categories	Number of occurrences	Cumulative occurrences	Cumulative percent (%)
Wrong part number	50	50	50.0
Wrong paperwork	20	70	70.0
Scratched or dirty	15	85	85.0
Broken	10	95	95.0
Other	5	100	100.0
Totals	100		

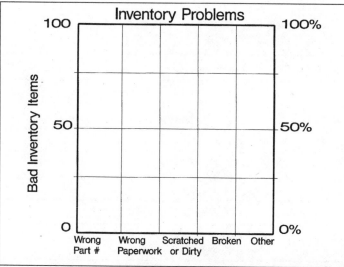

Now develop a rough grid showing percents (%) on the right side and numbers (sample size) on the left side of the diagram. The inventory problem categories are shown on the bottom of the grid.

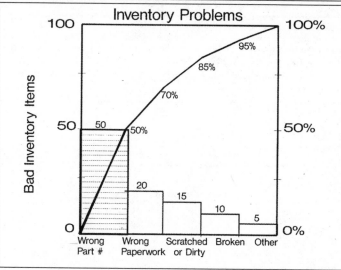

Now, complete the diagram by adding the appropriate bars, sample sizes percentages, and cumulative percent values. Then connect the cumulative percent values with a line to produce the final Pareto diagram previously shown.

Constructing a Pareto Diagram

Let's take a closer look at how check sheets are used to gather data which can then be displayed in a Pareto diagram to assist in problem identification. Our Friendly Texan Insurance Company consolidates purchasing for their 10 regional agencies at their Houston corporate office. Mr. John Jones is the Purchasing Manager responsible for procuring a broad base of items including computers, office furniture, and supplies of all types. (Corporate vehicles are leased and are not included in this study.)

A check sheet was created to keep track of problems users and suppliers experienced with purchasing from June 1 through August 31, 1994. The sheet was completed weekly, and then all the weekly sheets were summarized into the one grand check sheet shown.

Purchasing Problems: 6/1/94—7/31/94	
Item	Occurrences
Wrong product received	✓✓✓✓ ✓✓✓✓ ✓✓✓✓ ✓
Late shipment	✓✓✓✓ ✓✓✓✓ ✓✓✓✓ ✓✓
Payment complaints	✓✓✓✓ ✓✓✓✓ ✓✓✓✓ ✓✓✓✓ ✓✓✓✓ ✓✓✓✓ ✓✓✓✓ ✓✓✓✓ ✓✓✓✓ ✓✓✓✓
PO# not on outside of package [a]	✓✓✓✓ ✓✓✓✓ ✓✓
Damaged—usable [b]	✓✓✓✓ ✓✓✓✓ ✓✓✓✓ ✓✓✓✓ ✓✓✓✓
Damaged—not usable	✓✓✓✓ ✓✓✓✓
Other	✓✓✓✓ ✓✓

[a]Without a purchase order number clearly displayed on the outside of packages, it is difficult for the Receiving Office to know this is a purchased item.

[b]Damaged—usable items are items that should have been returned as not acceptable, but were used because of schedule pressures.

Total the check sheet and arrange frequency in descending order. Then develop cumulative frequencies and cumulative percentages.

Purchasing Problems: 6/1/94—7/31/94	
Item	Frequency
Payment complaints	49
Damaged—usable	24
Late shipment	18
Wrong product received	16
PO# not on outside of package	12
Damaged—not usable	10
Other	7

Purchasing Problems: 6/1/94—7/31/94			
Item	Number of occurrences	Cumulative occurrences	Cumulative percent (%)
Payment complaints	49	49	36.0
Damaged—usable	24	73	53.7
Late shipment	18	91	66.9
Wrong product received	16	107	78.7
PO# not on outside of package	12	119	87.5
Damaged—not usable	10	129	94.9
Other	7	136	100.0

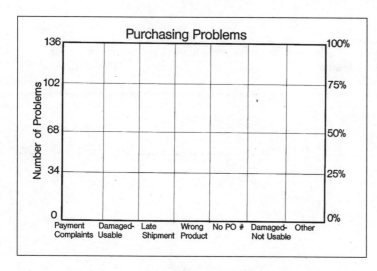

Now, layout the rough grid of the Pareto diagram as before.

Constructing a Pareto Diagram

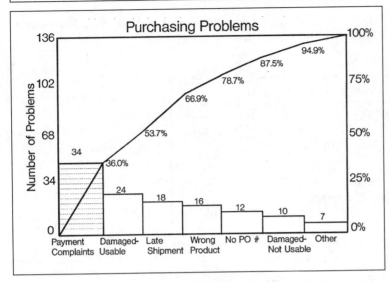

Purchasing Problems

Next, add the appropriate bars, sample size percentages, and cumulative percent values. Then connect the cumulative percent values with a line to produce the Pareto diagram for our procurement problems as shown.

You can "jazz up" a Pareto diagram to encourage people to think about the serious nature of the defects which have occurred. For example, suppose Sampson Upholstery Company collected data on the amount of scrap material (in square yards) produced during a recent two-month period. The *raw data* would appear as shown.

Material Waste—Sampson Upholstery 8/1/94–10/31/94			
Item	Square yards	Cumulative square yards	Cumulative percent (%)
Pattern repeats[a]	68	68	37.8
Wrong dimensions[b]	42	110	61.1
Cutting errors	30	140	77.8
Left overs	28	168	93.3
Other	12	180	100.0

[a]Pattern repeat: When matching patterns, fabric between the patterns is often scrapped.

[b]Wrong dimensions: Measurements are required of the product to be upholstered prior to cutting the fabric.

Are You a Total Quality Person?

I am proud of my achievements.   Seldom ☐   Sometimes ☐   Always ☐

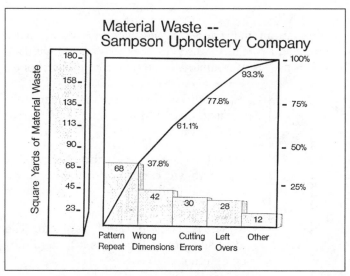

A Pareto diagram of Sampson Upholstery's material waste is shown. Note the use of the left-side bar showing that a total of 180 square yards of fabric were scrapped. Also note the rounding on the scale. That is, half of 180 is 90, and half of 90 is 45. But half of 45 has been rounded upward to 23.

Residental Water Usages—July 1994 Gallons			
Item	Gallons used	Cumulative gallons	Cumulative percent (%)
Lawns	1900	1900	38.8
Toilets	900	2800	57.1
Gardens	600	3400	69.4
Tub baths	500	3900	79.6
Showers	400	4300	87.8
Dishwashers	300	4600	93.9
Washing cars	200	4800	98.0
Other	100	4900	100.0

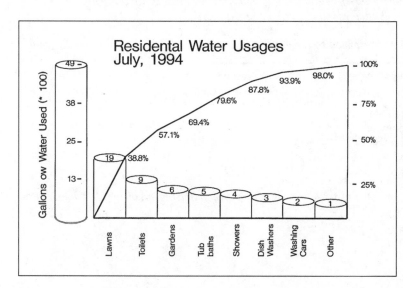

There are endless usages of Pareto diagrams. The raw data shown on residental water consumption will probably be ignored by readers. However, note the same data presented as a Pareto diagram. Do you "see" where water conservation efforts should be directed?

Constructing a Pareto Diagram

Be Careful!

When constructing a Pareto diagram, make sure that the categories are mutually exclusive. For example, if you had a category called "injuries," you could not have a second category of "broken bones" because injuries would include broken bones.

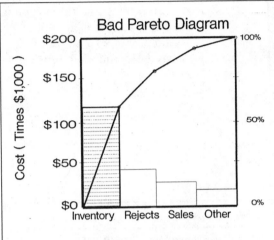

In addition, do not mix dissimilar problem categories. In the example of the Pareto chart shown:

- *Inventory* is a reduction problem. Although we cannot do without it, we would normally like to hold as little as possible.

- *Rejects* is a "zero-based" problem. The ideal situation is to reduce it to zero (i.e., no defects).

- *Sales* is an increase problem. We want to increase sales, not reduce sales to zero.

That is, the categories in the *bad Pareto diagram* are fighting each other and do not belong on the same chart. In addition, actual numbers are easier to compute if meaningful increments can be taken such as 100 units surveyed (instead of odd numbers such as 111 units).

Now It's Your Turn

1. *After we have constructed the Pareto diagram shown on insurance complaints, we need to take a closer look at the largest category of insurance complaints identified in the Pareto diagram as "claim payment delays."** *

    Use the grid provided in the appendix as a guide and develop a Pareto diagram.

Claim payment delay categories	Number of occurrences
Automobile	70
Homeowner	25
Apartment	15
Other	10
Totals	120

2. *After completion of the Pareto diagram on purchasing problems, Mr. John Jones,*

---

*The answers to these problems are in the appendix.

Friendly Texan Insurance's Procurement Manager, decided to take a closer look at the category of payment complaints. Unfortunately, he did not keep detailed records regarding payment complaints and had to take an additional study. As this now has become a corporate concern, he assembled a QI team of supervisors in accounting, accounts payable, and receiving and the scope of the study was changed slightly to include all payment problems.*

The team kept track of 50 payment problems beginning September 1. After 50 problems were encountered, they were tabulated and appear as shown. Construct a Pareto diagram of this data.

Payment Problems

Item	Frequency
Discount incorrectly taken	7
Not invoiced correctly	8
Invoiced quantity not same as quantity received	12
Yellow copy not received[a]	18
Other	5

[a]The recipient of the ordered merchandise signs and returns the yellow copy to Accounts Payable, verifying that the quantity and quality received is satisfactory.

3. *Thomas Industries recently received several complaints about the products sent from their Shipping Department. Ms. Janice Jones was asked to investigate and identify what needs to be corrected. She created a check sheet and recorded the following problems for the month of June. Using this data, create a Pareto diagram. You may use the general forms provided in the appendix as a guide.**

4. *A newspaper editor made a study of printed corrections that had to be made*

Shipping Problems: June, 1994

Item	Occurrences
Incorrect packing[a]	✓✓✓✓ ✓✓✓✓ ✓
Wrong container	✓✓✓✓✓ ✓✓✓✓✓ ✓✓✓
Documentation not correct	✓✓✓✓✓ ✓✓✓✓✓ ✓✓✓✓✓ ✓✓✓✓✓ ✓✓
Address label not correct[b]	✓✓✓✓✓ ✓✓✓✓✓ ✓✓✓✓✓ ✓
Other	✓✓✓✓ ✓

[a]Procedures for bubble wrap, shrink wrap, and dense packaging not followed.
[b]Includes illegible address, wrong address, incomplete address, and label not correctly affixed to package.

because of errors. He interviewed the reporter and/or editor responsible for the errors and asked them: "How could the error have been avoided?" A total of 103 errors were evaluated, and classified into the eight categories shown.*

1. Need to check more than one source	37
2. Incorrect information from "reliable" sources	23
3. Reporters or editors were inattentive (in a hurry)	19
4. Established procedures for checking accuracy were not followed	9
5. Assumed information was correct, when in fact, it was not correct	6
6. Faulty editing	6
7. Composing room error	2
8. Erroneous information in a clip file was never corrected	1
Total number of errors	103

5. *The Internal Revenue Service issued a news release regarding errors that occurred on the individual federal income tax returns filed by individuals. The purpose of the list was to indicate what individuals should consider to reduce the errors made. Read the paragraph shown, then develop a Pareto diagram to support your own article titled "IRS Blues."*

IRS Bulletin #94-21

The Internal Revenue Service reported that in 1993, individuals made numerous errors in their tax returns. There were the expected math errors, with 17,550 people making errors in figuring their taxable income. An additional 775,500 people made math errors in figuring refund or tax owed. But that's not the worst of it: 1,298,345 tax returns were in error because individuals copied the wrong number from the tax tables.

Furthermore, 312,377 people made mistakes in calculation of their earned income credit, and 389,902 itemized their medical and dental expenses incorrectly.

Constructing a Histogram

By now you should know how to identify problems using a Pareto diagram. If not, please go back and reread the last section. Another tool used in problem identification is a *histogram*. Although the end result is the same, Pareto diagrams and histograms are two entirely different tools, that are used for two entirely different data types.

**Rocky Mountain News*, October 6, 1986, p. 60

Histograms

- Gives a picture of the population.
- Displays continuous data.
- Displays variables in a data set.
- Develops logical groupings.
- Patterns of variability reveal underlying facts about process. (See section on interpreting distributions.)
- Patterns of variability can suggest theories to be tested.

Types of Data

The statistics to be used depend on whether the data is discrete or continuous.

Discrete (Attribute) Data
Discrete data is countable.
There are only that specific number of units. No decimals or further breakdown possible.
Defective/nondefective.
Pass/fail; Go/no go.

Continuous (Variable) Data
Measurable data.
Precision dependent on measuring instrument.
The data can be subdivided—length; weight; height.

Classification by Data Type

Weight/Height/Thickness
    Continuous
Average Service Time
    Continuous
No. of Unsatisfied Customers
    Discrete
Attitude Scale (Likert Type)
    Continuous
Rejections
    Discrete
No. of Customers
    Discrete
Average Failure Time
    Continuous
Defective Products
    Discrete

Pareto diagrams are used to display discrete data. *Discrete data* is countable in whole numbers. That is, there were five wrong parts, 30 complaints regarding insurance coverage, and so forth. Histograms are used to display continuous data to provide a picture that represents the distribution of the data. The larger the sample size, the clearer the picture of the population.

Continuous data (often called *variable data*) is measurable data that often contains a decimal point. For example, what is the width of a house? Forty feet? Are you sure? How about 40.2 feet? Perhaps someone else would measure the house with a sophisticated measuring instrument and conclude the width is 40.22 feet. The point being made is that data such as distances, height, and weight assume a range of measurements and, therefore, are not *discrete* (countable in whole numbers).

This will become clearer in a moment when we construct a histogram. Suppose Ms. Susan Jackson, our VP at Friendly Texan Insurance decided to "do some digging" and assembled the following traffic fines that were paid by Friendly's insurance adjusters (in dollars and cents) between March 1 and June 1, 1994. Notice two things about this raw data. First, it doesn't make any sense. Second, it contains decimals in terms of dollars and cents*, so we will treat the data as continuous.

---

*We will treat all data containing a decimal as continuous. However, a statistician could make an argument that the data are precise (countable in the hundredths) and, therefore, can be treated as discrete.

Constructing a Histogram

45.00	35.00	120.00	75.00	25.50
50.00	49.50	75.00	69.60	75.50
18.00	16.00	110.50	25.00	20.00
15.00	25.00	70.00	19.50	30.00
22.50	49.95	55.50	15.00	55.00
49.00	26.00	100.00	33.00	52.50

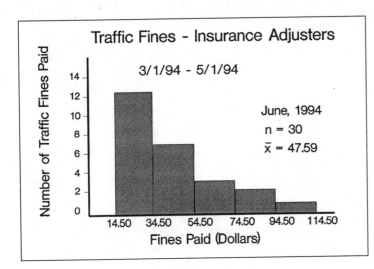

A histogram of the traffic fines is shown. Note that by organizing the data in meaningful groups, it's possible to make sense out of the data. Notice that there are a lot of relatively small traffice fines (under $34.50). Perhaps our adjusters are parking in restricted areas.

For the histogram shown, $\Sigma x = 1427.55$; $\bar{x} = 47.59$. A histogram permits us to understand the underlying structure of the data which can be very helpful in a QI analysis.

There are several steps required to construct a histogram beginning with computing the range (R) of the data.

Step 1: Compute the range (R) of the data:

$$R = X_{Max} - X_{Min}$$
$$R = 120.00 - 15.00 = 105.00$$

Step 2: Compute the approximate number of classes (k):

$$k = \sqrt{n} = \sqrt{30} = 5.48, \text{ round up to a } k \text{ of 6 classes}$$

We will treat all data containing a decimal as continuous. However, a statistician could make an arguement that the data are precise (countable in the hundredths) and can therefore be treated as discrete.)

The data groupings as shown in the Y axis label for the first group is read as 14.50 but less than 34.50. Then the next group is 34.50 but less than 54.50, and so forth.

Step 3: Compute the approximate class width (h):

$$h = R/k = 105/5.48 = 19.16$$

Step 4: Determine the unit of measurement (m):

1.00 (i.e., \$1)

Step 5: Finalize the class width (h) by rounding up to the next highest unit of measure. Even if h was 19.00, always round up to the next higher value so the highest value in the data set will be captured ($h = 20.00$).

Step 6: Compute the lower boundary of the first class (L_1):

$$L_1 = X_{Min} - (m/2) = 15.00 - (1.00/2) = 14.50$$

Step 7: Determine the lower boundaries of the remaining classes:

$$L_2 = L_1 + h = \quad 14.50 + 20.00 = \quad 34.50$$
$$L_3 = \qquad\qquad 34.50 + 20.00 = \quad 54.50$$
$$L_4 = \qquad\qquad 54.50 + 20.00 = \quad 74.50$$
$$L_5 = \qquad\qquad 74.50 + 20.00 = \quad 94.50$$
$$L_6 = \qquad\qquad 94.50 + 20.00 = 114.50$$
$$L_7 = \qquad\quad 114.50 + 20.00 = 134.50$$

Step 8: Using the class intervals, a frequency table is constructed as shown. Note the upper boundary for L_7 is also shown.

Class interval	Tally	Frequency
14.50–34.50	||||| ||||| |||	13
34.50–54.50	||||| ||	7
54.50–74.50	||||	4
74.50–94.50	|||	3
94.50–114.50	||	2
114.50–134.50			1
Total:		30

Frankly, developing frequency tables is a time-consuming process. If you have the software that is an optional companion to this book, please read the appendix and use the software. Differences in class intervals do not significantly affect the analysis.

Step 9: Develop a scale for the histogram as shown. Notice that the x axis layout was made to "take up" the available room to produce a wide-bodied graph.

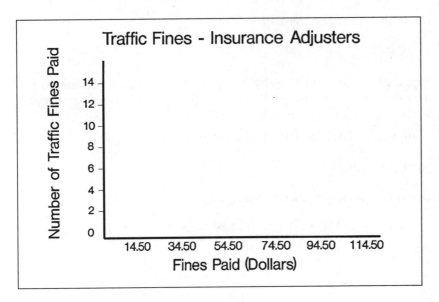

Step 10: Label and complete the histogram as previously shown.

Now It's Your Turn

1. *A QI team wants to use a histogram to display the time it took to process authorized travel reimbursements submitted by the claim adjusters at Friendly Texan Insurance. The team gathered data on 25 reimbursements after the authorized trips were completed and the employee received his/her expense payment. The data are for trips taken in July 1994. Day 1 begins when trip expense receipts are submitted to the departmental secretary. Ending time is the number of days that elapse until the adjuster receives payment for his/her expenses. Times (in days) are shown.**

30	40	102	45	44
109	80	95	84	108
107	76	64	104	78
44	60	47	35	59
94	70	41	32	60

*The answers to these problems are shown in the appendix.

To assist in labeling your histogram: n = 25, $\Sigma x = 1708$, $\bar{x} = 68.32$.

Step 1: Range: $R = X_{Max} - X_{Min} =$

Step 2: Approximate number of classes: $k = \sqrt{n} =$

Step 3: Class width $h = R/k =$

Step 4: Unit of measurement $m =$

Step 5: Final class width (Do not round this): $h =$

Step 6: First-class lower boundary $(L_1) = X_{Min} - (m/2) =$

Step 7: Lower boundaries of remaining classes:

$L_2 = L_1 + h =$

$L_3 =$

$L_4 =$

$L_5 =$

$L_6 =$

Step 8: Now, return to the raw data and construct a frequency table of the data in the space provided.

Class intervals	Tally	Frequency
Total:		25

Use the grid provided in the appendix (lengthwise) as a guide in developing your histogram.*

Are You a Total Quality Person?

I take personal pride and ownership in my job.

Seldom	Sometimes	Always
☐	☐	☐

*The answer to this problem is shown in the appendix.

2. *Fat & Sassy Ice Cream is a wholesale supplier of ice cream in prepackaged containers. Samples were taken by an independent testing agency and the weights shown (in ounces) were obtained.*

Fat & Sassy Ice Cream Supplier						
9.83	10.17	10.12	9.86	10.14	10.07	9.88
10.13	9.84	10.19	9.86	9.80	9.71	9.94
9.67	10.16	10.10	9.85	9.61	10.13	10.12
10.04	9.85	10.15	10.07	9.87	10.11	9.92
10.12	9.86	9.82	9.95	9.88	10.08	10.14

*Construct a frequency table of Fat & Sassy's data.**

Interpreting Distributions

Once a histogram or a frequency chart (to be discussed) is developed, the shape of the distribution can indicate something about the data. Four major distributions will be discussed:

1. Left-handed (i.e., skewed right) histogram.

2. Comb histogram.

3. Bimodal histogram.

4. Histogram with outlier.

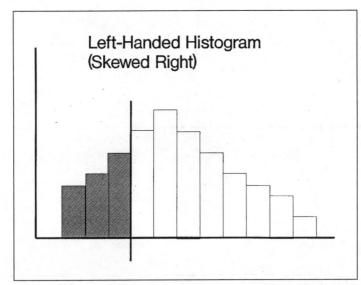

Left-Handed Histogram
(Skewed Right)

Left-Handed (Skewed Right) Histogram

The left-handed histogram shown on the left has several possible interpretations. First, perhaps we are viewing an output from a process that has been 100 percent inspected and some data (events) have been removed.

*The answer to this problem is explained at the end of the next section on interpreting distributions.

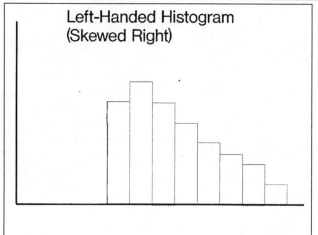

Left-Handed Histogram (Skewed Right)

In reality, we may have what is shown on the left before 100 percent inspection removed the lower shaded area. If this is the case, we need to reduce the dispersion in the process producing the output.

In the previous distribution of traffic fines received by Friendly Texan Insurance Company adjusters, a couple of people committed serious offenses, and the judge "threw the book" at them.

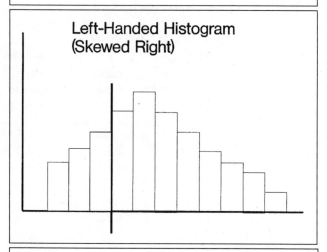

Left-Handed Histogram (Skewed Right)

A second interpretation of the left-handed histogram (shown again on left) is that perhaps small values cannot occur. If so, then no action is required.

Comb Histogram

Comb Histogram

More than likely, this histogram is not constructed properly. Perhaps the data was rounded incorrectly with someone always rounding up, and another person always rounding down.

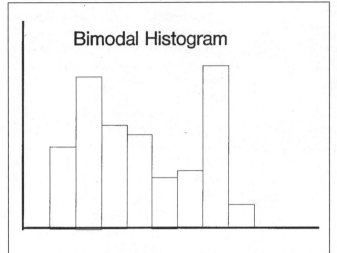

Bimodal Histogram

A possible interpretation is that two different data sets have been mixed. Each data set has a different mean and a different dispersion.

We need to stratify the data and determine if two different histograms should be constructed.

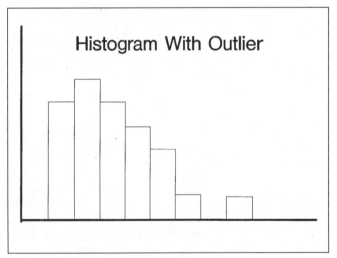

Histogram with Outlier

This outlier needs to be investigated.

If a logical explanation can be given for the removal of the outlier from the data set, then do so, and reconstruct the histogram.

Now It's Your Turn*

1. *Better Ice Cream (BIC) Company sells ice cream to consumers through 20 stores throughout the state. BIC buys many different ice creams for resale, but the largest purchase is a "base" vanilla ice cream container to which flavoring and "goodies" are added to meet a vast range of consumer ice cream demands. For example, any M&M candy combinations, popular candy bars, fruits, and so on are added to the "base" ice cream package upon request.*

   A major problem has just emerged regarding the net weight of the ice cream BIC sells in prepackaged containers. The ice cream in question is purchased in

*The answer to these problems are shown in the appendix.

small containers printed as 10 oz. net weight from suppliers. The state's consumer protection agency sampled package weights and found several containers that contained less than 10 oz. of ice cream.

Tremendous negative publicity about BIC "cheating" the public has emerged, and several papers ran editorials urging the Consumer Protection Agency to closely watch scoundrels such as BIC. To correct the problem, last month, BIC selected 35 samples from each of their three suppliers and submitted the samples to independent testing to determine weights. The results of these tests are shown. However, before all the data analysis could be complete, the statistician left to return to school. Complete the analysis, interpret the data, and advise BIC management on the course of action to be taken.*

Vendor	Total	Average	Low	High
Chubby[a]	353.39	10.10	9.96	10.19
Fat	349.04	9.97	9.61	10.19
Butter	347.16	9.92	9.81	10.07
Total	1049.59	10.00	9.61	10.19

[a]Supplier codes are:

Chubby: Chubby & Chunky Company

Fat: Fat & Sassy Company

Butter: Buttercup Company

BIC Ice Cream Company: Package Weight by Supplier						
C h u b b y						
10.16	10.09	10.15	10.17	10.18	10.18	10.14
10.16	10.11	10.18	10.19	10.17	10.13	10.01
10.09	10.16	10.02	10.18	10.08	10.17	10.04
10.13	10.09	10.09	9.96	10.14	10.02	10.00
10.14	10.05	10.06	10.06	10.01	9.96	10.01
F a t						
9.83	10.17	10.12	9.86	10.14	10.07	9.88
10.13	9.84	10.19	9.86	9.80	9.71	9.94
9.67	10.16	10.10	9.85	9.61	10.13	10.12
10.04	9.85	10.15	10.07	9.87	10.11	9.92
10.12	9.86	9.82	9.95	9.88	10.08	10.14
B u t t e r						
9.98	9.98	9.91	9.97	9.96	9.96	9.96
9.96	9.84	9.87	9.96	9.96	9.96	9.88
9.94	10.03	9.86	9.93	9.82	9.93	10.02
9.81	9.92	9.87	9.88	9.95	9.82	9.85
9.84	9.94	9.85	10.00	9.87	9.84	9.97

*Some of the possible interpretations of this problem are explained in the appendix.

Interpreting Distributions

To assist in developing a histogram, it was decided to plot all three firms on the same axis, starting with Fat & Sassy: n = 35, Σx = 349.04, x = 9.97. (See attached computer program.)

Step 1: Range: $R = X_{Max} - X_{Min} = 10.19 - 9.61 = .58$

Step 2: Approximate number of classes: $k = \sqrt{n} = 6$

Step 3: Class width $h = .58/6 = .0967$

Step 4: Unit of measurement $m = .01$

Step 5: Final class width: $h = .097$. Round up to .10

Step 6: First class lower boundary $(L_1) = X_{Min} - (m/2) = 9.61 - .005 = 9.605$

Step 7: Lower boundaries of remaining classes:

$$L_2 = L_1 + h = \quad 9.605 + .10 = 9.705$$
$$L_3 = \qquad\qquad 9.705 + .10 = 9.805$$
$$L_4 = \qquad\qquad 9.805 + .10 = 9.905$$
$$L_5 = \qquad\qquad 9.905 + .10 = 10.005$$
$$L_6 = \qquad\qquad 10.005 + .10 = 10.105$$

And, the upper boundary for $L_6 = 10.105 + .10 = 10.205$

Step 8: A frequency table of Fat & Sassy's data was constructed as shown.

Class intervals	Tally: Fat & Sassy	Frequency
9.605–9.705	| |	2
9.705–9.805	| |	2
9.805–9.905	||||| ||||| |	11
9.905–10.005	|||	3
10.005–10.105	|||||	5
10.105–10.205	||||| ||||| ||	12
Total		35

This data can then be graphed as shown on the next page. Please complete this graph as an aid in interpreting the data.

It is easier to solve complex problems using the software that is an optional companion to this book. Files on disk include:

HISTO_1	Fat & Sassy data
HISTO_2	Chubby & Chunky data
HISTO_3	Buttercup data

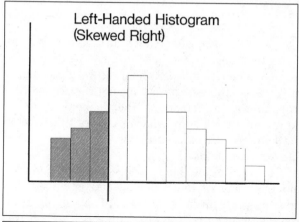

Left-Handed Histogram
(Skewed Right)

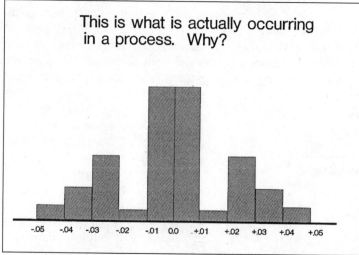

This is what is actually occurring in a process. Why?

2. *A product being produced by a process is measured for acceptance or rejection. The acceptance tolerance is 10.00 in. ± 1 in. Note that there is a low rejection between −.01 and −.02 as well as between + .01 and +.02. Why?*

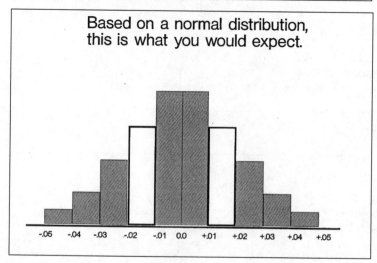

Based on a normal distribution, this is what you would expect.

If you consider a normal distribution, the areas −.01 and −.02 as well as +.01 and +.02 should appear as indicated with "boxed" area. That is, you would expect a far greater rejection that is actually occurring.

Why do you think this might happen in actual practice?*

*The answer to this problem is in the appendix. Please spend a moment thinking about why the histogram could appear as shown. Then check your logic.

Fishbone Diagram

Fishbone Diagram

Cause-and-Effect Diagram

- Helps identify root cause.
- Helps generate ideas.
- Is an orderly arrangement of theories.
- Is helpful in guiding further inquiry.
- The "head" is the effect
  at right of major spine.
- Major activities are in boxes
  at end of minor spines.

A *fishbone diagram*, often called an *Ishikawa diagram*, shows relationships between events. The diagram is useful as a cause-and-effect analysis to help in generating ideas, and in identifying the root cause of a problem for investigation. The fishbone diagram, named because it somewhat resembles the skeleton of a fish, provides a graphic display of the relationship between items.

This technique helps users reach a common understanding of the problem, and is constructed after the problem is identified. A fishbone diagram consists of a central "spine" with a fish's head (the box containing the main activity under discussion) on the right side. There are a number of diagonal ribs coming from the spine. At the end of each rib is a short horizontal box containing the major process steps.

The major process categories are recorded in the horizontal boxes at the end of the ribs. The causes of these categories (subideas) are recorded as short spines off the ribs.

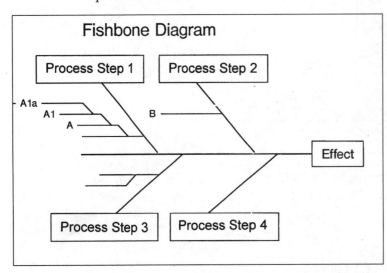

A general example of a fishbone diagram is shown. Notice the "fish head" on right. Ask "why" to identify the major process steps. Ask "why" again to identify the ribs.

Ask "why" five times to identify the fundamental root cause. This should be the last rib on the diagram.

Are You a Total Quality Person?

When in conversations, I make positive
comments that move the discussion forward.

Seldom ☐   Sometimes ☐   Always ☐

Constructing a Fishbone Diagram

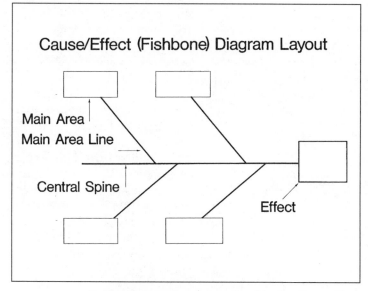

Cause/Effect (Fishbone) Diagram Layout

Main Area
Main Area Line

Central Spine

Effect

Layout the fishbone diagram as shown. Notice that the "effect" is always on the right, in the "fish head." The main area contains the main causes. These main area boxes are connected to the central spine (the main line).

The steps in developing a cause-and-effect diagram are as follows:

1. Start with the problem statement. Use single case boring to develop an understanding of the problem.

2. The "fish head" is the effect. Brainstorm possible causes.

3. Develop major categories (the horizontal boxes at the end of the ribs) by:
   - Stratifying into natural groupings.
   - Stratifying by steps of the process.

4. Write the problem (the effect) in the box on the right.
   - Build the diagram by linking the causes under the appropriate process steps.
   - Lines should flow toward the "effect."

5. Refine categories by asking:
   - What causes this?
   - Why does this condition exist?
   - Ask "why" five times, and build the fishbone until the causes are specific enough to take action on.

6. Walk through the fishbone logic developed in both directions. Little bones represent subclasses and reflect a chain of logic leading from step to step. Suppose A1a causes A1, which causes A, which causes the effect. If A1a is complex, it may be developed as a separate fishbone diagram.

7. The verified root causes are the last bone in the diagram.

Encouraging Employees to Use Fishbone Diagrams

Friendly Texan Insurance Company's Human Resource Department wanted to begin the process of installing TQM in their company. They felt that quality "lectures" were not enough to encourage significant employee involvement in process improvement.

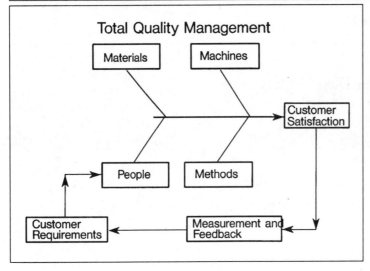

Total Quality Management

Ms. Susan Jackson was assigned the tasks of increasing employee involvement in quality improvement. After much thought she decided to host a series of luncheon workshops on selected quality improvement techniques. Agency employees were invited to a luncheon and were randomly seated, six people to a table.

The first workshop was an overview of TQM and the diagram shown was explained. That is, TQM involves looking at the way we do business with the one major objective in mind: to maximize customer satisfaction. In order to maximize customer satisfaction, we need to evaluate the materials we use, and we need to evaluate what machines, people, and methods are employed.

She then went over the five steps in a Quality Improvement (CQI) story to give the participants an overview of the QI system with the diagram shown. She asked each table to discuss what, in their experience, resulted in a high level of consumer satisfaction. These experiences were discussed, and the group went back to work.

At the second luncheon/workshop she asked the employees (who were sitting at six people to a table) to develop a fishbone application. The immediate question asked was "What process do you want us to develop a fishbone diagram for?" She used a technique called *nominal grouping* (see discussion of technique) where participants identified what they wanted to diagram. They selected the topic of "why does it take one and one-half months (about 45 days) to process an authorized travel reimbursement."

Each table had a transparency master and pens so that the various groups could develop their application. A half-hour was given the various tables to discuss the topic and to develop their fishbone diagrams. The groups then presented

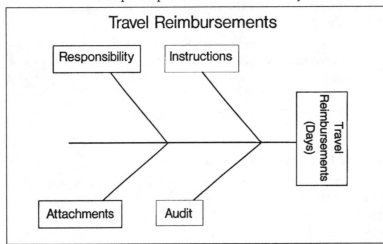

Travel Reimbursements

their diagrams. Major and minor topics varied enormously but no attempt was made to "reach a consensus." The transparencies were collected, photocopied, and distributed to participants a week before they attended the third workshop. The third workshop assignment was to review the the various fishbone diagrams to see if the groups could reach a general consensus on the major topics that "cause" travel reimbursements to consume an average of 45 days elapsed time. The general fishbone diagram shown on the major topics was constructed.

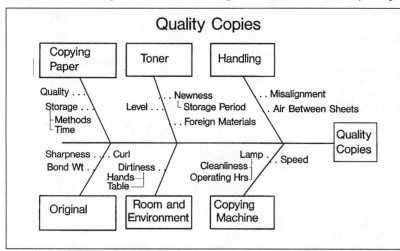

Quality Copies

The manager of accounting at Friendly Texan Insurance's corporate office attended the sessions, but didn't contribute much to the discussions. However, he began thinking. Would it be possible to develop a fishbone diagram to identify why they do not obtain good copies from their office copier? Employees are again complaining about poor quality copies, as they have done for the past decade. The manager thought the problem was solved last year when an expensive, new copier was purchased. Following the previous luncheon format, employees in the Accounting Department met and created the fishbone diagram shown on making quality copies.

Fishbone diagrams are a useful general analysis tool for identifying cause and effect relationships. For example, an attempt was made to identify the pounds of produce available at a farmer's market. On some days there was more produce than could logically be expected to be sold, and on other days, there was not enough produce to meet demand. You can have endless discussions on such an "elusive" topic, but once a fishbone diagram is presented to the group, the discussion becomes more meaningful in that people can focus on cause-and-effect relationships.

Getting Tired of Fishbone Diagrams?

Ishikawa introduced the fishbone diagram in the early 1950s as a problem-solving technique. Perhaps he chose a fish because it is a popular food source in Japan. However, whatever the reason for choosing a fish, we are not stuck with fish in all of our diagrams.

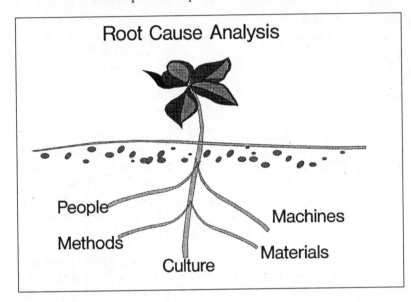

Why not expand the diagram, particularly if you are dealing with special interest groups. For example, gardeners think in terms of plants and weeds. If a weed diagram is used in place of a fish diagram, then the relationships might be easier for the "green thumb" person to understand. Just as you better "pull out the roots" to get rid of a weed, you had better remove the "root cause" to solve a quality problem.

If you are dealing with medical people, then "give them a hand" in solving a problem.

Or perhaps students want to receive a gold star. If so, ask them to fill in under the points of the star.

The opportunities are endless. The important thing to remember is to display relationships clearly.

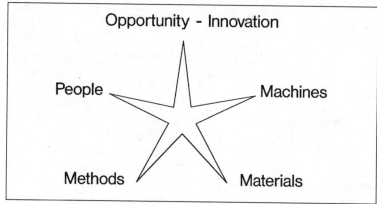

Opportunity - Innovation

People   Machines

Methods   Materials

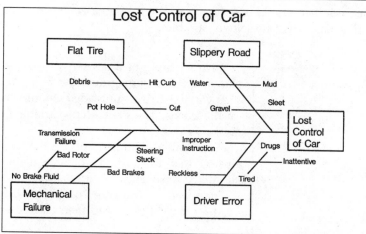

Lost Control of Car

Flat Tire   Slippery Road

Debris   Hit Curb   Water   Mud

Pot Hole   Cut   Gravel   Sleet

Transmission Failure   Improper Instruction   Lost Control of Car

Bad Rotor   Steering Stuck   Drugs

No Brake Fluid   Bad Brakes   Inattentive

Reckless   Tired

Mechanical Failure   Driver Error

Now It's Your Turn

1. *A QI team identified four major causes of urban problems, and sketched the skeleton shown. Develop subtopics (causes) for these categories. Please modify the diagram if you feel that a category should be added or eliminated.*

2. *The manager of a local automobile club is writing an article on driving safety for publication in their magazine. Recently, there have been a rash of accidents where the driver has lost control of the car. People were hurt in these single car accidents which cannot be attributed to driver intoxication.*

The manager felt that if the issues could be presented in a graphic manner, the article that might get their readers thinking about the problem. Please construct a fishbone diagram showing the major and minor issues involved in "the process" which results in a driver losing control of their automobile.*

Scatter Diagram

A *scatter diagram* shows the relationship between two variables; typically a cause and effect condition. Scatter diagrams are used to visually gauge how the change in one variable effects another. As such they are useful in developing problem solutions.

Scatter Diagram (Relationship Diagram)

- Shows relationship between two variables.
- Has high visual impact.
- Helps generate ideas.
- The cause (the independent variable) is shown on the x axis.
- The effect (the dependent variable) is shown on the y axis.

---

*The answers to these problems are in the appendix.

Scatter Diagram

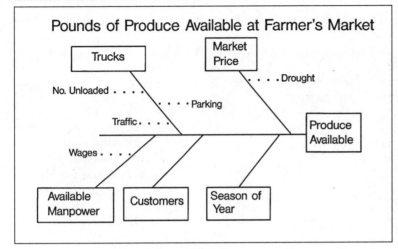

Pounds of Produce Available at Farmer's Market

Suppose a fishbone diagram was created to try to understand why the pounds of fresh produce varied at a farmer's market.

Perhaps the team suspects that the cause of the variation in the pounds of produce available was simply due to the number of trucks unloaded.* In other words, the availability of fresh produce is simply dependent upon the number of trucks unloaded, and neither demand nor weather has anything to do with availability.

If that were the case, they would use either the data available or collect more data to create a scatter diagram of these two variables.

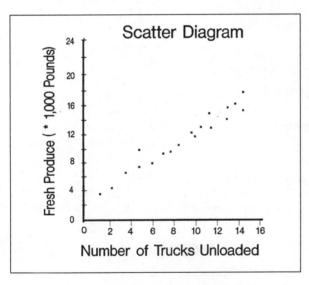

An example of a scatter diagram is shown. In scatter diagrams the independent variable (trucks unloaded) should be on the x axis. The dependent variable is on the y axis.

This scatter diagram supports the conclusion that fresh produce is available simply because trucks are unloaded. That is, independent truckers "drop by" the produce market to unload their trucks.

Steps in Construction of a Scatter Diagram

Step 1: Organize the data.

Step 2: Collect paired data (x, y) and arrange them in a table format. Statisticians prefer at least 30 pairs of data, however, we will accept a dozen or more.

*In reality, cause-and-effect relationships can be very complex.

Step 3: Set up your axis. The x axis is the independent variable. Time is *always* plotted on the x axis. The y axis is the dependent value. Scales should be selected for x and y that show your data without undue distortion.

Step 4: Plot the data. When a point is observed more than once, offset the points slightly.

Now It's Your Turn

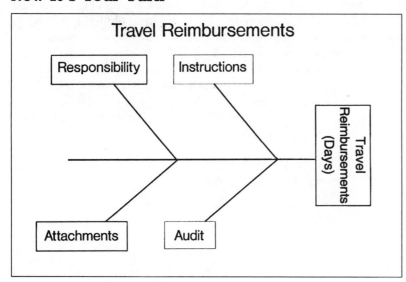

Suppose a QI team con-structed the fishbone dia-gram shown on travel reimbursements. They sus-pect that the cause of the lengthy time to process travel reimbursements is due to the number of expense receipts submitted.

That is, if there are 20 expense receipts, it stands to reason that it would take longer to process the reim-bursement than a reim-bursement with a single expense item such as air-fare.

A QI team then collected data on the number of days to process a travel reim-bursement along with the number of expense receipts (vouchers) attached to the reim-bursement form as shown.

Item number	Number of expense receipts	Days to process reimbursement
1	1	30
2	11	108
3	7	78
4	2	40
5	10	98
6	3	48
7	2	41
8	5	61
9	4	52
10	3	46
11	12	120
12	6	72
13	8	85
14	5	65
15	9	91

Using the grid provided in the appendix, construct a scatter diagram.

Scatter Diagram

Interpreting Scatter Diagrams

A relationship between two variables can take various forms. Our attention will be centered on a straight line relationship, called a linear relationship.

Strong Positive Correlation

If the relationship is such that when one quantity increases, the other quantity also increases, this is called a positive relationship. The previously plotted relationship between the number of expense receipts and the days to process a travel reimbursement shows a strong positive correlation.

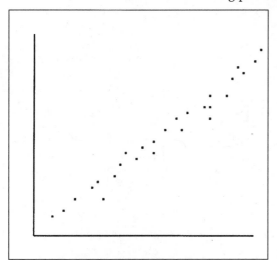

The general form of a positive correlation is shown.

Popular positively correlated variables include:

- Advertising costs and sales.
- High motivation and productivity.
- Speed and traffic accidents.

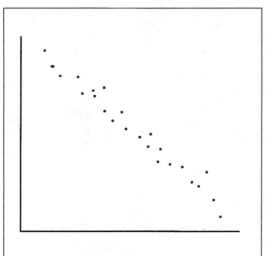

Strong Negative Correlation

If the relationship is such that as one quantity increases while the other decreases, this is a negative relationship.

The general form of a negative correlation is shown.

Popular negatively correlated variables include:

- Hours of training and rejects made.
- Money spent on maintenance and number of machine breakdowns.

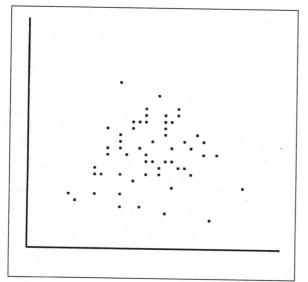

No Correlation

If the relationship between two variables is mixed such that a rise in one quantity may produce either a rise or a fall in another quantity, there is no linear correlation.

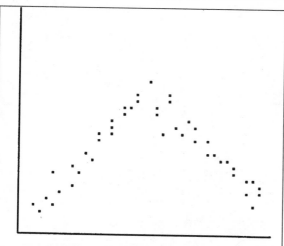

An example of a lack of correlation is shown in the two charts on the left. There may indeed be no correlation between the variables, or perhaps you need to take another look at how the data were stratified.

Run Chart

- Is a visual summary of data. ("A picture is worth a thousand numbers.")
- Shows output of a process over time.
- Shows trends over time.
- Is easy to understand.

All charts should have:
Consistency.
Good labels.
Standard methodology.

Run Chart

A *run chart* (often called a *line graph* or *trend chart*) is used to display output of a process over time. Errors per time period, machine downtime, and productivity are commonly displayed. The main point of any chart or graph is to "make your point" at a glance. Because run charts have a powerful visual impact, they are frequently used as a quality indicator to support a CQI Story.

Run Chart

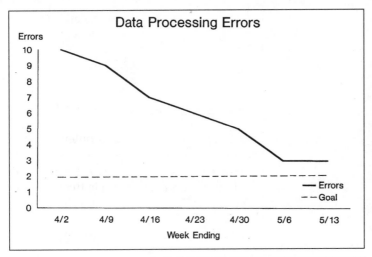

Data Processing Errors

Typical run charts for data processing errors and shipping document errors are shown. Both these charts highlight a trend in errors made over time (in this case, weeks). Also note that a benchmark is shown on both charts. Although both of these charts show a goal because we want to remind everyone that improvements are possible, on some charts it would be useful to show an *average line*.

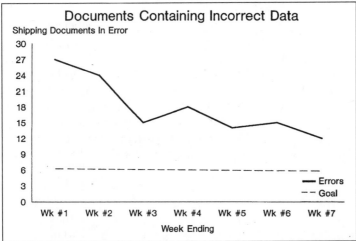

Documents Containing Incorrect Data

The general form of a run chart is shown. The important point is to clearly label all axes. The chart focuses attention on changes in output. At a glance, the chart should highlight meaningful trends or shifts in the output compared to the goal (or average) for the process. (See the section on control chart for tools to focus on statistically significant output changes.)

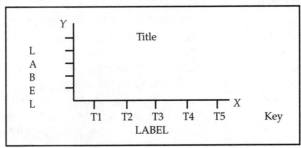

The "trick" in developing a good CQI story is to select the statistical tool that displays the data in a manner that reinforces our theme, problem statement, and analysis. As we often deal with events over time, let's take a closer look at creating a run chart in a standard format.

Format of Run Charts

Title, Date. All charts should have a title describing the graph contents. Often the date the chart was prepared is included.

y Axis. This is the vertical axis, which represents the quantity or frequency of what's being displayed. It must be labeled (have a title) and have a scale.

x Axis. The horizontal axis usually represents time, (normally days, weeks, or months). This is shown as Time1, Time2, etc. along a scale.

Key. A key (legend) explains the items on the chart such as number of errors, goals, etc.

Scale. A scale should be selected that permits the data movement to be clearly seen.

Selection of a meaningful scale, particularly the y axis scale, is often a problem. Here are a few suggestions.

1. Divide the y axis into equally spaced intervals. The range should cover all the existing data points and still allow a "cushion." A general rule when graphing, is to allow an extra 30 percent. That is, if your data ranges from 0 to 100, the top scale on the axis should be about 130.

2. Round off the values you are plotting, and never try to use more than a three digit number. If the actual data is in millions, you can always say (data in millions) but consider your scale to be in hundredths.

For example, suppose your data ranged from 300,000 to 1,200,000, a range of 1,200,000 − 300,000 or 900,000. Since this is close to 1,000,000, consider your scale to be from 1 to 130. Then values such as 300,000 would be plotted as 30. Values such as 875,750 would be rounded to 900,000 and plotted as 90.

A frequently asked question is, "Does the y axis always have to begin at zero?" No, choose your scale so the graph is easy to read. For example, suppose we wanted to display the number of customer complaints received by Friendly Texan Insurance. If we want to highlight the trend that the number of complaints is increasing, a run chart would be a very powerful tool.

Year	Number of complaints
1988	150
1989	170
1990	210
1991	225
1992	250
1993	300

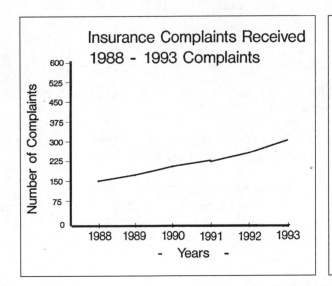

Poor Y Axis
Y value beginning at zero flattens trend.

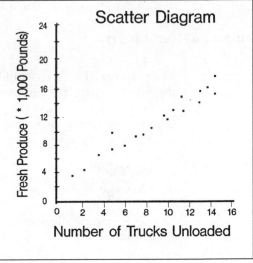

Note Obvious Trend
Y value beginning at 150 emphasizes trend.

Note the two run charts shown that display the data in the table on the number of complaints for years 1988 through 1993.

The graph beginning with a y value at zero flattens out the data too much to be useful. However, the graph beginning with a y value of 150 clearly shows a trend. If you are concerned with a trend in your QI theme, then the statistical tool selected must clearly show a trend in the data.

Rules to Follow When Preparing Run Charts

1. Clearly label all graphs with a title, x and y and axis "headings," scale, and, if appropriate, date prepared and key (legend).

2. Select a logical scale that shows the maximum variability in the data.

3. Explain the major point of the chart in the text, without duplication information unnecessarily. For example, a brief explanation accompanying the complaint chart might be: "Customer complaints have doubled since 1988."

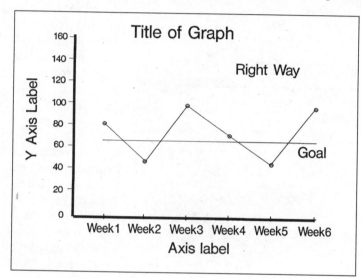

4. Keep the run chart simple. Don't include more than two lines of data on any chart. For example, the run chart shown displays data along with a goal. A display containing both the data and a goal is a reasonable way to show data.

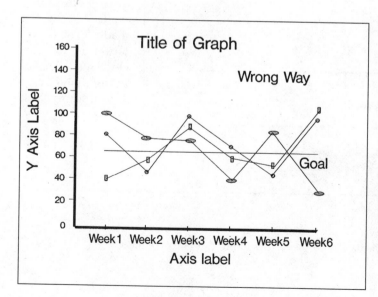

However, if more than two data categories appear on the same chart, the chart becomes difficult to read, which defeats the reason that you were displaying data in a run chart. A general rule to follow when using run charts is: Do not use more than two lines on the same chart because confusion will occur. The run chart shown is overwhelming because it contains too much data.

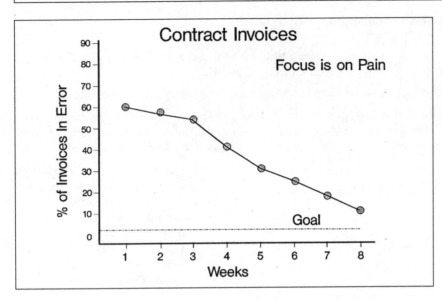

5. Decide which way to show performance indicators. The general rule of thumb is to concentrate on the pain on internal reports. Notice that the chart shown focuses discussion on the pain: There is a high percentage of invoice errors.

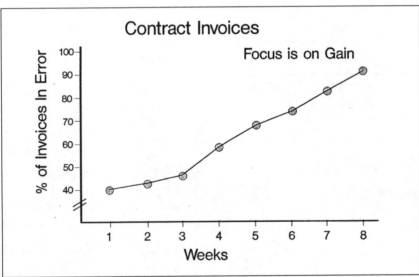

However, on external reports, you might wish to "paint a good picture." The run chart shown presents the data in a rosy picture that says, "look at the great improvement we've made." The temptation is to conclude that, "We are doing well and can afford to slack off."

Are You a Total Quality Person?

I improve the quality of life for others.

Seldom ☐   Sometimes ☐   Always ☐

Now It's Your Turn

The following data was collected on the number of customers who called our Accounting office about a question on their bill. Using the grid shown in the appendix as a guide, construct a run chart.

Months (1994)	Billing calls
January	250
February	300
March	300
April	330
May	333
June	400
July	420
August	420
September	450

Read the appendix to find out how to check your work using the software that is an optional companion to this book.

Control Charts

Control Chart

- Is a visual display of process.
- Helps organize process into manageable size.
- Promotes greater understanding and control of process.
- Shows if process is in statistical control.
- Shows trends over time.

This section requires an understanding of basic statistics. If you are rusty in statistics, then concentrate on developing an understanding of how control charts can be used in your organization. The examples presented will serve as guidelines for you in developing your own applications.

A *control chart* is used to identify statistically significant changes that may occur in a process. These changes, called *variations*, are inherent in all processes and result in variations in the products produced and the services offered. The variation may be large or very small, but it is always present. The trick is to identify the variation and either eliminate it or reduce the variation to a minimum.

The majority of the variation comes from factors which act on the process: changing raw materials and changes due to temperature or seasonality are typical. Many of these changes are slight and simply cause the process to vary in a natural or "normal" pattern. Such natural variations are referred to as *common causes*.

Occasionally, unusual factors will enter into the system, which cause a more severe variation, one that is much more important than all the other variations combined. This excessive variation is due to *special causes*, also called assignable causes. Special causes are the major sources of trouble in the production of a product or delivery of a service, and the variation makes the output pattern fluctuate in an unnatural manner.

Special causes are unpredictable. In service operations often can be traced to the attitude of the customer service representative who may have had "significant negative" variation, hopefully for a brief period.

Types of Variation

Common causes	Special causes
Normal	Abnormal
Typical	Untypical
Usual	Unusual
Small effect (by each)	Large effect (by each)
Predictable	Unpredictable

In manufacturing, process variation is handled by comparing the process output to engineering specifications. If the variation is within specifications, then the item is accepted. If the variations are not within specifications, then the item is either scrapped or reworked.

A service, once delivered, cannot be scrapped or reworked. However, service operations can benchmark customer perceptions and then take brief surveys to determine if significant variations are occurring from what is expected.

We will use control charts to distinguish between common causes (normal) variation and special causes (abnormal) variation in both service and manufacturing organization. Once the reasons for special causes of variation are identified, we can work to eliminate these variations from our processes.

If a process is operating under normal conditions, it will produce an output that will have only slight variations from time to time. (That is, special causes have been found and eliminated.) If these variations are put in graphic form, they will usually produce a bell-shaped curve, called a *normal curve*. The characteristic of this curve is the tendency of most of the data to cluster around some central value.

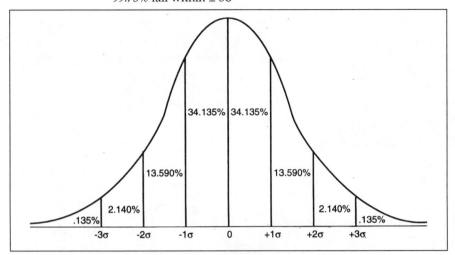

68.27% fall within ± 1σ
95.45% fall within ± 2σ
99.73% fall within ± 3σ

There are three ways of describing the central value: the *arithmetic mean* ($\bar{x}$ or average), the *median* (the middle value when figures are ordered), and the *mode* (the value which occurs most often). A statistic is used in control charts, called the *range R chart*. The *range* is the difference between the largest and smallest numbers in a set of data. This measure of dispersion is quick and easy to compute but has a drawback: an extreme value will distort the range.

Control charts used to measuring the output of a process, frequently both the average ($\bar{x}$) and range (R), are used for a series of samples. The output display is called a *control chart*. The x axis of all control charts contains a grid for the sample number (i.e., normally the day of the sample).

All control charts have three lines:

- A center line which provides the average line of the process.

- An upper line called the *Upper Control Limit* (UCL) drawn at a calculated distance above the center line. Points above the UCL indicate the process is out of control.

- A lower line called the *Lower Control Limit* (LCL) drawn at a calculated distance below the center line. Points below the LCL indicate the process is out of control.

Are You a Total Quality Person?

	Seldom	Sometimes	Always
I attempt to improve the quality of my personal life.	☐	☐	☐

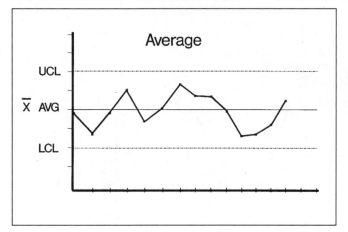

A typical mean $\bar{x}$ chart is shown. Mean charts are computed on process averages. That is, small samples are taken, often daily. The mean of the small sample is calculated and plotted on this type of chart.

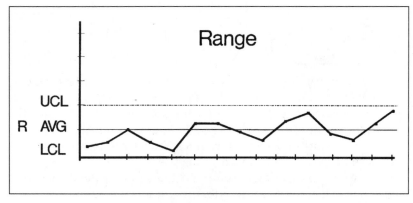

A typical range R-chart is shown. Range charts are computed based on the range (the difference between the highest and lowest values). Notice that the R-chart is "shorter." This is because the LCL of a range chart is typically zero, the x axis itself.

Control charts are used to monitor the performance of a process to determine if the process is in control. Control charts can be classified into two main groups:

1. Control charts for continuous variables.
2. Control charts for discrete (attribute) data.

Control Charts for Continuous Variables

$\bar{x}$ and R *charts* are used to monitor processes with continuous data. Typically both charts are used to monitor a process. The $\bar{x}$ chart reflects how the process average varies over time. The R-chart reflects the dispersion (variation) within the sample taken. Two examples employing $\bar{x}$- and R-charts would include charts to determine if the average weight of a package is in statistical control, or if the average daily sales is in statistical control.

Control Charts for Discrete (Attribute) Data

A *p chart* is used to monitor processes with discrete data output. This is appropriate for problems with percentages of items which are, or are not, meeting specifications. Two examples would include the percent of dissatisfied customers, or the proportion (percent) of damaged packages.

A *c chart* is used to monitor processes with discrete data output from a constant event. Two examples would include the number of errors per form or the daily returns at a service center.

What to Look for When Reading Control Charts

Before we get into the statistics involved in constructing control charts, remember that the purpose of control charts is to be able to interpret what is happening in the process being charted. A process that is in control is one that is stable with the process averages lying within the UCL and LCL limits.

Stable Process is displayed, the associated range *R*-chart

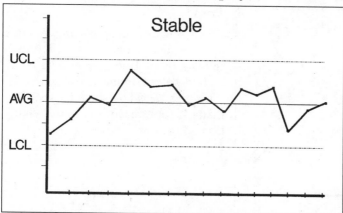

The example shown is for a *stable process* that is in statistical control. The process is in control because there are no points outside the control limits. Although a mean $\bar{x}$ chart is displayed, the associated range R chart would appear in a similar manner for a stable process.

Unstable Process

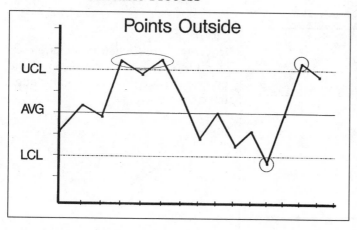

The example shown is an *unstable process* because there are one or more points outside the upper or lower control limits. The process should be stopped and corrected. Stopping and correcting a process can be expensive, so we want to carefully evaluate a control chart to see if we can detect problems likely to occur. The following are examples of unusual patterns within upper and lower control limits that would justify a closer investigation of the process.

Control Charts for Continuous Variables

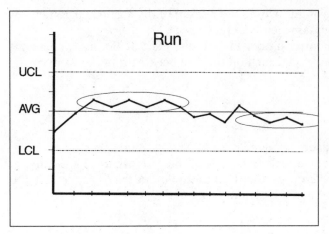

Run

When a series of points occur in sequence above or below the center line, the number of points is called a *run*.

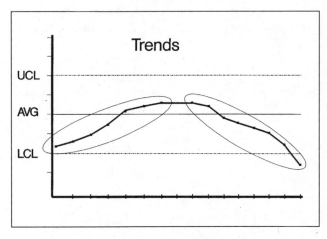

Trend

When a series of points move either upward or downward enmass, this is called a *trend*. Trends should be investigated to determine if the process is "slipping" and adjustments should be made before an out of control condition occurs.

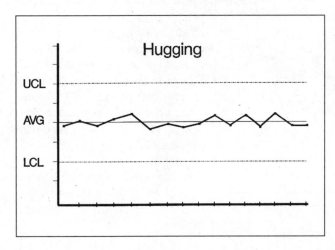

Hugging

Hugging occurs when points are constantly very close to the mean of the process. Notice that such points "hug" the center line.

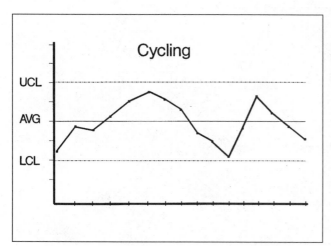

Cycling

Cycling occurs when the data points plotted repeatedly show the same pattern of changes over the same time intervals. External factors such as seasonality might attribute to such a condition.

Ideas for Consideration When Checking an Out of Control Process

✓ Are new or untrained people involved?
✓ Does operator fatigue occur?
✓ Are different methods used by different employees?
✓ Are operators consistently reporting all data, good as well as bad?
✓ Do the samples come from different operators on different machines, on different shifts?
✓ Has there been a change in raw materials?
✓ Have tools become worn?
✓ Has there been a change in maintenance procedures?
✓ Has there been a change in the environment (e.g., temperature, humidity)?

Constructing $\bar{x}$ and R Charts

There are two general types of data: *attribute data* and *variable data*. Attribute data deal with discrete data elements such as: good/bad; yes/no; or go/no go. We will later develop control charts for attributes using a *p* chart. However, our attention is now directed to developing control charts for variable data, the most common type of control charts. *Variable data* take on a range of measurements such as: weights, lengths; heights, and test scores. $\bar{x}$ and *R*-charts with UCL (Upper Control Limits) and LCL (Lower Control Limits) values are used to analyze variable data.

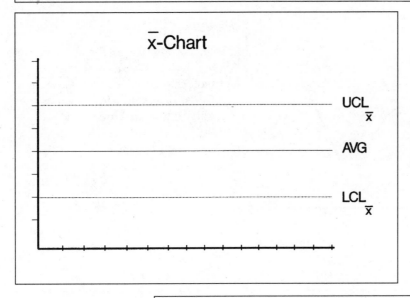

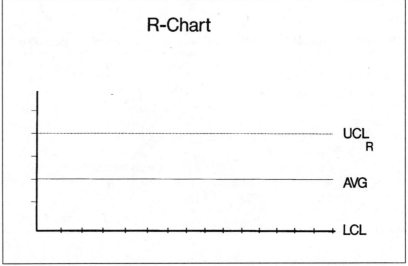

UCL and LCL values correspond to a statistical range of ± 3 standard deviations. That is, control charts detect if the variation is large enough to indicate that the process is out of control.

The values for D_3 and D_4 are from the table on the next page. They are used in the formulas below in computing the LCL_R and UCL_R lines in the R-chart. The LCL_R is often the y axis.

$LCL_R = D_3 * R$

$UCL_R = D_4 * R$

The A_2 value from the table is used in the formulas below to compute the $\text{LCL}_{\bar{x}}$ and $\text{UCL}_{\bar{x}}$ for the for the $\bar{x}$ control chart.

$$\text{LCL}_{\bar{x}} = \bar{\bar{x}} - A_2 * R$$

$$\text{UCL}_{\bar{x}} = \bar{\bar{x}} + A_2 * R$$

A table of standard values for these formulas has been designed to assist in creating control chart limits for the $\bar{x}$ and R chart. This table is used in establishing the UCL and LCL lines, which corresponds to ± 3 standard deviations.

Factors for Computing Control Chart Limits

Number of observations in sample n	Factors for $\bar{x}$ chart A_2	Factors for R-chart	
		D_3	D_4
2	1.880	0	3.268
3	1.023	0	2.574
4	.729	0	2.282
5	.577	0	2.114
6	.483	0	2.004
7	.419	.076	1.924
8	.373	.136	1.864
9	.337	.184	1.816
10	.308	.223	1.777
11	.285	.256	1.744
12	.266	.284	1.717
13	.249	.308	1.692
14	.235	.329	1.671
15	.233	.348	1.652

Sample Problem

For the past six days, samples (weights in ounces) were taken of a process. Using the data shown, create mean and range control charts for the process.

Day of sample	Sample values
Saturday	22, 19, 20
Sunday	21, 20, 17
Monday	16, 17, 18
Tuesday	20, 16, 21
Wednesday	23, 20, 20
Thursday	19, 16, 21

Constructing $\bar{x}$ and R Charts

After constructing the control charts, assume Friday's samples were 15, 14, and 21. Using the charts constructed, is the process in control?

Solution to Process Output Problem

Day	Sample values	R	ΣX	$\bar{X}$
Saturday	22, 19, 20	3	61	20.3
Sunday	21, 20, 17	4	58	19.3
Monday	16, 17, 18	2	51	17.0
Tuesday	20, 16, 21	5	57	19.0
Wednesday	23, 20, 20	3	63	21.0
Thursday	19, 16, 21	5	56	18.7
		22		115.33

$\bar{R} = 22/6 = 3.667;$ $\quad$ $\bar{X} = 115.33/6 = 19.22$

$LCL_R = D_3 * R = 0 * 3.667 = 0$

$UCL_R = D_4 * R = 2.574 * 3.667 = 9.44$

$LCL_{\bar{x}} = \bar{x} - A_2 * R = 19.22 - 1.023 * 3.667 = 15.47$

$UCL_{\bar{x}} = \bar{x} + A_2 * \bar{R} = 19.22 + 1.023 * 3.667 = 22.97$

It is a lot easier to develop control charts if you use the SPC disk that is an option companion to this book.

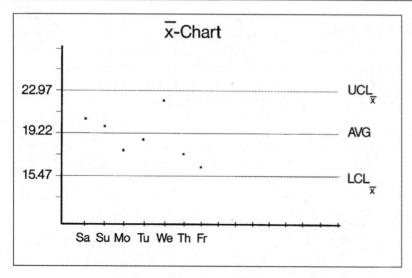

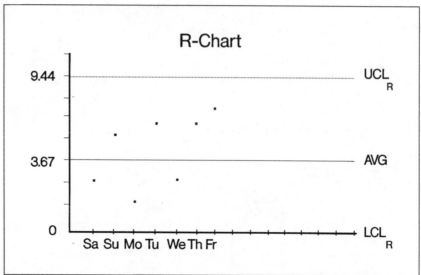

Friday's samples are 15, 14, and 21. $\bar{x} = 50/3 = 16.67$. $R = 7$. Friday's samples are within $\bar{x}$ and R chart ranges: the process is in control.

Now It's Your Turn*

Construct a mean and a range control chart for the problem assigned. Plot the LCL and UCL on the chart provided.

*The answers to these problems are in the appendix.

Constructing x̄ and R Charts

Workshop	Instructor's grade
November	4, 4, 4, 4, 4
December	3, 4, 3, 4, 4
January	3, 0, 4, 4, 4
February	4, 4, 4, 4, 4
March	4, 4, 4, 4, 4
April	3, 4, 3, 4, 3

1. A group of business people have completed a workshop to learn about quality management. At the end of the workshop, participants completed a questionnaire that graded the instructor on a grade range from A (received a lot out of the class) to F (received nothing out of the class). These grades were recorded and assigned the following numeric scores: $A = 4$; $B = 3$; $C = 2$; $D = 1$; and $F = 0$.

A sample of the data for the past six monthly workshops is shown on the left.

(a) Are any of the workshops out of control? Why?

(b) If May's workshop grades were 4, 1, 3, 4, and 4, is May workshop in control? Why? Record your analysis on the forms provided.

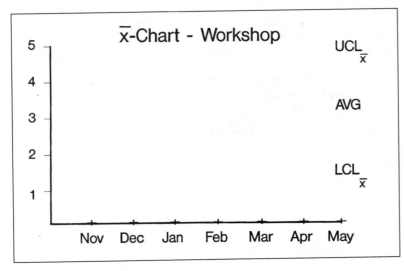

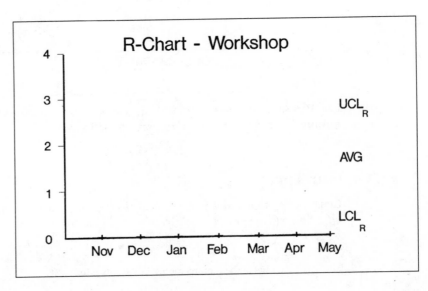

Day	Satisfaction scores
Sunday	18, 19, 20, 20
Monday	21, 20, 20, 20
Tuesday	19, 19, 19, 19
Wednesday	23, 17, 20, 20
Thursday	20, 20, 20, 21
Friday	19, 20, 21, 20

2. *Ajax Corporation monitors their customer satisfaction. Consumers complete a brief questionnaire and place it in a box labeled "How are we doing?" The box is emptied daily and a random sample of four questionnaires is selected. The satisfaction scores (summary of responses to three questions per survey selected) are as shown on the left.*

   (a) *Are any of the days out of control? Why? Record your analysis on the forms provided.*

   (b) *If Saturday's results are 20, 20, 14, and 20, is the process in control? Why?*

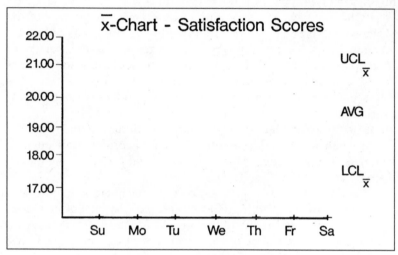

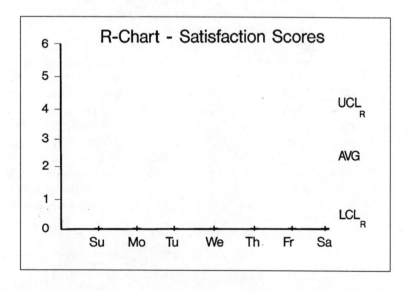

Process Capability

Now that you have learned how to use $\bar{x}$ and R charts to detect when a process is out of control, it is time to take a closer look at the capability of the process itself to produce quality products. Quality leadership stresses the need for continuous quality improvements of both the goods and services themselves, and of the process that produces the goods and services. Why design the best product in the world if the process being used is not capable of meeting product specifications? Deming highlighted the importance of continuous process improvement in his fifth point in which he states management must "Find the Problem." That is, management must focus on continuous improvements of the process itself.

Deming highlighted two types of process variations. The first type he called *common variations* which are system variations accounting for 94 percent of the total variation. The second type of variation identified by Deming was called *special variation* which is under the operator's control and accounted for 6 percent of the total variation. These special variations tend to be unpredictable and account for massive, rapid changes in variation. Management must work with the employee to help them bring their portion of the process under control by eliminating special variations.

Only after all special variation has been eliminated can management turn its attention to the problem of process variation. That is, a process can only be brought under statistical control after the individual special variations are identified and eliminated.

Process capability is the ability of a process (people, machines, materials, and methods) to produce a product or service that will consistently meet design specifications. It is a measure of the capability of the process after all special causes are eliminated and the process is in a state of statistical control (i.e., only exhibiting common variations).

In our previous histogram example on ice cream, assume the design specification for the ice cream cup is a net weight of 10 oz., ± .01 oz. (The words "design specifications" are used interchangeably with "product" or "service" specifications.) The Lower Specification Limit (LSL) weight is 9.99 oz., and the Upper Specification Limit (USL) weight is 10.01 oz. If an ice cream scoop is used to place the product in a cup, there will probably be a large percent of rejections (i.e., cups that do not conform to the LSL and USL specifications).

The process is not capable of meeting design specifications because an ice cream scoop is too crude a device to hold these tight specifications. The only way to achieve the desired LSL and USL limits is to 100 percent inspect (weight) each package and to adjust those packages outside the specification limits. Even then, inspection errors will undoubtedly result in some products "slipping" through the system. We need to either widen the specifications or invest in a new technology.

There are three components to process capability:

1. The product specifications.

2. The centering of the natural process variation.

3. The range (spread) of the variation.

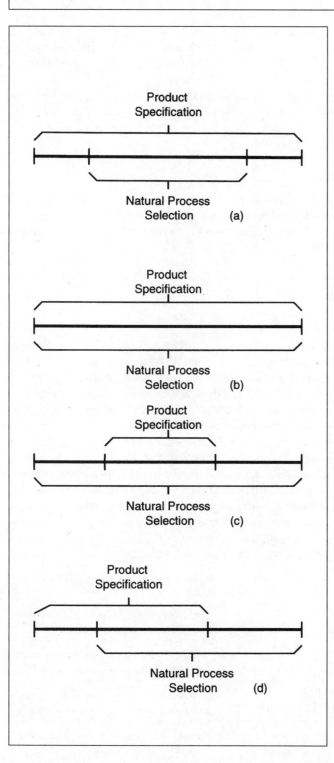

For example, in Fig. (a), the product specifications are such that the natural (common) process variation occurs within the product specifications. This process will be able to produce products that conform to specifications as long as the process remains in control.

In Fig. (b), the product specifications are the same as the natural process variations. Most of the products produced will be acceptable but there will still be a small percentage of nonconforming products. The process will have to be monitored closely.

In Fig. (c), the product specifications are tighter than the natural process variations. It is impossible for this process to meet product specifications, even when the process is under control. If the product specifications cannot be relaxed, then the process must be improved so that it is consistently capable of producing within specifications.

In Fig. (d), the product specifications are the same as the natural process variations, but the process average is off center. A large portion of the output will not meet specifications, although the process itself may seem to be in control. Adjustments should be made to move the process to conform to specifications. You might be tempted to conclude that a process should be established such as shown in Fig. (b), where the product specifications are the same as the natural process variations. However, remember a normal distribution ($\pm 3\sigma$) contains 99.73 percent of the output. This means that 0.27 percent of the output will fall outside the tolerance range, which translates 2.7 defects per thousand. A car with 5000 parts would then contain an average of 13.5 defects. Or consider a space shuttle with 1,000,000 parts. A "seemingly acceptable" defect rate of 0.27 percent is actually 2700 defects per million, an obviously unacceptable number of defects in a shuttle.

Companies are now talking design tolerances of six sigmas ($\pm$ 6σ). This six-sigma quality level translates into 3.4 defects per million. A six-sigma level has become the goal of world class quality systems, and to achieve this goal, we will have to closely analyze process capabilities.

Measurements of Process Capability

We will be using four process capability measurements: C_p, C_{pu}, C_{pl}, and C_{pk}. These process capability measurements relate the spread of the product specification limits to the natural process variation. The measurements can be used with the following process assumptions:

1. The process is stable and all special variations have been eliminated.

2. The process is normally distributed.

3. Variable data is used.

C_p is concerned with a centered, two-sided process. That is, if our ice cream net weight specification was 10 $\pm$ .01 oz., then this statistic could be used. However, if the supplier was only concerned with *not* exceeding the upper specification limit (i.e., giving too much product) they would have a specification of 10 +.01 oz. This is a one-sided process with an USL of 10.01 with no lower specification. In this case, a C_{pu} measurement would be used.

However, if the Consumer Protection Agency reads that an ice cream has a net weight of 10 $\pm$ .01 oz., their concern might be that the vendor is not shipping less than 9.99 oz. This again is a one-sided process, with a LSL of 9.99 but with no upper specification. In this case, a C_{pl} measurement would be used.

C_{pk} is a more common overall process index than C_p and is used to summarize a process's ability to meet a two-sided specification limit. C_{pk} penalizes the process if it is not centered by taking the minimum of C_{pl} and C_{pu}.

The equations used for these measurements are as follows:

Index	Equation	Purpose
C_p	$\dfrac{USL - LSL}{6\sigma}$	Summarize process potential to meet two-sided specification limits.
C_{pu}	$\dfrac{USL - \bar{\bar{x}}}{3\sigma}$	Summarize process potential to meet a one-sided upper specification limit.
C_{pl}	$\dfrac{\bar{\bar{x}} - LSL}{3\sigma}$	Summarize process potential to meet a one-sided lower specification limit.
$C_{pk} = Min\ (c_{pl},\ c_{pu})$		Summarize process potential to meet two-sided specification limits.

The formula for the standard deviation of a population (σ) is shown. As it is often not practical to study a population, the standard deviation of a sample (s) is used to approximate the standard deviation of a population.

$$\sigma = \sqrt{\dfrac{\displaystyle\sum_{i=1}^{n}(X_i - \bar{x})^2}{n}} \qquad\qquad s = \sqrt{\dfrac{\displaystyle\sum_{i=1}^{n}(X_i - \bar{x})^2}{n-1}}$$

If the standard deviation of a sample (s) is not available, then σ can be used to approximate s. An example of this is shown using C_p.

$$C_p = \dfrac{USL - LSL}{6\sigma}$$

where $\hat{\sigma} = \dfrac{\bar{R}}{d_2}$

$\bar{R}$ = the average of the subgroup ranges

d_2 = a tabled value based on the subgroup sample size

Factors for Estimating $\hat{\sigma}$

n	d_2
2	1.128
3	1.693
4	2.059
5	2.326
6	2.534
7	2.704
8	2.847
9	2.970
10	3.078

Let's take a closer look at what the various C_p values mean. A C_p value of 1.0 occurs when the spread of the design specifications equals the natural process variations. As can be seen in the graph, the process is meeting specifications, but the process will be making a minimum of 0.27 percent rejects.

A C_p < 1 indicates the process variations are exceeding the spread of the design specification. Defects are being produced. A C_p > 1 indicates the process variation is less than the spread of the design specifications. However, defects may still be made if the process is not centered on the target value.

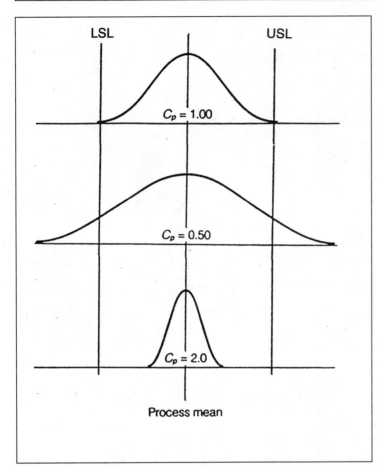

LSL   USL

$C_p = 1.00$

$C_p = 0.50$

$C_p = 2.0$

Process mean

Process meets specifications, with .25 percent rejects.

Numerous defects are produced.

Few defects are produced, provided process is centered.

This brings up an important point. Although C_p relates the spread and the product specification to the process variation, the index does not take into consideration how well the process average $\bar{X}$ is centered on the target value. That's why we use the C_{pk} index, which is the minimum of C_{pl} and C_{pu}.

An example will help demonstrate how these statistics are used. Suppose a control chart was maintained on a process and the following statistics were produced:

$$\bar{X} = 212.1 \qquad \bar{R} = 1.3 \qquad n = 6$$

Product specifications are 211 ± 2 (LSL = 209, USL = 213).

$$\hat{\sigma} = \frac{\bar{R}}{d_2} = \frac{1.3}{2.534} = .513$$

$$C_p = \frac{USL - LSL}{6\hat{\sigma}} \qquad \frac{213 - 209}{6\,(.513)} = \frac{4}{3.078} = 1.30$$

So far the process is "looking good." Technically, a C_p or for that matter, a C_{pk} value of 1.33 is considered very good, and a value of 2.0 or higher is excellent. Now let's take a closer look at the capability of the process to meet its lower specification limits.

$$C_{pl} = \frac{\bar{X} - \text{LSL}}{3\sigma} = \frac{212.1 - 209}{3\,(.513)} = \frac{3.1}{1.539} = 2.01$$

This is an excellent statistic. The process is capable of meeting its lower specification limit. Finally, let's take a look at the capability of the process of meeting its upper specification limit.

$$C_{pu} = \frac{\text{USL} - \bar{X}}{3\sigma} = \frac{213 - 212.1}{3\,(.513)} = \frac{.9}{1.539} = .58$$

Oops, the process is not capable of meeting its upper specification limit. What happened is that the process is not centered and rejects will be produced as shown by the shaded area. C_{pk} = min of C_{pl} and C_{pu} which is .58. That is, the process as it exists is not statistically capable of meeting product specifications.

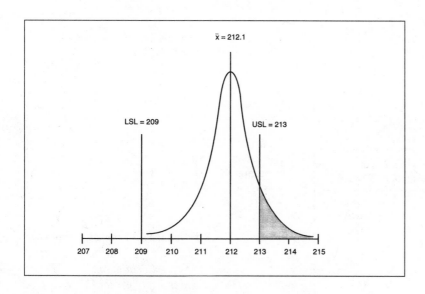

Are You a Total Quality Person?

I set personal goals.

Seldom   Sometimes   Always

☐   ☐   ☐

Now It's Your Turn*

1. *Fishing For Fun Company (FFF) produces graphic shafts for specialized manufacturing needs as a sideline to their basic business of manufacturing fishing rods and reels. The production process produces rods that are normally distributed with a mean of 12.00 in. and a standard deviation of .11 in.*

   Alpha company wants to buy these shafts for use in their products. They require rods between 12 in. ± .1. What is the capability of FFF's process to meet Alpha's needs?

2. *Burpie, a national bottling company of private brand soft drinks wants to make Big Gulp, a local firm, the bottler of their new 16 oz. drinks. Burpie obtained a sample of 100 bottles of the 16 oz. soft drinks that Big Gulp currently bottles and subjected them to an analysis. The mean net liquid ounces was 15.9 with a standard deviation of .1 oz.*

   Burpie's specifications are 16 oz., ± .3 oz. Will Big Gulp be able to meet Burpie's needs? Support your answer.

3. *Delphi Foods company produces prepackaged frozen foods in bulk for wholesaler to add to their packaged frozen foods. These are bulkpacked, but individually frozen so they can be "scooped" out and added to industrially produced products such as TV dinners. Delphi's product lines and their specifications are:*

Delphi's Product Statistics

Product prepackage	Mean weight (oz.)	Standard deviation (oz.)
Peas	2.1	.1
Carrots	3.1	.1
Potatoes	3.0	.02
Hamburger	6.0	.1

Food Weight Specification
US Government Specification WW-10

Product	Mean weight (oz.)	Lower weight Specification[a] (oz.)
Peas	2.0	−.1
Carrots	3.0	−.2
Potatoes	3.0	−.1
Hamburger	6.0	−.4

[a]This is how much "less" than the mean weight that is acceptable.

Eat Well Institutional Foods wants to purchase from Delphi for use in their TV dinners they sell to institutional buyers (notably state and governmental food services). These agencies buy food that is purchased to weight specification WW-10 which is shown.

What problems can Eat Well anticipate if they use Delphi's prepackaged foods? Defend your answer.

*The answer to these problems are shown in the appendix.

Constructing *p* Charts

A *p chart* is used for attribute data such as percent defective, where a large number of potential defects can occur, but the actual number that do occur tend to be small. This includes applications such as blemishes on an appliance surface or typographical errors on a page of text.

A *p chart* is typically drawn at $p \pm 3\sigma_p$. *p* represents the average defects for the process, and *n* is the small sample size.

$$\sigma_p = \sqrt{\frac{p\,(1-p)}{n}}$$

p charts are used for attribute inspection and the 99.7 percent of the data lie within the LCL_p and UCL_p of $\bar{p} \pm 3\sigma_p$. A range chart is not required when using *p* charts. For example, suppose 100 records entered by the data-entry people processing medical forms were sampled daily for 20 days. A table was then constructed to identify the number of errors (shown as errors) and the percent defective (shown as %).

Data Entry Errors: Insurance Forms

S#	Errors	%	S#	Errors	%
1	5	.05	11	1	.01
2	0	.00	12	8	.08
3	6	.06	13	6	.06
4	1	.01	14	7	.07
5	4	.04	15	5	.05
6	2	.02	16	4	.04
7	5	.05	17	11	.11
8	3	.03	18	3	.03
9	3	.03	19	0	.00
10	2	.02	20	4	.04

Total: 80

Are You a Total Quality Person?

I have specific plans to improve the quality of my personal life.	Seldom ☐	Sometimes ☐	Always ☐

Constructing *p* Charts

A *p* chart with control limits that include 99.7 percent of the variation in the medical data entry can be computed as shown.

$$\bar{p} = \frac{\text{Total number of errors}}{\text{Total number of records examined}} = \frac{80}{100 * 20} = .04$$

$$\sigma_p = \sqrt{\frac{p\,(1 - p)}{n}}$$

$$\sigma_p = \sqrt{\frac{(0.04)\,(1 - 0.04)}{(100)}} = \quad 0.02$$

$$\text{UCL}_p = \bar{p} + 3\sigma = .04 + 3(.02) = .10$$

$$\text{LCL}_p = \bar{p} - 3\sigma = .04 - 3(.02) = 0.0$$
(We cannot have below zero)

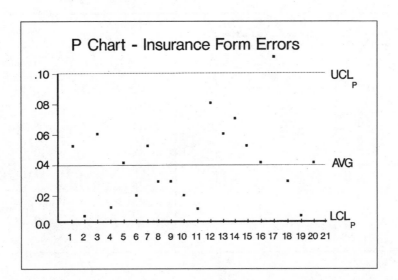

Are You a Total Quality Person?

	Seldom	Sometimes	Always
I personally attempt to master something new, at least quarterly.	☐	☐	☐

Now It's Your Turn*

Pretty Lady: Hosiery	
Sample	Defects
1	1
2	0
3	1
4	1
5	1
6	5
7	0
8	1
9	1

1. *Pretty Lady Clothing store sampled incoming shipments from their hosiery supplier. Nine samples of 10 dozen packages (120 products) where taken and the defects were recorded as shown. record your analysis on the form provided to determine if any of the samples indicated the vendor was "out of control."*

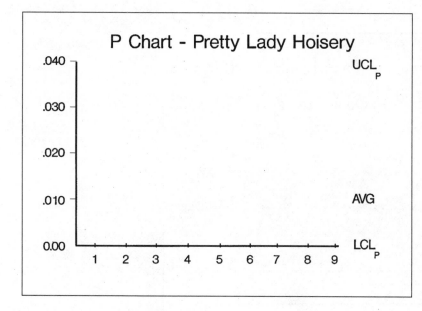

2. *Fresh Products, Inc. produces frozen products using highly automated processes. They sampled individual cartons of frozen products daily to identify if the products are packed according to specification GL12.4. The sample size is one gross (144 packages) for each of the 30-day period shown on the next page. (S# is Sample Number, Errors is the packaging errors found). Record your analysis on the form provided.*

*The answers to these problems are shown in the appendix.

Constructing *p* Charts

Packing Errors

S#	Errors	S#	Errors
1	0	16	0
2	1	17	0
3	1	18	1
4	0	19	0
5	1	20	1
6	1	21	0
7	0	22	0
8	1	23	0
9	1	24	0
10	0	25	4
11	1	26	1
12	3	27	0
13	0	28	0
14	0	29	0
15	0	30	1

Develop the appropriate control chart. After establishing this chart, was the process out of control for any of the days? Suppose the following packing errors were encountered. Is the process out of control for either day 31 or day 40? Record your analysis on the form provided.

(a) Day 31: 2 packing errors
(b) Day 40: 4 packing errors

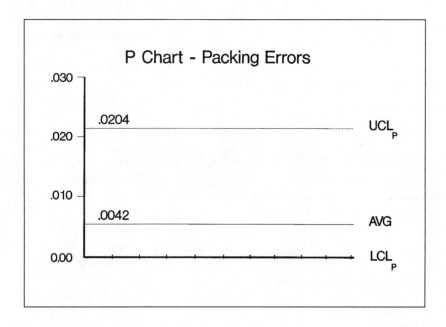

Supporting Quality Improvement Tools

Pie Chart		
Description	Purpose	Method
Divided circle with pieces arranged in descending order starting with the largest at top	Shows percent each item (piece of the pie) makes up of the whole.	Develop "pieces" by multiplying percent times 360° to aid in plotting.

The basic Quality Improvement (QI) tools previously discussed are general tools that can be used in all QI improvement applications. This chapter offers more specialized tools that are designed to enhance your QI skills.

Excessive Paperwork Categories

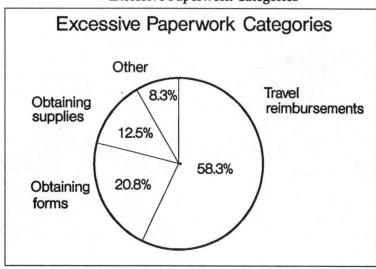

Supporting Quality Improvement Tools

Bar Chart

Description	Purpose	Method
Shows data as separated rectangles (bars) of equal width and of different heights.	Compares differences in quantities for discrete data.	x axis shows categories and y axis shows the measurement.

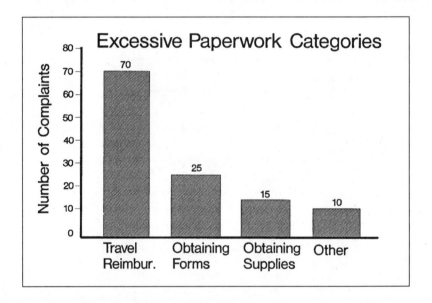

Horizontal Bar Chart

Description	Purpose	Method
Compares "before" and "after" using separate rectangles (bars) of equal width and of different lengths.	Compares differences in quantities for discrete data.	x axis shows measurement. y axis different categories.

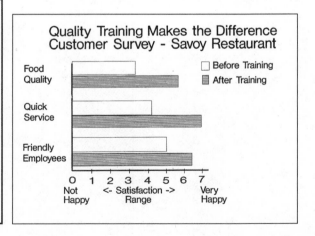

Stratification

Description	Purpose	Method
Separates data into categories of concern.	Adds meanings to a seemingly random group of data.	Trial and error approach where categories are identified and totaled.

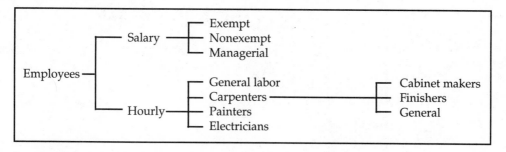

Frequency Chart

Description	Purpose	Method
Used with discrete data to show distribution of data.	Compares Differences in quanatities for discrete data.	x axis shows categories. y axis shows quantity.

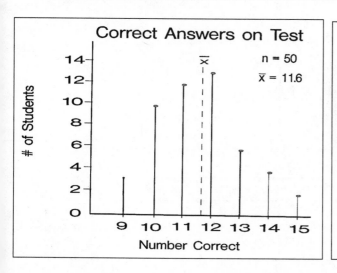

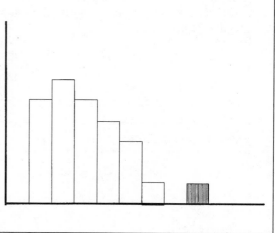

Supporting Quality Improvement Tools

Single Case Boring

Description	Purpose	Method
Conduct an in-depth evaluation of an unusual single case.	To develop an understanding of the event in question.	Investigate what caused the unusual case.

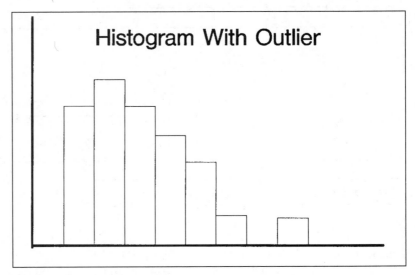

Likert Scale

Description	Purpose	Method
A seven-point scale ranging from strongly disagree to strongly agree used in questionnaires.	To measure subjective data.	Questionnaire is administered to identify strengths of opinions.

Likert Rating Scale

		← Disagree	Neutral	Agree →		
1 Disagree Very Strongly	2 Disagree Strongly	3 Disagree	4 Neither Agree nor Disagree	5 Agree	6 Agree Strongly	7 Agree Very Strongly

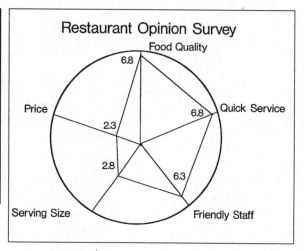

Radar Chart

Description	Purpose	Method
A circle divided into "slices" representing questions. Answers plotted along slices from center.	Represents relative strengths of important activities.	A line from the circle's center represents an activity. Particularly useful to show Likert scales.

Pie Chart

Pie Chart

- Is a circular graph used to compare the relative magnitudes of items by slices of the pie.
- Shows proportions (arrange items in descending order starting with the largest at the top).
- Furnishes a quick, visual indicator of relative importance of items shown.

A *pie chart* is a circular graph which compares the relative magnitudes of the parts under discussion by slices of the pie. The chart shows the percentage an item contributes to a whole.

A pie chart is constructed by first converting a table of events into cumulative percentages, beginning with the largest category and proceeding to the smallest. A pie chart can be visualized as a clock with 12:00 noon at the top (0 percent), 3:00 at 25 percent, 6:00 at 50 percent, and 9:00 at 75 percent. If there is an "other" category, it should be shown as the last slice of the pie chart.

Plot the cumulative percentages which occur and label each wedge. It's often helpful to multiply the cumulative percentage times 360 (360° in a circle) as an aid in plotting the chart.

Excessive paperwork categories	#	%	Cum. %	Degrees
Travel reimbursements	70	58.3	58.3	210°
Obtaining "standard" forms	25	20.8	79.1	285°
Obtaining supplies	15	12.5	91.6	330°
Other paperwork	10	8.3	100.0	360°
Totals	120			

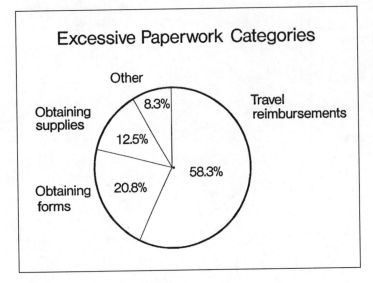

Excessive Paperwork Categories

Other
Obtaining supplies
8.3%
12.5%
Travel reimbursements
58.3%
Obtaining forms
20.8%

Now, you are ready to plot your pie chart, using the excessive paperwork categories identified.

Begin the first line at the 12:00 noon position and proceed around the clock as shown.

Now It's Your Turn

Suppose a QI team wanted to use a pie chart to show the type of parking tickets issued to claims adjusters.

Types of parking tickets	Number of tickets in 1993
No permit	90
Unauthorized area	50
Handicap space	30
Out of area	20
Other	10
Total	200

Construct a pie chart of the types of parking tickets. Use the blank pie chart form provided in the appendix as a guide.

Are You a Total Quality Person?

I volunteer to help others in need.

Seldom	Sometimes	Always
☐	☐	☐

Bar Chart

Bar Chart

- A graph that compares different quantities by means of rectangles (bars) whose length is proportional to the number represented.
- Used with discrete data.
- Bars are arranged vertically.
- Provides order to the activity.
- Provides a quick visual reference.

A *bar chart* is a graph which is used to compare different quantities by means of bars (rectangles). All the bars have the same width, but the bar height is proportional to the number being represented.

A bar chart is made by displaying the items being compared on the horizontal (x) axis. Frequencies are shown on the vertical (y) axis. A typical y axis include discrete data such as the number of rejects and/or occurrences of the items shown in the bars.

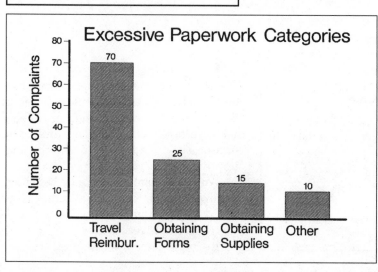

An example of a bar chart is shown for our previous discussed categories of excessive paperwork. Note that the bars do not touch and that each bar is labeled.

A bar chart begins with the highest occurrence on the left, proceeding to the smallest occurrence on the right.

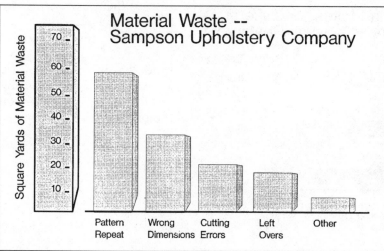

With a little ingenuity, bar charts can be used to display data in an eyecatching manner. For example, notice the material waste from Sampson Upholstery Company. It is easy to see that problems involving pattern repeats (repeating pattern designs) is creating the largest scrap.

Now It's Your Turn

Develop a bar chart to display the type of parking tickets received by Friendly Texan Insurance Company's adjusters. Use the forms provided in the Appendix (lengthwise) as a guide in developing your chart.

Types of parking tickets	Number of tickets in 1993
Parking without a permit	90
Parking in unallowed area	50
Parking in handicap space	30
Parking over line; and/or taking two spaces	20
Other	10
Total	200

Horizontal Bar Chart

> **Horizontal Bar Chart**
>
> - Chart that compares different quantities by means of rectangles (bars) whose length is proportional to the number represented.
> - Used with discrete data.
> - Bars are arranged horizontally.
> - Provides order to the activity.
> - Provides a quick visual reference, useful when comparing two items.

A *horizontal bar chart* is a specialized bar chart used to compare items, such as a "before" and an "after" condition. When making a horizontal bar chart, often one condition is shaded to highlight the "improvements."

An example of a horizontal bar chart is shown. In this case, a restaurant conducted a consumer survey before and after their employees received training in quality improvement techniques.

When two items are shown such as this before and after condition, make sure your shading is "drastically" different to allow for variations in photocopying (more on this in the section on Radar Charts).

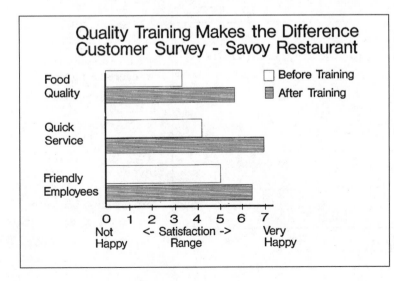

Now It's Your Turn*

1. *Develop a horizontal bar chart to display the miles per gallon (MPG) increase in cars using the new RoadMaster carburetor. Use the form provided in the appendix (lengthwise) to display the data shown below for the performance boost experienced by cars using the new carburetor.*

Car make/model	MPG from factory	MPG with new carburetor
Pontiac Grand Am	18	24
Ford Probe GT	21	26
Nissan 240 SX	17	21

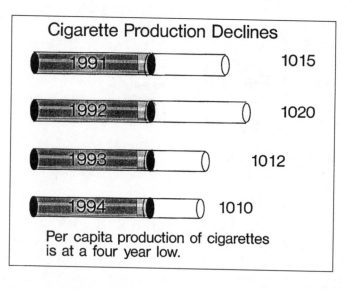

2. *What's fundamentally wrong with this horizontal bar chart?*

Frequency Chart

Frequency Chart

- Displays dispersion of discrete data and when there are < 20 unique values.
- Data displayed using "spikes," not bars.
- Number on x axis are whole numbers.
- y axis contains number of occurrences.

Frequency charts are used to display the dispersion of data in a distribution. They are used with small numbers (less than 20 unique data values) of discrete data. Histograms were also used to display data, however, continuous data was used.

For example, suppose 50 people completing a QI workshop were given a 15-item test on the concepts they studied. A table was then constructed with the students having the number of correct

*The answers to these problems are shown in the appendix.

answers as shown. That is, 3 students scored 9 correct answers, and 2 students answered all 15 answers correct.

Note that there were only seven discrete events. That is, the categories of correct answers were 9, 10, 11, 12, 13, 14, and 15. Also note there can only be a whole number in a category (i.e., such as a person answering 9 correct answers). That is, the data is discrete.

Correct answers	Number of Students with That Number Correct
9	3
10	10
11	12
12	13
13	6
14	4
15	2
n =	50

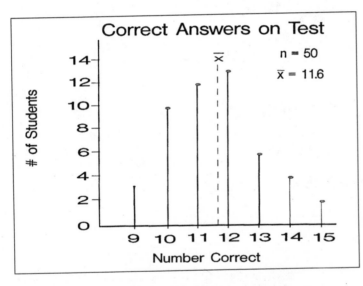

Whenever exact whole numbers are to be displayed, a frequency chart, not a histogram is technically preferred.

When constructing a frequency chart:

- Use with discrete data with less than 20 different values.
- Use "spikes," not "bars."
- Use a title that describes the data.
- Show $\bar{x}$ and n.
- x axis lists whole numbers (counts).
- y axis contains the number of occurrences. Use whatever increments that are appropriate.

Using Frequency Charts Versus Histograms

Frequency charts: Use for discrete data *and* the number of unique values is < 20.

Histograms: Use for continuous data *or when* the number of unique values is ≥ 20.

Always use a histogram for continuous data. For discrete data, the value of 20 is an approximate range, that in reality is from 10 to 20. The key issue for discrete data is not to get "hung up" on statistical rules. Use the chart that gives the best picture of the data.

Now It's Your Turn*

Suppose a QI team wanted to use a frequency chart to display the type of parking tickets received by Friendly Texan Insurance Company's adjusters. Develop a frequency chart using the form provided in the appendix.

Types of parking tickets	Number of tickets in 1993
No permit	90
Unauthorized area	50
Handicap space	30
Out of area	20
Other	10
Total	200

> Read the appendix, and use the software that is an optional companion to this book to check your answers.

Are You a Total Quality Person?

I have a healthy, positive outlook on life.

Seldom ☐   Sometimes ☐   Always ☐

---

*The answer to this problem is shown in the appendix.

Stratification

Stratification
<ul><li>Breaks down a general category into smaller, related subgroups.</li><li>Permits a more precise analysis of the data by focusing on subgroups.</li><li>Encourages problem evaluation from different "angles."</li><li>Useful in identifying which subcategory contributes to the problem under analysis. (A bar chart is often used to display the subcategory.)</li></ul>

Stratification involves the separation of data into categories. It breaks down a whole category (total area of concern) into smaller, related subgroups to identify possible causes of a problem. Stratification can be used throughout a CQI story to identify which categories contribute to the problem under analysis.

Stratification is a natural way of adding logic to a semingly random group of data. A building company might stratify their employees as shown.

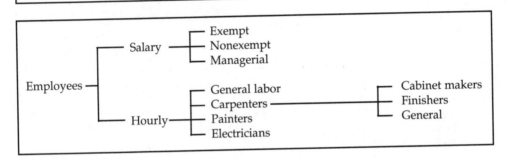

Let's take a closer look at our builder. The builder sells a house to a real estate firm only if the house passes inspection. An inspection consists of a professional inspector who carefully goes over the house and makes a record of the defects that must be corrected. These defects are expensive for the builder to correct, because final payment for the house does not occur until all problems are resolved.

Suppose a QI team looked into the problem to see if anything could be done to reduce the defects which have increased 20 percent in the past year.

Now It's Your Turn*

1. *Write the theme for this builder's CQI story.*

Next, write the problem statement for this QI team.

How might the analysis proceed?

*The answer to this problem is shown in the appendix.

After construction of the appropriate theme and problem statement, an analysis might begin by developing job categories for workers (carpenter, plumber, electrician, painter, etc.). The defects identified could then be classified into the appropriate job category. Defect rate by category can then be computed as an aid in interpreting the data.

Steps in Stratifying Data

Step 1: Select the variables to be stratified.

Step 2: Establish categories to be used (either discrete or a range of values).

Step 3: Count the number of observations for each category.

Step 4: Display the results. Bar type of graphs are a quick method for displaying stratified data. Perform a second-stage stratification when needed.

Although data stratification can point to possible causes of a problem, further investigation is needed to determine if the subclass is the actual cause of the problem.

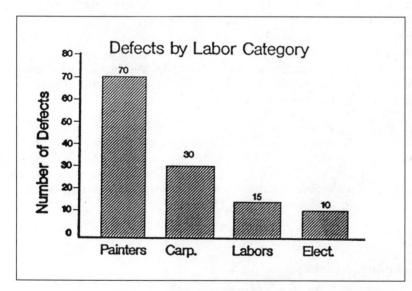

Suppose the builder's QI team collected data on the defects that occurred over the last year. A single stage stratification was then performed and the chart shown was constructed.

Key:

Labors: General Laborers

Carp.: Carpenters

Painters: Painters

Elect.: Electricians

After analyzing the data, the QI team remembered that the builder has two construction teams. There is the East team who has worked together for the past eight years, and there is the new West team that was developed last year in response to an increase in business.

A two-stage stratification was calculated and a chart was constructed as shown on the following page. This indicates that further investigation should be made of the West team's painters to identify the root cause of the problem.

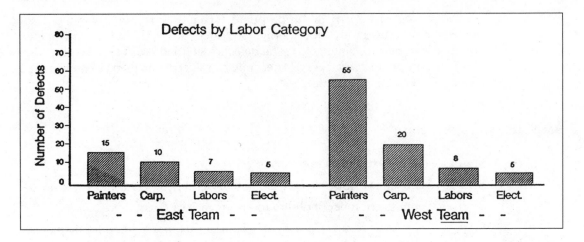

Defects by Labor Category

Stratification can be used in many different instances to assist in problem analysis. Let's take another example to demonstrate this point. Suppose a bank continuously collects data regarding deposit errors. Last year, the bank deposit error rate was 2 percent per month, but this year, deposit errors averaged 4 percent a month. A QI Team was formed, and they stratified the data by type of deposit: window tellers, night depository, and mail deposits.

Most errors occurred with window tellers, so this step was further broken down into deposits with preprinted slips and deposits with generic slips. Although generic slips accounted for only 20 percent of the deposits, they accounted for 80 percent of the errors. Thus stratification and substratification focused attention on where improvements should be made.

Now It's Your Turn*

2. *The bank's QI team gathered the data shown on the next page regarding bank deposit errors. Write the theme for this CQI story.*

Next, write the problem statement for this CQI story.

Next, stratify and graph the data. Your time is limited, so study the data before developing your graph. Use the grid provided in the appendix to construct a graph of the stratified data.

*The answers to these problems are in the appendix.

Survey number	Type of deposit	Forms	
		Generic	Preprinted
1	W	x	
2	N		x
3	W	x	
4	M	x	
5	W	x	
6	W		x
7	W		x
8	W	x	
9	W	x	
10	M	x	
11	W	x	
12	W	x	
13	M	x	
14	W	x	
15	W	x	
16	N		x
17	W	x	
18	W	x	
19	M	x	
20	W	x	

Type of Deposits:
W   Window Teller
N   Night Deposit
M   Mail

Forms:
Generic: Forms obtained
at the "counter"
Preprinted by bank

3. *Field failures were occurring on Ajax Corporation's new automatic coffee making machines. This machine is produced at one of three factories (A, B, C) by one of two operators (1 or 2) at each factory. The suppliers for the units are X, Y, Z.*

   Factory repair personnel completed the table on the following page that was provided to the QI team. Stratify and graph the data using the grid provided in the Appendix. Is there a factor that can be associated with the majority of the failures? (Note: To save time, select the most appropriate stratification scheme before graphing the data.)

Are You a Total Quality Person?

I take control of my life and I do not rely on others to plan my future.

Seldom ☐   Sometimes ☐   Always ☐

Unit number	Factory	Operator	Supplier
1	B	1	X
2	A	1	Z
3	C	2	Y
4	B	2	X
5	C	2	Y
6	A	1	Z
7	C	1	X
8	B	2	Z
9	A	1	Y
10	C	2	Y
11	A	2	Z
12	B	1	X
13	C	2	Y
14	A	1	Z
15	C	2	Y

4. *Friendly Hotel Corporation operates a well-known hotel in a midwestern city. Lately the number of repeat customers has diminished, and in an attempt to iden-tify why some customers were not returning, a feedback card was initiated. The guests were asked to complete a feedback card (a brief questionnaire), and drop it in a "How Are We Doing" box after checking out of the hotel. At the end of the month, 25 cards were randomly selected, and the card comments were tabulated.*
  The categories on the card were:

Have you previously been a guest at our hotel?
1 (Yes)   2 (No)

Are you primarily a business or vacation traveler?
B (Business) or V (Vacation) traveler

A comment section allows patrons to make additional comments. Four major categories of comments (complaints) were identified. Each response card may have more than one category.

1   Poor quality food

2   TV: Didn't work/reception poor

3   Lengthy check in and check out time

4   Room not clean

The hotel manager completed the table on the next page which was then given to the QI team. Note that a check mark in the question boxes indicated the patron identified as an area of dissatisfaction. Stratify and graph the data using the grid provided in the appendix.

Survey number	Previous guest (Y/N)	Traveler: Business Vacation	Question number 1	2	3	4
1	Y	B	✓	✓		
2	N	V	✓			✓
3	Y	B			✓	✓
4	N	B		✓	✓	
5	Y	V		✓		
6	N	B			✓	✓
7	Y	B			✓	✓
8	Y	B		✓		
9	Y	V		✓		
10	Y	V		✓		
11	N	B			✓	✓
12	Y	B	✓			
13	N	V		✓		
14	Y	B	✓		✓	
15	Y	B	✓	✓	✓	✓
16	N	B	✓			✓
17	Y	B			✓	
18	N	V		✓		
19	Y	B		✓	✓	
20	Y	B			✓	
21	N	V		✓		
22	N	B	✓		✓	
23	Y	B	✓		✓	
24	Y	B			✓	
25	Y	V	✓	✓		

Single Case Boring

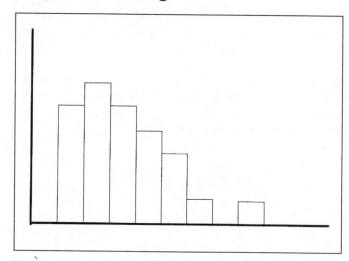

Single case boring is an in-depth analysis into one or a few sample cases. The purpose of single case boring is to concentrate on a limited number of cases so that you can spend the time needed to understand all of the relationships within an event.

There is no single format for single case boring. For example, note the shaded outlier in the histogram shown on the left. (Refer back to the section on interpreting distributions for an expanded discussion.)

Why did this occur? What caused this outlier? Suspicious data should not be discarded or ignored without using single case boring to "bore" into the case at hand.

Do not limit your investigation to an outlier case. You are trying to get an understanding of the data, so be sure to take a "typical" case. For each case under examination, a detailed analysis should be conducted to identify what happened, why it happened, when, where and how. This analysis should be conducted by someone familiar with the process and aware of unusual conditions that might occur.

Likert Scale

Likert Scale

- Used in measuring attitudes and perceptions.
- Has a simple, check-off scale.
- Is easy to administer.
- A five-point or seven-point scale measures strengths of disagreement or agreement.

Likert scales are used in developing questionnaires to measure attitudes and perceptions. By interpreting answers to Likert scale questions, an understanding can be gained regarding consumers' feelings about the quality of goods and services. A seven-point Likert scale structure is shown. This can be abbreviated to a five-point scale if desired.

Likert Rating Scale						
		← Disagree	Neutral	Agree →		
1 Disagree Very Strongly	2 Disagree Strongly	3 Disagree	4 Neither Agree nor Disagree	5 Agree	6 Agree Strongly	7 Agree Very Strongly

Before developing the actual questions to be asked, define the objective of the study, which should closely match the problem statement. Then, precisely define the consumer you are concerned with. Keep the survey's objective and the consumer in mind when developing specific survey questions.

Now It's Your Turn

Develop a brief questionnaire to measure some aspect of consumer quality. Use the forms provided below as a guide.

This questionnaire asks your opinion about issues regarding _____ at our firm. Please choose the one number that best matches how you feel about the statement. The further away from the middle (4), the stronger is your feeling about the statement.

For example, if you were asked about the quality of our food, and if you felt the quality was high, but could be better, you might cross through the number "6" as shown.

Our restaurant offers high quality food.	Strongly Disagree						Strongly Agree	Unknown
	1	2	3	4	5	6̶	7	0

In My Opinion:	Strongly Disagree						Strongly Agree	Unknown
1.	1	2	3	4	5	6	7	0
2.	1	2	3	4	5	6	7	0
3.	1	2	3	4	5	6	7	0
4.	1	2	3	4	5	6	7	0
5.	1	2	3	4	5	6	7	0
6.	1	2	3	4	5	6	7	0
7.	1	2	3	4	5	6	7	0
8.	1	2	3	4	5	6	7	0

Identify technical and "human" questions.
Develop the specific demographic questions that should be asked.
Clearly specify the objective of the study and your definition of a consumer.

Radar Chart

A *radar chart* is a combination of a circle and line graph that is used to portray relative strengths (or weaknesses) of activities. These charts are particularly useful in showing changes from period to period for items measured on a Likert scale.

Radar Chart

- Combination circle and line graph are used to represent relative strengths of activities.
- Is particularly useful in displaying changes in intangible activities.
- Is an eye-catching and unusual method to display changes in a small number of items.

Radar Chart

Before constructing a radar chart, let's review the questionnaire developed for a resturant.

This questionnaire asks your opinion about the quality of services at our restaurant. Please choose the one number that best matches how you feel about the statement. The further away from the middle (4), the stronger is your feeling about the statement.

For example, if you were asked if your food was served quickly, and if you felt the service was fast, but could be better, you might cross through the number "5" as shown.

	Strongly Disagree						Strongly Agree	Unknown
The food was served quickly.	1	2	3	4	~~5~~	6	7	0

In My Opinion:	Strongly Disagree						Strongly Agree	Unknown
1. Size of the servings were ample.	1	2	3	4	5	6	7	0
2. The food quality was high.	1	2	3	4	5	6	7	0
3. The price was reasonable.	1	2	3	4	5	6	7	0
4. Employees were friendly.	1	2	3	4	5	6	7	0
5. The food was quickly served.	1	2	3	4	5	6	7	0

Please write any comments/suggestions you might have below. Place the completed survey in the suggestion box on your way out. Thank you.

Four surveys were randomly collected and summarized in the chart shown. In actual practice, averages should be developed on a minimum of 24 randomly selected surveys to assure statistical accuracy.

Surveys	Q1	Q2	Q3	Q4	Q5
1	4	6	3	6	7
2	2	7	1	7	7
3	3	7	2	7	6
4	2	7	3	5	7
Total	11	27	9	25	27
Average:	2.8	6.8	2.3	6.3	6.8

Before proceeding, the data should be organized from highest to lowest average response as shown.

Surveys	Q2	Q5	Q4	Q1	Q3
	Food quality	Speed	Friendly service	Serving size	Price
Average	6.8	6.8	6.3	2.8	2.3

Based on the survey, our customers felt we have high quality food (Q2), that was served quickly (Q5) by friendly employees (Q4). Our customers did not like the size of their servings (Q1) and the price they were charged (Q3).

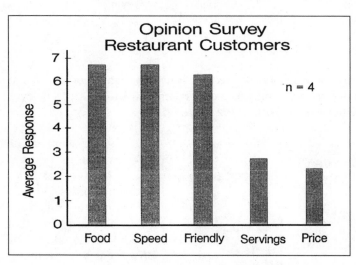

A bar chart of the data is shown. Note that the data were organized from highest to lowest. This serves as a powerful incentive for management to evaluate the serving sizes and the prices charged.

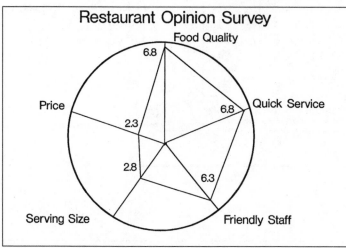

The same survey data can be plotted on a radar chart as shown. Note that the data are laid out, equally spaced from the center.

A radar chart is constructed by dividing the circle into as many "slices" as there are questions to be plotted. In this case, divide five questions, into 360° to obtain 72° per "slice." The "slices" range in values from 0 to the outermost rim value of 7.

Chart off the degrees in the circle, beginning at 12:00 noon. Draw the lines and label the end of the lines with the question being asked. Plot the values (0 to 7), label the values, and draw a line connecting the various points. When the points are joined, a pattern is formed which represents the cumulative responses.

In the example shown, there is no particular advantage to using a radar chart over a bar chart. However, what about when the next survey is completed? How can results be shown from one survey to the next?

Let's take a look at how a "before" and "after" condition can be displayed. Suppose the restaurant survey was repeated, and the results shown were obtained.

Surveys	Q2	Q5	Q4	Q1	Q3
	Food quality	Speed	Friendly service	Serving size	Price
Average	6.8	7.0	6.6	6.0	4.2

A second bar chart could be constructed to show the changes on each item from the first time period to the second. The data taken in the follow up survey is shaded differently than the data taken in the first study.

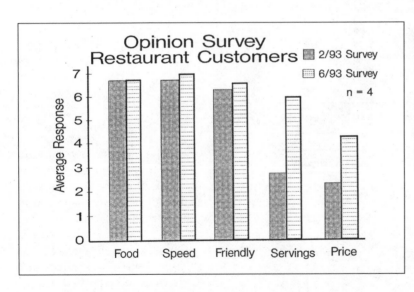

The bar chart on the left "seems to permit" comparisons over two different studies.

However, this type of display is a trap that should be avoided. The shading is so close that it is difficult to interpret the findings.

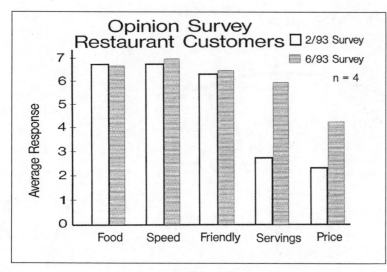

Look at the bar chart on the left. This is the same data, but only the most recent study is shaded. Visual comparisons are easer when only one bar is shaded.

But, even with one bar shaded, the results are not easy to interpret.

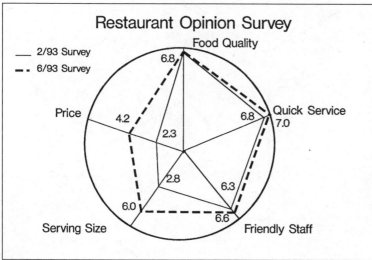

The same data displayed in a radar chart format is shown. Now, which one do you like?

Some people like radar charts because they are a unique and interesting way to display data.

Others do not like radar chart and want to stick with bar charts. It's your choice: Either a bar or radar chart can be used to display data.

Now It's Your Turn

*Get together in your assigned team and construct a radar chart of the following summarized data developed from surveys conducted on shoppers at a specialized men's clothing store. Use the form provided on the next page to record your chart.**

Surveys	Q1	Q2	Q3	Q4	Q5	Q6
	Friendly service	Clothing quality	Alterations: quality	Alterations: speed	Selection	Price
Average:	6.1	7.0	6.6	1.9	3.2	4.2

*The answer to this problem is in the appendix.

113

Radar Chart: Clothing Store Survey

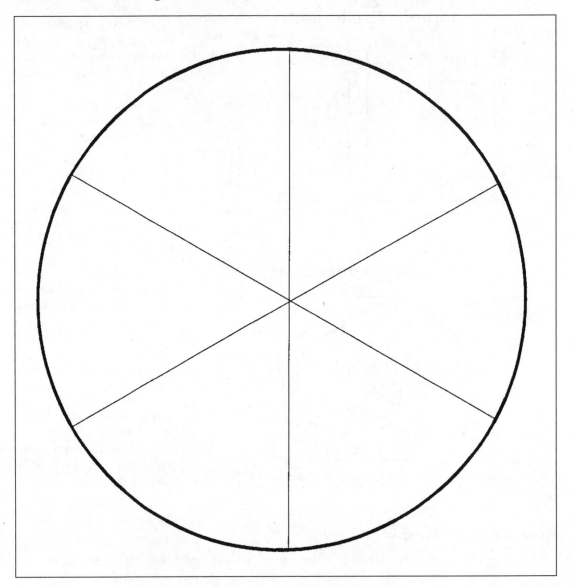

Use of Charts and Graphs to Support a CQI Story

Let's look at a few of the reasons for using various charts in a CQI story.

1. To Provide an Exploded View of a Quality Indicator

For example, if our theme involved traffic fines received by Friendly Texan Insurance adjusters, a trend chart might be useful, particularly if it highlights increasing pain (i.e., the trend indicates more fines are likely in the next year). The bar chart shown encourages a closer inspection of the category of tickets issued.

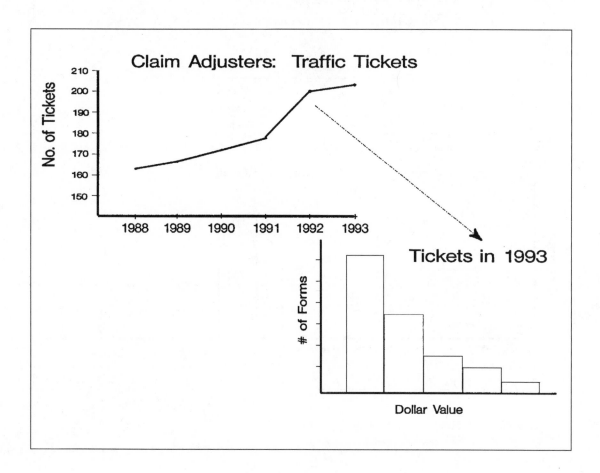

2. To Use With Stratification As a Step in Verifying a Root Cause

Note the use of a fishbone diagram to aid in root cause identification. Then a scatter diagram was used to identify possible cause and effect relationships. This was followed by a histogram showing the dollar value associated with the number of forms (i.e., travel reimbursements) processed.

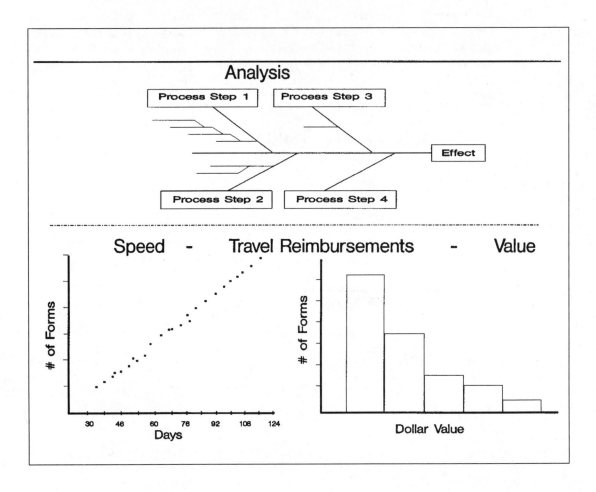

3. To Set Goals for Continuous Improvement

A "before" and "after" trend chart is shown to highlight the goal of reversing the trend of increasing traffic fines for adjusters. This is followed by a histogram highlighting the high dollar fines we wish to eliminate with a policy change, such as having the adjuster's supervisor discuss the reason the fine was incurred with the offending adjuster.

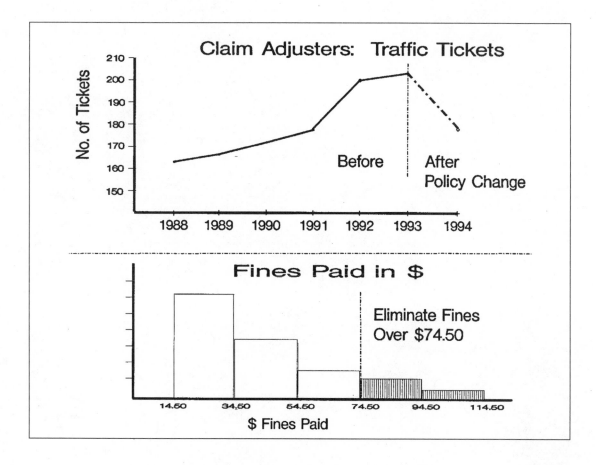

Of course, these are only a few of the many applications. You are basically limited only by your creativity.

Basic QI Techniques

Several basic Quality Improvement (QI) techniques will be presented in this section. These techniques are different than the previously discussed tools in that they often do not deal with quantitative issues. Fundamental QI issues such as planning and control are discussed, and application of the technique are by nature general. Hence, there are very limited problem solutions in this section.

A brief overview follows. Refer to the appropriate section for more details.

Technique: Plan-Do-Check-Act

Provides an overview of the activities required for quality improvements.

Useful when a simple framework for planning activities is needed.

Limitations: None.

Technique: Personal Quality Checklist

Provides a structure by which you personally can improve the quality of any activity undertaken.

Useful when obtaining "buy-in" into the concept of continuous quality improvement. That is, if you first improve yourself, organizational improvement will soon follow.

Limitations: None. Frankly, this is one of the most powerful quality improvement tools in this book.

Technique: Vision and Mission Statements

Defines a future state—what an organization is trying to become. Visions need to be innovative and reaching, and the companion mission statement should identify what is needed to accomplish the vision.

Useful when planning, and focusing the future thrust of the organization. People are more likely to be personally committed to quality improvements if they believe in the organization's vision, and if they want to help the organization to accomplish its vision.

Limitations: Although needed for planning, often the vision is so "idealistic" that some groups do not understand: the vision statement; how they can contribute to such "lofty" goals, and how the vision can be realized (attained).

Technique: Deployment Chart

This is an action plan often used in step four of the CQI story. The plan identifies the steps needed to complete a project, and who is responsible for each step.

Useful when developing a simple plan and a quick visual reference is needed to identify assignments.

Limitations: Difficult to use with complex projects containing interrelated activities, or with projects containing subactivities.

Technique: Kaizen

A concept of continuous improvement in all aspects of work, family, and life.

Useful when developing an understanding that continuous quality improvement is a broad philosophy applicable to any activity.

Limitations: It is difficult for an organization to obtain employee commitment on such a strong philosophical concept that has a commitment bordering on a religious belief.

Technique: Kanban

Appearance of an empty production case is the authority needed to manufacture to fill the case. A card is often attached to the case to facilitate part ordering.

Useful when simple production loops are involved and it is desirable to use a "demand pull" type of production.

Limitations: Becomes difficult to plan and control if products re involved that have subassemblies.

Technique: Poka-Yoke

Often called mistake proofing or "idiot proofing," products are designed to eliminate mistakes in assembly and use.

Useful when designing a product to reduce manufacturing defects, and to reduce chance of misuse.

Limitations: None. All products and services should be designed to minimize potential misuse, and to minimize errors in manufacturing (or delivery of the service).

Technique: SMED

Single Minute Exchange of Dies (SMED) seeks to reduce set-up time from hours to minutes.

Useful when numerous small runs are encountered in repetitive manufacturing environments.

Limitations: The flexible manufacturing and support equipment needed is often very expensive.

Technique: Nominal Grouping

A structured technique to generate ideas by encouraging input from group members. In the open version, ideas are submitted in round-robin fashion. In the anonymous version, ideas are anonymously submitted. In both versions, after ideas are clarified, voting is anonymous.

Useful when there is a need to generate ideas on a topic which may be difficult to openly discuss (such as personal policies).

Limitations: It is still difficult to tackle very sensitive issues, and a neutral facilitator is needed to conduct the process.

Technique: Brainstorming

A well-known technique in which a group is encouraged to generate as many ideas as possible. Ideas are offered without critique, or without consideration of practicability.

Useful when there is a need to develop "breakthrough" thinking.

Limitations: It is difficult to get members to open up and actively participate because there are often hidden agendas and vested interests in the issue being discussed.

Technique: Multivoting

A method to reduce a lengthy list of ideas into a smaller, more manageable list.

Useful when a voting procedure is needed whereby the group understands how they will reduce the number of ideas down to a manageable proportions.

Limitations: Does not obtain group consensus.

Technique: Force Field Analysis

Used to identify the driving forces and the restraining forces in a situation.

Useful when there is a need to understand the restraining forces that are attempting to maintain the status quo.

Limitations: A good, simple way of developing a beginning understanding of the forces "involved" in a situation. It is not likely all forces can be identified, nor can the interaction (reinforcement) between the forces be identified.

Are You a Total Quality Person?

	Seldom	Sometimes	Always
I understand my values, which I follow in my personal life.	☐	☐	☐

Technique: Classifying Quality Problems

Used to identify and classify quality problems into major categories of internal and external problems. These problems are then further divided into small and large problems.

Useful when the result classification clarifies the different problems in terms of the action required. That is, a small internal problem can be tackled easier than a large external problem.

Limitations: This technique assumes quality problems can be clearly identified and easily classified.

Technique: Improving Perceived Quality

Defines perceived quality as actual quality minus expected quality.

Useful when there is a tendency to overadvertise (raise consumer expectation so high that actual quality cannot possibly meet expectations). This results in a negative perception.

Limitations: Few. This is a useful technique of identifying how positive perceptions of quality occur.

Technique: Effective Presentations

Identifies major factors involved in conducting an effective presentation.

Useful when presentations have to be given, particularly to upper management on quality improvement projects.

Limitations: None.

PLAN—DO—CHECK—ACT

The CQI story previously explained serves as a guide for planning, doing, checking, and acting. The PDCA was originally proposed by Walter Shewhart as the *Plan-Do-Study-Act* cycle, and was modified by Dr. Deming into its present form. The PDCA (Plan, Do, Check, Act) cycle is a concept that can be applied to the management of any process.

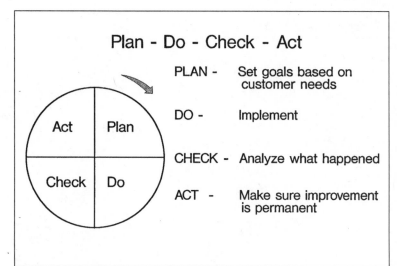

Plan - Do - Check - Act

PLAN -   Set goals based on
           customer needs

DO -   Implement

CHECK -   Analyze what happened

ACT -   Make sure improvement
           is permanent

Act | Plan
Check | Do

Plan. Begin by setting goals based on customer needs. Your plan is how you will meet these needs.

Do. Try out (implement) the plan to see how it works.

Check. During and after implementation find out what happened. Are you actually closer to your planned target? Or did something not work out as planned?

Act.   Make sure the improvements made are permanent. That is, make whatever adjustments are necessary to assure the improvements remains in place.

Personal Quality Checklist

Who has the responsibility of installing TQM? Is it solely the organization's responsibility, or does the employee share some of the responsibility for implementing TQM? Well, if you view the TQM process in a narrow-minded focus of continuous "organizational" improvement, then it's the organization's responsibility to install TQM.

However, if you take the broader view that TQM is a philosophy involving continuous improvement on the behalf of everyone (society, the community, the organization, and the employee), then everyone should share the responsibility for installing TQM in their organization and in their personal lives.

A *personal quality checklist* is an excellent way to get both management and employees personally involved in continuous quality improvement. The checklist encourages participants to keep track of job performance failures (defects). The mere act of itemizing the personal defects that you want to improve upon is a step toward improvement. Then, keeping track of the defects serves as a reminder to pay attention to those important items, and improvement tends to "automatically" follow.

The hardest part in developing a personal quality checklist is in identifying the items that should be on the checklist. I'll share my personal checklist with you, but remember: this isn't your checklist, it's mine; so your items will undoubtedly vary.

Personal Quality Checklist

Personal Quality Checklist: Peter Mears

Week of _____

Defect category	Mon	Tue	Wed	Thr	Fri	Sat	Sun	Total
Excessive handling of paperwork								
Delayed return of forms								
Not prepared for meeting								
Office not clean at end of day								
Not answering phone within two rings								
Typos in correspondence								

I'm a university professor, and teaching is the "fun" part of my job. The "hard" part is that, in addition to research, a lot of coordination with students and higher administration is required. I handle an immense amount of paperwork. Therefore, my primary improvement item is that I want to stop the excessive handling of paperwork. What often occurs, is that instead of immediately answering a message left in my mail box, I "think" about it, and place the message in my attache case. Then I carry the message around, look at it a couple of times, and after a number of weeks pass, the message stack builds up, so I am "forced" to finally answer them.

Undoubtedly, some messages require a lot of thought; but most messages in my job are simple requests that can be handled immediately. I am "making a mountain out of a mole hill" by the excessive handling of these messages. Hence, every time I handle the same request, I will count it as an error. Some complex messages will indeed require double handling, but they are very few in number. Of course this means I will never get to zero, but I never thought of myself as a zero-defects person. However, my goal is to become a more efficient person.

The second checklist category, "delayed return of forms" (including official correspondence), is related to the first category, but again, my checklist is concerned with my personal improvement items. Many forms and official correspondence require that a statistic be referenced before responding (grades, students no longer in class, meeting times, requests for information, etc.) which, of course, means the correspondence will have to be handled several times. This category is not included in the first tally, and my goal here is to answer all such correspondence within one working day. This goal may be unreasonable, because some correspondence requires that I obtain input from other people who may not respond quickly to my request. However, I need a simple working definition of what is, or is not acceptable, so I'm going to leave the goal at one day for the time being.

Another personal improvement item involves my habit of not answering a phone call quickly. I have a reason for this: when the phone rings, I am either talking to someone who is in my office, or I am busy, and I try to complete what I'm doing before answering the phone. But why wait? My thought process is effectively destroyed by the ringing phone, and since I'm going to have to answer the phone sooner or later anyway, I am going to try answering it within two rings.

The category "office not clean at end of day" is the result of poor work habits. At the end of a day, I simply stop what I'm doing and leave. That is, leaving everything in a mess or partially completed. That must stop! My goal is to have everything completed and delivered (i.e., no out basket, I'll take it to the mail room on the way out). Or, if something absolutely cannot be completed, it will be placed in an in-basket. By doing this, there will be no half-completed work, and no stacks of paper on my desk facing me when I come in the morning. If there is, it will be recorded as an error.

Although we have secretaries, they are monopolized by administrators, and I have to type my own correspondence. I learned how to type, but I have not learned how to spell. I am embarrassed by my typos, so I have purchased a pocket dictionary and will use it if in doubt about any spelling. Recording these errors will be difficult, because if an error can be detected, it will be corrected immediately, hence it is not an error because it has been corrected. I'm sure psychologists could have a "field day" with this type of logic, but it's my checklist, and I'm going to keep track of errors as something that I did wrong, after the item left my control. I know this isn't a good "working definition" so I made this item last in my personal checklist.

Did the Personal Quality Checklist Work?

I'm not a psychologist, so I don't know if the personal quality checklist modified my behavior. However, I feel more in control than before on most items. But frankly, some days the phone rings so many times, particularly on Monday mornings, and so many defects were recorded that I gave up. (The weekends must be used by students to think up new ways to confuse directions, while administrators use the time to think up new forms for faculty to complete.) Anyway, I revised my checklist to temporarily remove that item until I can figure out how to organize those "high-volume" days better. However, I know I am working smarter on handling paperwork, and I am "forcing myself" to respond quicker, particularly on routine forms and correspondence.

I am thinking of another revision in which a "very" personal checklist will be created by adding personal improvement items. I know that I should read at least one article a week from each of two leading journals that I subscribe to, but I procrastinate. The articles are inevitably poorly written by some frustrated statistical person who likes to flaunt their mathematical knowledge, rather than simply explaining the point they are trying to make. However, the articles do represent innovative thinking, so perhaps I should "bite the bullet" and read the articles.

And, speaking of biting, I've been biting into food so much lately, that I am a few inches "wider around the beltline." So I joined a health club, only to find that joining wasn't enough: I have to *go* to the club on a routine basis and work out in order to reduce the waistline. As I paid for membership, I had better keep track of how many times a week I actually go to the club.

And where will it all end? Will I ever construct a good personal quality checklist I can live with? I doubt it because continuous quality improvement is a never-ending process.

Now It's Your Turn*

Using one of the forms shown as a guide, construct your own personal quality improvement checklist.

Personal Quality Checklist

Week of								
Category	Mon	Tue	Wed	Thr	Fri	Sat	Sun	Total

Short Pocket Form:

Personal Quality Checklist

Week of	
Category	Total

*See Harry V. Roberts, "Using Personal Checklists to Facilitate TQM," *Quality Progress*, June, 1993, pp. 51–56.

Vision and Mission Statement

Whoever said that "nothing in this life was certain, except death and taxation," must have been thinking about current organizational changes. Organizations everywhere are experiencing massive changes due to downsizing, responding to changing markets, or adjusting to competitive pressure. Change is everywhere and is a fact of life. Unless care is exercised by organizational leadership, the firm can get so bogged down responding to immediate conditions that a sense of direction is lost.

Vision Statement

Vision defines what we want to be.

Envisioning the future is not the same as predicting what will occur. A vision statement is a statement that defines what we want to be. A well-written statement can provide a stable sense of direction to guide an organization through numerous changes. The leader who is a visionary can create a self-fulfilling prophecy in that others will have a sense of direction that will help make the vision come true.

A *vision statement* should be:

1. Brief.

2. Inspiring.

3. Challenging.

4. Descriptive of an ideal condition.

5. Appealing to employees and stockholders.

6. Provide a direction of the future business.

Health care, educational organizations, and volunteer groups can develop powerful vision and mission statements. Health care vision statements such as "Provide for the health and well-being of our people" accompanied by a mission statement "Our business is saving lives" are powerful motivational tools.

Ford Motor Company has a no-nonsense vision: "...to be the maker of the highest quality cars and trucks in the world." In other words, they plan on being the best. One way to develop a vision statement for your organization is to get an executive team together for an exercise. Ask them to pretend that reporters from *Business Week* and *The Wall Street Journal* are interviewing your company five years from now. Ask each member of the team to write the lead paragraph for the article. In the lead paragraph (written five years from now), what can they say about the organization? What does it do? Who are its customers?

Write the major themes that are represented in the different paragraphs on a flipchart. Then craft a vision statement with these ideas as a course of action. Think in terms of headings, and subheadings as an aid in organizing your thoughts to develop a vision that everyone can buy into. Mission statements are not designed to "nail everything down" and some vagueness is desirable. Concentrate on developing a general direction, image, and a general philosophy to guide the organization.

Mission Statement

> *Mission* defines the accomplishments needed that will result in realization of the vision.

A vision without a mission statement is often a "pipe dream." A *mission statement* describes the accomplishments that are necessary to move the organization toward the vision. Factors addressed in a mission statement state what is needed to realize the vision. That is, a mission statement addresses the achievements needed in major areas of importance to your organization.

A mission statement is often the most visible part of a strategic plan. A good mission statement should include all of the essential components of an organization's future "thrust" and it should communicate a positive feeling that will guide others to action. The vision and philosophy can be included in the mission statement or stated separately.

Key Components of a Mission Statement

Customers: Who are the customers of the organization?

Markets: Where does the organization compete geographically?

Products or services: What are the major products or services?

Technology: What is the organization's basic technology?

Economic goals: What is the organization's attitude towards growth and profitability?

Self-concept: What are the organization's strengths and competitive advantage?

Image: What public image is desired?

Philosophy: What are the fundamental beliefs and values?

Effectiveness: Does the mission statement address the wishes of key stakeholders

Inspirational: Does the statement motivate people?

There is no single, textbook mission statement for all organizations, nor do they have to be lengthy statements. Differences will occur, but perhaps the key point is that an effective mission statement specifies the fundamental reason why an organization exists. By doing this, it provides a guidance for strategic plans.

Guiding Principles

The vision statement is what we want to be, while the mission statement identifies what needs to be accomplished in the key areas that affect our business. The gap between these will undoubtedly be difficult for some people to accept. Principles help bridge the gap by identifying the fundamental, underlying beliefs that guide our actions. Many Malcolm Baldrige National Quality Award winners have stated that without employees working together in empowered work groups, the organization would not have been successful in their pursuit of improved quality.

That is an underlying belief in basic human values is needed for an organization to "come together." Beliefs such as treating customers and employees with respect, dignity, and honesty cannot be mere words, but should guide actions.

A clear vision and mission statement, along with a statement of organizational beliefs provides the basis by which departments can focus their quality improvement efforts. Make sure your organization not only has a meaningful vision and mission statement, but that such statements are known to your employees.*

Now It's Your Turn

1. *Read the excerpt which follows regarding the Saturn Division of General Motors (GM).** Then develop a vision and mission statement for the Saturn Division of GM. Be able to support your answer.*

   Background. The Saturn facility was established as a strategic response to pressure from Japanese automobile manufacturers in 1986. It was the first time that GM attempted to design and manufacture its own cars using Designs for Flexible Manufacturing and concurrent manufacturing technologies in a United Auto Worker facility. However, GM previously undertook joint ventures with Toyota including manufacturing the GEO Prizm.

   Over the past six years, the Saturn project has experienced several setbacks, including a major redesign of the car prior to its initial release. Initial union negotiations were very difficult as several new concepts were negotiated.

   Current Situation. Saturn has now achieved remarkable success, and is operating slightly below its present manufacturing capacity of 325,000

---

*Recommended readings: John Pearce and Fred Davis, "Corporate Mission Statements: The Bottom Line," *Academy of Management Executive*, 1987, Vol. 1, No. 2, pp. 109–116.
**Excerpted from *Business Week*, August 17, 1992.

per year. It will take an additional $1 billion to expand manufacturing and dealer capacity to 500,000 cars per year. Several encouraging events have occurred recently. Dealers report minimum inventories, and they are able to charge sticker price. In a study involving perceived automobile quality, J.D. Powers ranked Saturn third of all major car manufacturers.

However, Saturn has not yet returned a profit, mostly due to its high initial investment of $5 billion. Furthermore, the parent firm has a large inventory of Chevrolets and is evaluating which facilities to close. Senior GM management must make a decision on the future of Saturn as well as the development of larger cars using Saturn successes. GM management has always assumed that Saturn buyers will trade up to large GM cars as their next purchase, in the same manner that Japanese car buyers have done. However, this assumption may be false since there is little early evidence of repeat purchasing behavior, and no evidence of a tendency to "upgrade" into higher priced GM cars.

2. *Read the excerpt which follows regarding American Telephone and Telegraph Co. (AT&T).* Then develop a vision and mission statement for AT&T. Be able to support your answer.***

Background. AT&T with $68 billion in 1993 sales, just purchased the largest cellular phone company, McCaw Cellular Communications. AT&T paid heavily for their late entry into the cellular phone market. The cost was $12.6 billion for McCaw's stock, and AT&T is assuming $5 billion in McCaw debt. Their purchase of McCaw is approximately $300 per potential subscriber, making it one of the most expensive cellular buy out ever.

The specter of a nationwide cellular phone service has competitors nervous. AT&T is banking that the purchase of McCaw could be a boon to their bottom line as they find a way to link cellular customers directly to their long-distance networks, by-passing local phone systems. This will reduce the $14 billion a year AT&T currently pays to local phone companies (called *Baby Bells*). AT&T will then be able to proceed with building a network expanding the globe and fill that network with every kind of communication including: voice, data, video, computer, and entertainment.

Some insiders called the deal "gutsy," others felt AT&T has finally overextended themselves. Even AT&T's chairman Robert Allen concedes this is a risky deal. The AT&T-McCaw link will give Baby Bell's the argument they need to sway regulators to let them enter long distance services, particularly if they give up their monopolies in local service.

So, AT&T is taking a calculated risk: They could lose the savings if the Baby Bells are granted the right to enter the long distance market.

*Excerpt from *Business Week*, August 30, 1993.
**The answer to this question is in the appendix.

However, insiders agree that the McCaw deal will increase AT&T's business outside the United States Allen hopes to increase internal revenues from 25 percent to 40 percent of the total business in the next five years. Cellular service is particularly popular in developing countries such as China, which can utilize cellular technology to modernize their phone service far more rapidly than with wired systems. And in the developed countries in Europe, most regulations do not apply to cellular affording AT&T a large advantage over local phone companies.

There is also a possibility that a new wireless system called *personal communications service* (PCS) will emerge as a major rival to cellular phones. Cellular networks use powerful transmitters to relay signals across towers 20 miles apart. The PCS territory is far smaller, and since callers are closer to transmitters, the handsets need less power, making them smaller, cheaper and they have a longer battery life. Furthermore, the small territories enable PCS systems to carry a greater communication capability, making the per call cost more economical, which should attract more customers.

Additionally, the Federal Communications Commission (FCC) is considering regulation that will increase competitors in the market. That means, if PCS is the dominate communication media of the future, major investments will be needed by AT&T in the cellular network purchased from McCaw to install numerous transmitters. For example, a PCS network to cover Chicago will require 200 cells (towers and relays) at a cost of $250,000 per cell.

Allen says he and his staff have considered all the arguments and agonized over the purchase decision. Not all major purchase decisions have gone well for AT&T. Sun Microsystems, Inc. and Olivetti cost billions in investment but have produced little in the ways of revenue. Allen agrees not all purchases were wise, and has since divested the majority of noncommunications business. AT&T must make this purchase "work" if they are to be a viable firm in the next century.

Deployment Chart

A *deployment chart* is an easy-to-read action plan that identifies who has primary and secondary responsibility for key planning steps. (An *action plan* was presented in the CQI story, fourth step.)

A deployment chart is constructed by listing the major action steps vertically. On a horizontal grid, list the name of the person who is responsible for completion of each step in the action plan. Then mark the appropriate symbol to denote who has primary responsibility and who is assigned a helper/advisor role. Completion dates can be written in the symbols if desired.

An example of a deployment chart is shown. Notice that its simplicity helps reduce later misunderstandings.

Deployment Chart

Steps	Jackson	Thomas	Smith
Train secretaries	� primary		⬭ helper
Standardize forms			▮ primary
Train accountants		▮ primary	
Develop electronic mail	▮ primary		
Train all employees		▮ primary	⬭ helper

 Primary responsibility
 Helper/advisor

Kaizen

Kaizen includes

✓ Total Quality Management
✓ Continuous Quality Improvement
✓ Just-in-Time
✓ Poka-Yoke
✓ New product design
✓ Zero defects
✓ Kanban
✓ Quality circles
✓ Customer service agreements
✓ SMED
✓ Consumer orientation
✓ Empowered teams

Kaizen means improvement. The Kaizen philosophy assumes that our way of life deserves to be constantly improved. It is a broader philosophy than TQM because it embraces the necessity for ongoing improvement as managers, workers, and in all aspects of our life. Kaizen, often called "the improvement movement" is a philosophy that extends to constant improvement in our working life, our social life, and our home life.*

*For a better understanding of Kaizen, read the Kaizen® Communique published by the Kaizen Institute of America, Austin, Texas.

The Kanban

In Japanese, the word *Kanban* means card or visible representation. The Kanban system is a case with a card attached. The arrival of the case at the production unit is the authority to initiate production of enough units to fill the case. Although the card is often used to control inventory, the card is optional. The Kanban system revolves around an empty component case with slots. The case itself is all the authority the employees need to meet production needs.

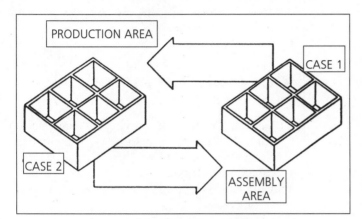

The Kanban system is trickier if subassemblies are involved. A slotted case has to be created for each item to be produced. Then, usage patterns have to be observed so that there are a minimum number of cases.

A typical two-slotted case Kanban system is shown. The timing of the assembly process dictates the number of cases needed.

In a restaurant serving donuts, an empty donut tray that holds a dozen specialized donuts, when given to the kitchen, is the authority for the kitchen to "fill the tray." Note that the Kanban system is a *demand pull system.* More than one tray of common, high-usage donuts might be needed to meet demand.

A Kanban system for an office supply store might be as simple as attaching a card to an expensive office item. When the item is sold, the card is removed, which forms the basis for a reorder of the product.

Poka-Yoke

Poka-yoke is mistake-proofing. A process or product should be designed to eliminate the possibility of any anticipated defects. Automatic test equipment shoud be designed that "inspects" the operations performed when manufacturing a product to prevent the product from proceeding unless everything is correct. Poka-yoke can make it possible to attain the goal of zero defects in production.

Are You a Total Quality Person?			
I measure whether I am meeting my personal goals.	Seldom ☐	Sometimes ☐	Always ☐

Let's take a look at how poka-yoke could be applied to an assembly operation consisting of bolting two parts together. Part A has four centered bolts that protrude from a square, flat metal surface. This is to be bolted to part B, which has four matching holes that the bolts fit into. If the holes are centered, the parts can be bolted together in a number of different ways, but perhaps only one way is correct.

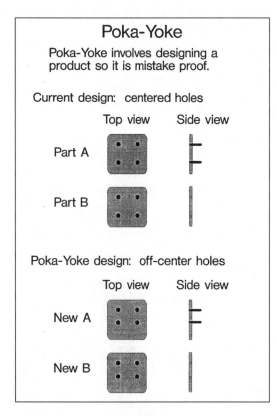

Poka-Yoke

Poka-Yoke involves designing a product so it is mistake proof.

Current design: centered holes

Top view   Side view

Part A

Part B

Poka-Yoke design: off-center holes

Top view   Side view

New A

New B

A poka-yoke design would not leave anything to chance. The holes could be designed off-center so that there is only one possible way parts A and B can fit together.

The Problem with 100 Percent Inspection

The old approach to improving quality was to increase the number of inspectors at the end of the line, thus catching the "bad" products. By catching more bad products, it was assumed that the quality of the products being shipped would increase.

However, just because you 100 percent inspect all products, does not mean you catch 100 percent of the errors. Even if the errors are obvious, your mind "plays tricks" on you and you simply do not "see" the error. Spend a couple of minutes and work through problem 1.

Now It's Your Turn*

1. *How many times does the letter* a *occur?*

All the king's men, and all the awful people assisting King Author, couldn't put him back together again. Our answer to any and all problems involving arithmetical analysis: About face!

The answer to this problem is contained in the appendix, but don't peek: Spend a few minutes and count the number of times the letter a *occurs.*

SMED

In repetitive manufacturing environments, production occurs in small runs called *lots*. Production of a particular lot requires that one or more machines have to be *setup* (changed over) to perform the particular operations needed. These repeated setups are very costly because during the setup time, neither the operator or the machine(s) are producing anything. Hence, to save on this "wasted time," many production runs are longer than desired simply to avoid incurring multiple setups. This larger lot size increases the amount (volume) of the work in process, which ties up more funds in production, and requires larger facilities.

A concept called SMED *(Single Minute Exchange of Dies)* has been developed that concentrates on reducing setup times from hours to minutes.* Before SMED, production management was more concerned with planning around lengthy setup times than with reducing the time required. The concept arose in Japan when Toyota's management found that they were spending four hours for a press die change, but a similar setup only required two hours at a German Volkswagen plant. An industrial engineer, Shigeo Shingo, was assigned the problem of reducing Toyota's setup time[†] to at least the German's time.

Mr. Shingo was successful in his assignment and initially reduced Toyota's setup time from four hours to one and a half hours. However, instead of being content with the reduced setup time, Toyota's management asked Mr. Shingo to determine if an EOQ *(Economic Order Quantity)* approach could be used in handling the now more manageable production lots. This was a seemingly impossible assignment due to the EOQ's square root formula. In the *EOQ formula*, to reduce the inventory costs and lot sizes by tenfold, the setup cost must be reduced by a hundredfold (i.e., 10 squared).**

Mr. Shingo then reduced the setup time from the initial four hours to three minutes! His breakthrough was simple, yet brilliant: Make the setup outside the press, yet parallel to its operation. Then "swing" the setup into the press when required. Hence the setup becomes a "remove and replace" operation. Interestingly, the EOQ formula approach could now be ignored because inventory costs became too small to be a major consideration. Furthermore, there is so much additional machine capacity, the machine may no longer be a bottleneck. Thus, SMED was the seed of JIT (Just-in-Time) approach to manufacturing.

Technically, Shingo's acronym SMED meant "single digit exchange of dies" because all die changes should require a single digit number of minutes (such as

---

*Trietsch, Dan. "Focused TQM and Synergy: A Case Study," Paper Number 92-06, Monterey, CA: *Naval Postgraduate School*.

[†]Shingo, S., *A Revolution in Manufacturing: The SMED System*. Productivity Press, 1985.

**Trietsch, Dan. "Some Notes on the Application of Single Minute Exchange of Die (SMED)," NPS-AS-92-019, Monterey, CA: *Naval Postgraduate School*.

9 minutes, not 10 minutes.) Through time, the acronym became know as "single minute exchange of die."

SMED can be applied outside the manufacturing environment. For example, a practical application of SMED was reported by a student who applied the concept of setup reduction to a personal setup operation of getting the shower to the required temperature in the morning. He simply marked the optimal tap position on the shower walls, so he did not have to repeat the same operation daily. The tap then only had to be opened to the hot setting until the hot water arrives, then adjusted to the second marked position. This saves time, water, energy, and the likelihood of getting scorched or chilled. Exercise caution when applying this to your own life as the improved process requires considerable explanation to others as to why there are strange markings on the shower walls, during which time the listener tends to have a weird grin on their face. (See Trietsch's SMED notes, page 135.)

Conceptual Stages of SMED	
Stages	Description
Preliminary	Mixed internal and external setups
First	Separate internal and external setups
Second	Convert internal setup to external setups
Third	Streamline both internal and external setups

Preliminary Stage: Mixed Internal and External Setups

An *internal setup* consists of operations that can only be done while the machine is stopped, such as mounting or removing fixtures. *External operations* consist of operations that can be performed while the machine is running, such as assuring the correct parts, fixtures, and tools are on hand. Perform an indepth evaluation of all setup operations and classify each step as either internal or external.

First Stage: Separate Internal and External Setups

Setup time cannot be less than the internal setup time, nor should it be more than the internal setup time. Care should be taken to perform all external setups while the machine is running. After classification the setup operations, develop a time for the activities. Your initial goal should be to reduce the total setup time to less than the internal setup time.

Second Stage: Convert Internal Setup to External Setups

Analyze the internal setup activities to identify which can be transformed to external setup. One case was quoted involving the use of an extra metal table on wheels so that the operator could setup a new job while the old job was running. Then the setup on the table was exchanged (swapped) for the internal setup when the production lot was produced.

Third Stage: Streamline Both Internal and External Setups

Reduce the total setup by streaming both internal and external setup. A lot of ingenuity has occurred in the past 10 years in this third stage of developing innovative devices to speed up the setup operation. A few of the hundreds of possible labor-saving ideas are:

- Provide stops that locate the new dies at the right spot.
- Use dies with standardized external dimensions.
- Use one-turn fasteners and ball-locks (thumb screw fasteners).
- Use "automatic positioning" chucks.
- Use standardized fixtures containing specialized setups that are secured using ball-locks.
- Use tables with rollers, not cranes to roll dies in or out.
- Use prepositioning templates.

Group Interaction Techniques: Nominal Grouping and Brainstorming

There are two major interaction techniques used to obtain data from groups: *nominal grouping* and *brainstorming*. Nominal grouping is a structured interaction technique used to capture a group of ideas by "encouraging" input from all group members.

Are You a Total Quality Person?

	Seldom	Sometimes	Always
I am open to changes in my life that will assist me to learn new things.	☐	☐	☐

Stages in Nominal Grouping

Stages	Description
1	The facilitator presents an issue for analysis. Example: What are the major problems that prevent us from offering high quality services at our organization?
2	Individual members silently and independently write down their ideas. This is a nominal (noninteracting) stage.
3	Each group member presents one of their ideas: This is presented one at a time, in a round-robin fashion. Each idea is written on a blackboard.
4	After everyone presents their ideas, there is a discussion of the recorded ideas for the purposes of clarification and evaluation. This is the interaction stage.
5	The meeting ends with a silent independent voting on priorities by a ranked order. The group decision is the total of the votes. (See multivoting.)

Nominal grouping is particularly useful with topics which may be difficult to discuss openly. Such topics include changing or developing policies on activities where feelings may become involved, such as smoking, drinking (coffee) on the job, and personnel policies.

Nominal Grouping: A Step-by-Step Approach

Step	Description
1	The facilitator presents an issue and explains that ideas will be anonymously submitted.
2	Individual members write down their ideas.
3	Ideas are "shuffled" and recorded on the board.
4	After all ideas are recorded, there is a discussion for the purpose of clarification and evaluation.
5	Individuals anonymously rank order the ideas. The "group decision" is the pooled outcome.

We will concentrate on the *open version* of nominal grouping.

Nominal Grouping—Open Version

- Facilitator presents issue.
- Begins with silent (noninteracting) stage.
- Members write their ideas.
- Ideas presented round-robin fashion until end.
- Ideas are clarified.
- Anonymous voting.

Nominal Grouping—Anonymous Version

- Used for sensitive issues.
- Encourages the quiet/shy.
- Facilitator presents issue.
- Members anonymously write their ideas.
- Ideas are shuffled and written on board.
- Ideas are clarified.
- Anonymous voting.

Now It's Your Turn

1. *Select an organization for analysis. Then using nominal grouping, identify what prevents the organization from offering high quality services.*

   Brainstorming is a process of group decision making. When brainstorming, the group is encouraged to explore as many alternatives as possible. "Wild" ideas are encouraged, and negative ideas are not permitted. A brief description of the ideas offered are written on the board.

Brainstorming

- Encourages creativity.
- Encourages involvement.
- Obtains a variety of new ideas.
- Is a source of alternate solutions.
- Provides a method to identify resistance.
- Results must be analyzed and processed.

Brainstorming—Rules

Conceptual Rules
- No criticism or evaluation allowed.
- Be open; innovative and daring.
- Aim for quantity.
- Hitchhike on other ideas.

Practical Rules
- Contribute in turn.
- Accept one idea per turn.
- You may pass.
- Do not explain ideas.

2. *Get together in your assigned teams. Brainstorm ways retailers could make shopping easier.*

   Multi-voting is a method of reducing a long list of ideas into a smaller list. A facilitator should be used to record the ideas on a blackboard or on a flip chart so they will be easy to understand. In addition, the facilitator should provide paper to the team members for recording their votes on. If the team is large, someone should assist the facilitator in vote tabulation.

Steps in Multivoting

Steps	Description
1	Review list of ideas generated and eliminate duplications.
2	Number the remaining ideas to facilitate recording votes.
3	Each team member should vote on approximately 30 percent of the total items. Hence if there are 20 items, vote on the top six choices.
4	Members should privately vote by placing the number corresponding to the ideas they feel are most beneficial. The paper the votes are recorded on should be provided by the facilitator.
5	Tabulate votes. Remove items that receive one or no votes.
6	Repeat the process a second time to reduce the long list to a few major ideas.

Other voting schemes are equally as useful but exercise caution. Do not *use a voting scheme if you are trying to generate consensus.*

3. *Use multivoting to reduce the previously brainstormed issues into a few manageable ideas.*

Force Field Analysis

Force field analysis is a technique developed by Kurk Lewin for identifying the forces that are present in a situation. Once the driving and restraining forces are understood, then plans can be developed for implementing change.

Change is a dynamic process and suggests movement from one time to the next under given conditions. However, how does change occur? Mr. Lewin views change as the outcome of a struggle between driving forces that are seeking to upset the status quo and restraining forces that are attempting to maintain the status quo.

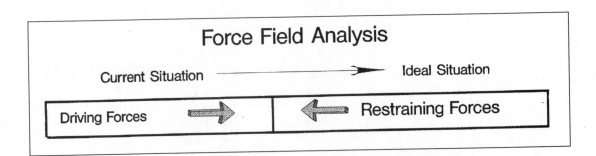

That is, driving forces attempt to move (change) a situation, while restraining forces attempt to maintain the current situation. If the driving forces are stronger, the restraining forces will be overcome, and change will occur. However, when the restraining forces are equal to or stronger than the driving forces, there will be no movement.

Our attention is directed to using force field analysis in a small group to identify a situation which needs to be changed. Brainstorming can be used to identify driving forces and restraining forces in the situation. After eliminating duplications, voting (see nominal grouping) can be used to identify the most important points.

Consider a practical example of a problem statement confronting many parents: "teenager not eating balanced meals." The current situation is that the person continuously eats junk food. The ideal situation is to get the young adult to eat balanced meals at established times. Driving forces are identified (i.e., forces as to why they should eat balanced meals) and restraining forces (why they do not eat balanced meals) are identified. A sample force field analysis is shown.

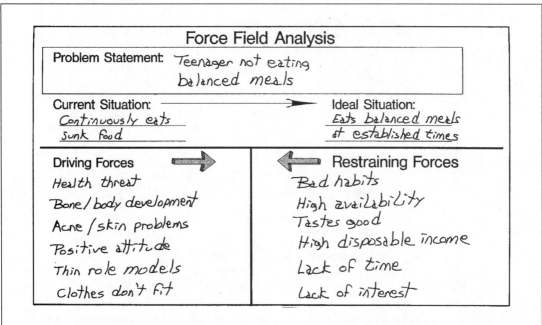

Force Field Analysis

Problem Statement: Teenager not eating balanced meals

Current Situation: Continuously eats junk food

Ideal Situation: Eats balanced meals at established times

Driving Forces
Health threat
Bone / body development
Acne / skin problems
Positive attitude
Thin role models
Clothes don't fit

Restraining Forces
Bad habits
High availability
Tastes good
High disposable income
Lack of time
Lack of interest

How Force Field Analysis Facilitates Changes

✓ It forces people to identify and to think through the specific facets of a desired change.
✓ It identifies the relative priority of the specific driving and restraining forces.
✓ It provides a priority action plan.

A force field action plan to change from a current to an ideal situation can be in terms of either strengthening the driving forces or in terms of reducing the restraining forces. This plan permits action to be taken with the understanding of the possible negative consequences.

How can a negative consequence occur when attempting to strengthen a driving force? Consider a simplistic response to the teenager's problem by a parent who consistently points out that eating junk food is bad for your health. Instead of achieving the desired results, reinforcing the point might actually strengthen resistance. A two-part attack is needed: provide multiple reasons for the change (highlight several driving forces) and eliminate some of the restraining forces (perhaps work with the habit, lack of interest, and high availability). Thus, when the driving forces outweighs the restraining forces, changes will occur.

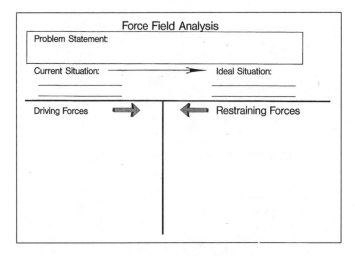

Now It's Your Turn

1. *Select a topic and then complete the blank force field analysis form shown.*

Classifying Quality Problems

Sometimes the techniques discussed in this book work too well: So many quality problems are generated that the issues seem overwhelming. One method to make the number of issues more manageable is to classify the quality problems on the quality quadrant shown.

Small quality problems are caused by failure to observe standards. Large quality problems refer to the poor supply of requested services and products. Large internal problems involve improving services supplied by one department to another.

Classifying Quality Problems

Classification	*Description*
Small internal:	Meetings without a pre-published agenda which do not start or end on time; internal communications are not clear; poor atmosphere, and mistakes in records
Small external:	Waiting/lines for customers; customer grumbling, and unkept building/grounds
Large internal:	Timely and accurate completion of work from other departments; caring and involved employees, and quality of workmanship
Large external: product	Lengthy delivery time; low customer satisfaction; high returns, and numerous customer complaints
Large external: service x	Access time; complaints; customer empathy, and poor atmosphere

Now It's Your Turn

1. *Identify and record a quality problem for each of the quality quadrants on the form provided. After recording the quality problem, which problem do you feel should be solved first? Why?**

Classifying Quality Problems
Quality

	Internal	External
Small Problem		
Large Problem		

Quality

*For a complete discussion on classifying quality problems, see Masterbroek, Willem, *Managing for Quality in the Service Sector*, Cambridge, MA: Basil Blackwell, Inc., 1991.

Improving Perceived Quality

There are two types of quality: the tangible quality that can be measured in terms of the usefulness it provides. The traditional approach to quality embraces this tangible, measurable approach. Product or service attributes are quantified in terms of performance, features, reliability, and serviceability. However, often ignored is that quality is a subjective attribute that is "assigned" to a good or a service by the consumer.

It is the consumer's definition of quality that counts. They are "paying the bills" and although objective quantitative quality measurements are useful, they are of secondary importance. If a product or service is actually of high quality, but if the consumer doesn't "like" the quality, then by definition, the quality is poor.

Measurements of quality such as Likert scales, are fine, but think through the degree of contact the customer had with the product or service under measurement. This is particularly important before investing in new systems to change the output, if the opinion of the consumer is based on a "casual" contact with the product or service.

Degree of Customer Contact

Customer contact	Attribute measurement
Low contact	Supermarket type of survey, with "shallow" inferences. "Taste this sausage: Does it taste good? Did we process you quickly?"
Medium contact	This is concerned with consumer satisfaction, and questions are more personal. "Does your car run Ok after repair? Are you satisfied?"
High contact	We are concerned with a more knowledgeable viewpoint, and how the customer relates to multiple points of interaction. In a hospital environment, opinions are the sum of many different interactions.

Perceived Quality = Actual Quality – Expected Quality

Perceived quality is the customer's opinion regarding what they received. Customers are satisfied if they feel the actual quality received was more than they expected.

Actual quality is what the consumer feels they received. It is a composite of subjectively assigned likes and dislikes, and objective measurements that can be expressed in terms of hours between breakdowns, ease of use, and costs to operate. A common mistake in quality measurement is to assume this is the same as perceived quality.

Expected quality is what the consumer expects upon use of the product or service. Advertising and word-of-mouth has a large influence on this. If expectations are too low, customers will go elsewhere. If expectations are too high, consumers will not be satisfied no matter how high the actual quality.

We can "toot our horn" and advertise that we have the best quality products in the world, but be careful. If expectations are raised too high and customers expect too much, they will be disappointed even if they are given a high quality service. Try creating a perception of high quality by positioning a firm so that it is perceived as offering a defined range of high quality services. That way, the firm avoids implying that "we are the best in the world."

The standard rule of thumb for quality professionals is: Underpromise and overdeliver. Get the customer to use your services without promising them a rose garden, but once they use your services, make the experience equal to paradise.

Now It's Your Turn

1. *Select a good or a service and attempt to define that "product" in terms of both objective and subjective measurements. Study the definitions of actual and expected quality, and develop ideas for improving the perceived quality.*

Effective Presentations

Presentation Criteria

Content Organization
Identifiable objectives
Explanatory introduction
Clear structure
Decisive conclusion

Teamwork
Attentiveness to speaker
Organized supportive material
Smooth flow between speakers

Visual Aids and Handouts
Creativity
Clear, simple, and neat
Equipment setup and operative

Delivery of Individual Presentations
Personal appearance
Voice projection
Articulation: *Do not read materials*
Handing of notes and visual aids
Eye contact with audience

Impact
Were there questions after your summary?
Was audience paying attention?
Was objective accomplished?
Was audience convinced?

It takes a lot of work to put together a top quality presentation. Perhaps the most important thing to remember when giving a presentation is to practice first. When you know your material, you can relax, and presentation quality will be enhanced. It is a good idea to employ visual aids and handouts to reinforce presentation content. A few additional ideas are shown.

Advanced QI Techniques

Several advanced Quality Improvement (QI) techniques will be presented in this section. An application of any of the techniques in this section requires both thought and careful planning. A brief overview of the techniques discussed follows. Refer to the appropriate discussion for more details.

Technique: Focus Groups

Groups brainstorm product or service features within a structured condition.

Useful when there's a need to obtain input into either the design of a new product or service, or a review of an existing product or service. Moderators can then perform a "linking" function with appropriate departments.

Limitations: It is often difficult to summarize general brainstorming findings into a single, coherent action report.

Technique: Benchmarking

Identify how other firms perform their functions.

Useful when a breakthrough approach is needed. Benchmarking can demonstrate that others have solved the problems in providing high quality products and services on a timely basis.

Limitations: There is a tendency for people to reject comparisons by rationalizing "but our process is different."

Technique: Process Ownership

Get employees to "buy into" the part of the process that they can control.

Useful when an "emotional" commitment to quality of a process is desirable.

Limitations: May be difficult to apply to subprocesses when employees are not permanently assigned to the same subprocess.

Advanced QI Techniques

Technique: Customer Needs Mapping

Categorizes customer wants (needs) and identifies the internal processes required to those needs.

Useful when an understanding is needed of the production processes required to meet consumer needs.

Limitations: Exact needs must be identified, which are often unknown.

Technique: Quality Functional Deployment

A formal process for translating customer requirements into the appropriate technical requirements.

Useful when customer requirements (both needs and product specifications) must be transferred into either an organizational design or a technical product design.

Limitations: Exact needs must be identified in complete detail. However, despite this difficulty, this is an excellent tool for reducing "off the shelf" designs that are made before understanding requirements.

Technique: Hoshin Planning Techniques
(Often Called the Seven Management Tools)

Breaks down the planning process into general, intermediate, and detailed planning. Seven management tools are used to assist in planning from studying consumers, to detailed policy deployment.

Useful when breakthrough thinking is needed in the planning process.

Limitations: Many of the specific techniques involved suffer from "data explosion" in that alternatives too numerous to evaluate may be generated.

Technique: Gap Analysis

Develops an understanding of services offered from different viewpoints.

Useful when an understanding is needed between different views of services.

Limitations: Although the gaps provide a useful indicator of different viewpoints regarding services, the gaps should be taken only as a general indicators. Recent academic studies have shed doubt about the existence of, and ability to, quantify all five gaps.

Technique: Taguchi Methods

Extends quality improvement activities to include product design and process design.

Useful when developing an understand of the multitude of different factors affected by the quality of goods and services.

Limitations: You better understand statistics.

Focus Groups*

The term *focus groups* is used to describe a method by which a group of people gather in a structured environment to offer their opinions. The opinions given can be about either a product or a service, and opinions can be offered by consumers or nonconsumers alike. Particular attention will be devoted to the process used to gather opinions regarding a service, however, product opinions can be gathered in the same manner.

The facilitator is the person who is in charge of the total focus group study. Conducting multiple focus groups is a large and demanding task, so the facilitator is often assisted by one or more moderators. The moderator, in such instances, is the person actually conducting the focus group meeting. The moderator follows a discussion guide prepared by the facilitator to assure that the group stays "on track" and that the desired questions are discussed by the group.

The information gathered by focus groups serve a dual purpose: to be able to improve organization's marketing/design efforts and to "educate" the organization's facilitator and moderators. There is nothing like "hearing it first hand" from the consumer to sharpen one's opinions, which in turn can be relayed to quality improvement teams. Scheduled follow-up discussions with fellow employees will enhance the firm's internal consumer orientation.

Depending on the objective of the focus group, participants can be a cross-section of society or be comprised of a specific age and sex. For example, manufacturers of women's hair spray would probably not want the opinions of bald, middle-aged males mixed in with a focus group of potential female users. Hence, such subgroups would be excluded. However, other services, such as marketers of television advertisements, or manufacturers of convince foods, may want focus groups comprised of a mixture of ages, sexes, income levels, and viewpoints. Furthermore, these marketers and manufacturers might wish to include nonconsumers as well as consumers of the service (or product) being discussed to encourage a wide range of comments.

Since opinions vary widely, often numerous focus groups are conducted by several different moderators. The discussion guide created by the moderator is vital as it's all too easy to have several moderators go off on different tangents, resulting in focus group meeting that cannot be summarized into an overall report. Hence the focus group discussion guide assists moderators in "staying on track."

In addition to coordinating the moderators, it is the facilitator's job to be sure that he/she understands the mindset of the decision makers. Instructions to construct focus groups to find out more about XYZ are not enough: The facilitator must understand how the information will be used and, if possible, meet with potential users to understand their requirements.

After issues are discussed and understood, the facilitator can assemble the moderators and begin developing a discussion guide. Once the guide is created,

*Thanks are due to Dr. Glynn Mangold, Professor of Marketing, for sharing his focus group studies.

149

the facilitator must assure that moderators follow the guide so that there is a uniform method of conducting the various focus group sessions. During and after the focus group sessions, the moderator gathers the data called for in the discussion guide, summarizes the results of the focus group sessions they conducted, and presents their write-up to the facilitator.

The opinions of any group of people regarding what is important will naturally vary, and there is never enough time in a relatively brief focus group session to cover all the desirable topics. However, unless the moderators closely follows the discussion guide, the results from different moderators cannot be written up into a single, logical, coherent analysis.

Steps to be followed by the facilitator when creating a focus group discussion guide are shown. The third step, the development of the actual questions to be asked in the focus group, is itemized separately.

Creating a Focus Group Discussion Guide

Step 1: Write the problem statement in one sentence. If you cannot state the issue in one sentence, you probably do not have the specific direction needed to successfully complete the focus group.

Step 2: Make sure you understand the mindset of the key manager(s) who will use the report.

Step 3: Develop the questions to be asked to obtain the needed information. (See developing the focus group questions.)

Step 4: Print copies for facilitator and moderator so that questions are easy to read at a glance. Leave room for answers to be written on the guide.

The method used to develop the actual questions asked to focus group participants shown in Step 3. Note that in order to organizes the focus group activities, the facilitator must prepare two documents: the participant's demographic questionnaire which is completed privately by focus group participants, and the moderator's discussion guide with blanks under each question to record key ideas.

Are You a Total Quality Person?

	Seldom	Sometimes	Always
I attempt to improve my home/family life.	☐	☐	☐

Organizing Focus Group Activities

Step 1: Develop the participant's demographic questionnaire containing questions that explain variations in opinions between different focus groups. These questions generally include: sex, age, income range, education, and general buying preferences.

Step 2: Develop the moderator's discussion guide containing the major questions to be asked to focus group participants. Think through how possible answers will shed insight into the problem statement. Be creative in your questions.

Step 3: After a few days, review your focus group questions, combine similar questions together and arrange into a rough discussion guide. (It is difficult to cover more than 10 questions in an hour period and allow sufficient time for discussion.)

Step 4: Circulate drafts of the participant's demographic questions and the moderator's discussion guide. Ask for feedback from the moderators and from interested people on the participant's questionnaire as well as on the discussion guide.

Step 5: Incorporate revisions and ask yourself: "When these questions have been answered, has the central issue been adequately addressed?"

Step 6: Finalize the two documents: The participant demographic questionnaire which will be completed by focus group members before the group discussion, and the moderator's discussion guide with space for the moderator to write key items offered by participants.

Step 7: Conduct a "dress rehearsal" with the moderators. Then have the moderators conduct the focus groups.

Step 8: Have the moderators communicate their findings to other employees.

The facilitator will have to develop a plan for obtaining focus group participants. In addition, suitable testing sites will have to be arranged, which is often difficult for commercial firms. Finally, it is a good idea for the facilitator to ask a moderator to volunteer to test the procedures and questions developed before widespread use.

Friendly Texan Insurance's Focus Group

The executive committee at the Friendly Texan Insurance Company decided they did not know enough about current and future insurance needs for people in their business area. The assignment was given to Ms. Joyce Jackson, who initially felt that focus groups could be used to identify current and future insurance needs in Dallas and Houston.

Mr. Tom Martin in the Dallas corporate office was assigned the task of being the main facilitator because of previous focus group training. He would be assisted by the following people from the Human Resource Department who would serve as moderators: Mr. Jerry Adams of the Dallas office and Ms. Susan Smith from Houston. These people also work with Friendly Texan Insurance's quality council composed of agencies in their city. It was felt that the information they obtained could be communicated to the council on a "first-hand" basis. All people were contacted, and they agreed to get together in a meeting in Ms. Jackson's office to discuss how the focus group activities would be coordinated.

When the facilitator and moderators met, Ms. Jackson circulated the preliminary action plan shown and asked: "Who can do what, when?" It was decided to first make a rough draft of participant's demographic questionnaire, and the focus group discussion guide before finalizing dates.

Focus Group: Preliminary Action Plan

Activity	Description
Problem statement	Identify current and future insurance needs in the area we service.
Facilitator assigned	Tom Jackson, Dallas Office.
Moderators assigned	Jerry Adams, Dallas; Susan Smith, Houston.
Participant's questionnaire	See attached.
Group discussion guide	See attached.
Obtain participants	Contact market research firms in Dallas and Houston.
Location	Houston and Dallas—2 groups each.
Moderator's report	Separate reports summarizing focus group findings for Dallas and Houston.
Facilitator's report	Combine write-up of moderator's reports.

Mr. Martin was able to quickly locate reputable marketing research firms in both Dallas and Houston. However, both firms warned him that obtaining participants would be difficult because people would perceive any meeting by Friendly Texan Insurance Company as simply an "excuse" to sell them insurance.

After discussing the problem with Ms. Jackson, they decided to broaden the scope of the study. The problem statement was finalized as: "The objective of the focus group study is to identify current and future community needs for health, safety and welfare issues in the Dallas and Houston areas."

The decision was made not to telephone people to obtain focus group participants, but to resort to the relatively standard method of "mall intercepts." That is, people shopping in a mall would be approached by a professional facilitator and asked if they would be willing to share their ideas for a study conducted by Longhorn Research to identify future community needs. (The sponsor, Friendly Texan Insurance, was not mentioned.) Potential participants were promised that this is not a sales or promotional meeting and that no firm or products would be mentioned.

Once the objectives of the study were identified and the type and selection of focus group participants qualified, a focus group discussion guide was developed. Draft copies were circulated by the facilitator to interested parties in Friendly Texan Insurance and to the moderators that would be employed by Longhorn Research. Comments were incorporated and the focus group discussion guide shown was produced. Room was left on the actual form for the moderator to make notes and record comments (although the discussion was also tape recorded).

Focus Group Participant's Questionnaire

Thank you for agreeing to participate in a focus group. In a moment this group will be asked their opinions regarding future needs in our community. All information is confidential, in fact we are not even requesting that you state your name.

Please answer the following questions so that we can be sure we are obtaining participants that represent a cross-sectional view of our community.

How long have you lived in the area?

Please check the answer that best applies.

Do you:
- ☐ Own your home?
- ☐ Rent?
- ☐ Other?

Are you:
- ☐ Married/living with another?
- ☐ Single?
- ☐ Divorced/separated/widowed?

My yearly family income is:
- ☐ Under $15,000
- ☐ $15,001–$25,000
- ☐ $25,001–$40,000
- ☐ $40,001–$75,000
- ☐ $75,001+

Actual participants in the focus group sessions were "qualified" in two ways. First, they must look like they were "over 21" in that people of high school age were not approached. Second, they must have resided in the Houston (or Dallas) area for one year or more prior to the study. If these qualifications were met, they were accompanied to a room in the mall, where there was snack food and nonacholic beverages, provided by a local restaurant. They were told that a moderator would join them shortly and they were given assistance in completion of the focus group participant's questionnaire shown. Questions about the session were sidestepped by stating that the moderator would answer the questions in a few moments. This had the dual function of building suspense and permitting a flexible staging of participants in an enjoyable atmosphere (i.e., it could take 20 minutes or so to obtain enough qualified participants).

Focus Group Discussion Guide

Please make sure that every participant has completed the focus group participant questionnaire. Introduce yourself and ask each participant to give their name, which area of the town they are from, and their major hobby.

Restate that the purpose of this focus group session is to identify present and future community needs, and that this is not a sales meeting. Simply provide us with your ideas. There are no right or wrong answers, and their frank opinion is appreciated.

Ask participants to complete the participant's questionnaire. Point out that the information is confidential and that we are not asking for their name. This information will only be used to assure we obtain a cross-section of community viewpoints.

1. What are the biggest threats confronting residents of our city?
2. What kinds of health, safety, and welfare issues can you insurance against?
3. Did you every have to "use" your existing insurance?
4. What was your experience when you "used" your insurance?
5. After initial comments, ask: What were you satisfied about in the interaction? Where were you dissatisfied about?
6. Assume we are trying to come up with "ways" of meeting the community's insurance needs. What should be made available?

Note: It is unlikely more than six questions can be discussed in an hour, particularly if everyone expresses an opinion. An optional question, time permitting is:

7. Suppose you were advising the President of the United States and he asked: "What are the future community needs for health, safety, and welfare issues?" What would be your response?

The first focus group session was in Dallas, so Mr. Jerry Adams was in attendance. Because sessions also would be conducted in Houston, Ms. Susan Smith also attended. Both people stayed in the next room and were not seen by participants. After the focus group session was completed, they meet with the moderator from Longhorn Research to discuss refinements to the participant's questionnaire and to the focus group discussion guide.

Now It's Your Turn

Design a focus group study to obtain information about a product or service of your choice.

Benchmarking

Benchmarking is a strategy of copying the best practice of a company that excels at a given business function. The company doesn't even have to be in the same industry: a wide, broad-based comparison can be used. For example, suppose a retailer is concerned about excessive inventory levels because items are carried in inventory for several months before they are sold. Benchmarking a firm in a different industry might provide ideas that otherwise would be overlooked. You might find a firm that ships orders directly from the factory to the consumer, virtually eliminating the need for inventory.

There are five different types of benchmarking:

1. Internal

2. Competitive

3. Shadow

4. Industrial

5. World-class

Internal benchmarking occurs when a firm looks within its divisions or branches and compares repetitive operational functions. Although it might not be fair to compare inventory turns in a heavy equipment division to a retail division, other processes are more universal. For example, why does it take one division two days to fill a backorder for an item, yet another division takes two weeks. What is the average time it takes to answer a phone? In other words, those functions common to operating an ongoing business can become the basis for internal benchmarking.

Competitive benchmarking involves identifying key competitive characteristics of a product or service and then comparing these characteristics to your competitors. For example, fast food restaurants, particularly ones serving hamburgers would be well advised to send a QI team to study the time it takes for a competitor to service a customer. In addition to "hard" objective data, subjective aspects of quality need to be identified and analyzed. Often market research firms are contracted to use "mystery shoppers" and to undertake extensive surveys to benchmark your performance against key competitors.

Shadow benchmarking involves monitoring key product and service attributes of a successful competitor and meeting changes as they occur. That is, if a dominant firm in a competitive industry comes out with a new product or service, immediately find out why. More likely than not, firms practicing shadow benchmarking immediately offer that same product or service. Shadow benchmarking is obvious with some gasoline stations and fast food restaurants selling major brands. Often when a successful industrial leader opens a retail facility at a new location, within months a competitive store appears next door.

Industrial benchmarking, often called *functional benchmarking*, involves a comparison of functions within the same industry. Some industrial associations exchange information to facilitate this comparison (such as the Aerospace Manufacturers Association's sharing of direct and indirect ratios for numerous labor categories). If the industrial average for a production control function is 15 percent of direct manufacturing hours, why is our ratio 18 percent? Or, if there is an average of one secretary per 20 accounting people, why do we have one secretary per 15 accountants?

World-class benchmarking involves comparisons of processes across diverse industries. For example, General Motors might compare the time required to fill a customer order with a small mail order firm that is world renown for its outstanding success. That is, a comparison is made of your process to the best in the world, no matter what the industry. A retail sales firm might ask why a particular restaurant has such a large repeat business? Is there anything we can learn from them? What are they doing right?

Getting Started in Benchmarking

Beginners in benchmarking would be wise to concentrate on *cycle time reduction* has the beneficial effect of quickly transferring improvements to the "bottom line." External measurements include factors such as responding to customer demand. However, do not ignore internal measurements of *support department responses*. Why does it require: a month to purchase an item; three months to process capital expenditure requests, and three trips to a University for a student to register for a class? Why can't sales personnel be empowered to make many on-the-spot refunds or exchanges?

Benchmarking Steps	
Needs Assessment Team	Benchmarking Team
1. Identify internal and external customer needs.	1. Develop operational definitions for critical indicators
2. Identify key customer needs:	2. Baseline your own process
Not met	3. Identify best in class
Met but can be improved	4. Gather data
Met better by competition	5. Analyze and communicate findings
	6. Develop strategies

Two teams are required for benchmarking: a *needs assessment team* and the *actual benchmarking team*. The needs assessment team begins by identifying internal and external needs, independent of the ability to find "data" on these needs. That is, the needs assessment team concentrates on the firm's critical success factors and what is needed to monitor performance on those factors. Their output provides direction so that the benchmarking team does not run off "half-cocked" to visit a competitor without thinking through what is really needed. (See the sections on needs mapping, surveys, and focus groups.)

Needs Assessment Guidelines

What are the critical success factors of strategic importance to your organization?

Which factors differentiate your firm in "the eyes of the customer"?

What data is needed to determine the effectiveness of your critical success factors?

Which factors significantly impact quality, costs, or cycle times?

Where is there the greatest room for improvement?

There are several factors the needs assessment team should consider. A brief summary is shown.

The needs list generated should be reduced to six or less needs so that the benchmarking team will not divert their attention from the key issues. Benchmarking teams typically follow a six-step process.

1. The benchmarking team* begins by taking the critical success factors identified. A clear operational definition is needed for each factor. For example, suppose a fast-food, drive-in restaurant is developing an operational definition of responsiveness. *Responsiveness* would probably be defined as the time (in seconds) from when the customer arrives on the premises to when they leave the premises.

   That is, the team is concerned with the time required for the customer to decide on an order, relay the order to the order taker, wait while the order is filled, pay for the order, and then leave the premises. On the other hand, a QI team developing a definition of responsiveness for an expensive restaurant might have an entirely different definition. Responsiveness might be defined in terms of a total dining experience which would include the chiefs' ability to accommodate varying customer requests in the way food is prepared.

   Benchmarking is an ongoing process. Detailed operational definitions help ensure that the findings can be replicated by other teams. It is a good idea to internally circulate the definitions developed prior to undertaking a study. Ask respondents to use their own words to explain the definitions. This will help assure that meaningful definitions are clearly stated.

2. Baseline your own operations using the operational definitions developed. In addition to providing an internal reference point, operational problems in the definition can be corrected before visiting other organizations.

---

*In actual practice, the same people can be on both teams. The use of two different teams highlights the importance of needs assessment prior to undertaking a benchmark study.

3. Brainstorm ideas to identify best in class. Practical issues suggest you should concentrate on organizations willing to cooperate with you.

4. Gather data in whatever way that is appropriate. In addition to visits, try plant tours, interviews, and conversations with reliable sources.

5. Analyze and communicate findings. Set up a series of employee meetings to discuss the team findings. Encourage employee inputs into the process so that everyone understands what is required to create a high quality product or service.

If desired, a quantitative measurement can be developed that indicates the gap between your performance and the benchmark process. Suppose we were concerned with response time and your firm required 120 seconds for a customer to be processed while the benchmark firm required 60 seconds. One way to convert this performance difference to gap figures is shown in the following formula. The minus indicates a negative (adverse) performance gap exists.

$$\text{Gap} = \frac{\text{Your Performance}}{\text{Benchmark Firm}} - 1 \qquad \frac{60}{120} - 1 = -50\%$$

This formula is not useful in all conditions. Perhaps your performance was higher in terms of customer complaints (including order errors, cold food, and returns). That is, 5 percent of your customers complained, versus 10 percent of the benchmark firm. A formula for showing this could be:

$$\text{Gap} = \frac{\text{Benchmark Firm}}{\text{Your Performance}} - 1 \qquad \frac{10\%}{5\%} - 1 = 2 - 1 = +100\%$$

6. Develop strategies by implementing procedures to reduce the cycle time. Then benchmark the process again.

What's So Complicated About Benchmarking?

If you have been following the discussion of benchmarking, by now you might be asking the question: "What's so complicated about benchmarking?" Everything we've said is rather obvious and is based on common sense.

The reason for the difficulty is because there is a vast number of different potential outcomes for each type of benchmarking undertaken. Remember, five types of benchmarking were mentioned: internal, competitive, shadow, industrial, and world-class benchmarking. Each of these types has varying impacts on the major benchmarking characteristics shown.

Common Benchmark Characteristics

Speed and cost of conducting benchmark

Types of processes being studied

Difficulty of collecting data

Difficulty of selling improvement ideas to management

Transferability of lessons learned

Adoption risk

Expected benefits

For example, internal benchmarking studies can be quickly and economically conducted. On the other hand, world-class benchmarking might take the longest to conduct and may well be the most difficult to gather data on because many of the firms simply do not share their data. However, the benefits of world-class benchmarking might be immense: as a new way of viewing your products and services might emerge.

Not only is it difficult to gather first-hand personal data on world-class firms, there is seldom an easy way to apply the findings to your firm, hence the adoption risk might be extremely high. On the other hand, data from internal benchmarking is easily verified and has a minimum adoption risk.

With so many possible interactions, what's a person to do? Frankly, benchmarking is more of a science than an art. When beginning, benchmark a process that you can control and that has the highest probability of success. After an initial success, even a small one, you can branch out and try riskier benchmark studies.*

Now It's Your Turn

Benchmark a fast-food firm of your choice.

Process Ownership

The purpose of conducting a *process ownership review* is to have everyone think through the processes they use to perform their jobs. Begin by first identifying the customers of their process, then identify the suppliers that enable them to do their job, and finally, identify the data they need to personally control the process. Ideally, everyone should own a "piece" of the process.

Are You a Total Quality Person?

	Seldom	Sometimes	Always
I personally attempt to master something new, at least quarterly.	☐	☐	☐

---

*For an excellent treatment of the concept of benchmarking, see John J. McGonagle's article, "New Options in Benchmarking." Printed in the *Journal for Quality and Participation*, July/August, 1993, pp. 60–67.

Process Improvement Checklist		
✓	1	What is your job?
	2	What processes do you own?
	3	Describe and flow chart the process. Identify critical steps. Remove nonvalue-added steps. (Use a separate sheet of paper.)
	4	Determine the customers for each process. (See this page.)
	5	Determine the supplier for each process. (See page 161.)
	6	Define output quality for each process and identify data source. (See page 162.)
	7	Determine total cycle time (process flow time): A. Compute cycle time for subprocesses and total processes. B. Identify slack time/queue time. C. Establish theoretical cycle time. (No constraints, no bottlenecks, no excess queue time.) D. Eliminate nonvalue-added activities.
	8	Follow QI steps to identify area with greatest improvement potential and to improve the process.

Steps 1, 2, and 3 are relatively straightforward. Difficulty is sometimes encountered with step 4, which requires that the customers for each process be identified. A closer evaluation of this step follows.

Process Improvement Checklist		
✓	4	Determine the customers for each process.

The purpose of this exercise is to encourage all of us (individually and as work teams) to think about customer relationships. Your customer is the next phase in the process and their needs must be understood so that high quality output can be delivered. Some of those needs are universal such as a desire to be treated with respect and to feel good about themselves. Other needs are specific because of job requirements.

Who Is My Customer?

What is the next phase in the process? When I complete my job, what is the next job that has to happen?

Customer	Needs
Name and describe process	Give specific product/process requirements
1. _____	_____
_____	_____
_____	_____
2. _____	_____
_____	_____
_____	_____
3. _____	_____
_____	_____
_____	_____

Process Improvement Checklist		
✓	5	Determine the supplier for each process.

The purpose of this exercise is to encourage all of us (individually and as work teams) to think about supplier relationships. Your supplier is that phase of the process which precedes your phase of the process. It is that job which should occur before you do your job. You are the customer for that supplier.

Are You a Total Quality Person?

	Seldom	Sometimes	Always
I admit my mistakes, and then move on with the goal of not making the same mistake again.	☐	☐	☐

Process Ownership

Supplier	My needs
1. _____	_____
_____	_____
_____	_____
2. _____	_____
_____	_____
_____	_____
3. _____	_____
_____	_____

How well is my supplier meeting my needs as a customer?

Process Improvement Checklist		
✓	6	Define output quality for each process and identify data source.

The objective of Step 6 is to bring your process under control. Identify the data available and the data to be gathered so that you can prove the output quality of your process. An example of the type of data needed to define the output quality of a sample process is shown. Using this as a guide, identify the needs of your process and complete the form shown.

Data: Needed and Source—Example

Data Needed	Type of Data	Source of Data
Waiting time	Quantitative	Take a weekly timestudy
Billing errors	Quantitative	Review bills and record complaints/inquiries
Customer satisfaction: Immediate term	Quantitative	Brief "How am I doing" survey
Customer satisfaction: Long term	Qualitative	Letter to home asking opinion

Now It's Your Turn

1. *Complete the form shown for your own process.*

Data: Needed and Source		
Data Needed	Type of Data	Source of Data

Customer Needs Mapping

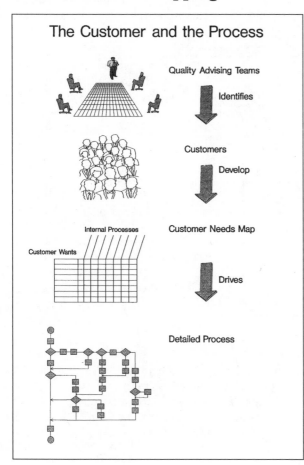

The Customer and the Process

Customer needs mapping is a technique used to identify consumer wants and then to identify the ability of internal processes to meet those wants. The technique begins by first identifying the customers of a process. There are two major customers of any process: the external customer and the internal customer. The external customer is the person or group who buys the product or service. The internal customer is the next step in the process that receives the output. This concept of an internal customer is frequently overlooked by support departments such as facilities, inventory control, accounting, and the computer group. Because they have "captive customers" they often behave as if there is no need to worry about quality, courtesy, and rapid delivery.

Suppose we have selected our customer as an external customer who uses our services. Then develop a list of customer wants through a combination of focus groups, brainstorming, and customer interviews. Group these wants into logical categories.

Then identify the processes required to meet these wants. Concentrate on identifying the "major" processes needed to meet the customer needs. If you go into detail and attempt to flow chart all the activities in a firm that interface with the customer's wants, you will become so overwhelmed with detail that you will never complete the task.

After the general customer needs (often called *wants*) are identified and grouped together, assign an importance ratings on a scale of 1 to 5, where 1 is the least important and 5 is the most important customer want. Next, list the internal processes required to meet these wants across the top of the grid. Then evaluate the effectiveness of each specific internal process in meeting the customer's wants. This effectiveness is evaluated in terms of: High (H), Medium (M), and Low (L).

A beginning customer needs map for a fast-food restaurant is shown. As with any map or text, it is read from left to right with the items on the left being what the customer wants. How these wants are satisfied (the internal process steps) are shown across the top of the chart.

Note there is a problem with the internal process of filling an order as the process has a low effectiveness in meeting customer wants. This evaluation score was not assigned by a QI team, but is the concensus of the opinions of the customers who were interviewed. When such a condition exists, further investigation to determine the cause of such low scores is definitely warranted.

Customer Needs Mapping—Benefits

Increased understanding of who the customer is

Awareness of customer requirements

Transforms customer requirements into design features

Focuses on process steps critical to customer

Identification of customer requirements not addressed

Customer Needs Map: Fast Food Restaurant
Internal Processes

Customer Wants			Importance Rating	Take Order	Fill Order	Prepare Food	Display Food
Service	Quick	5	M	L	L	L	
	Clean	3	M	L	L	L	
	Friendly	2	H	L	L	H	
	Inexpensive	4	M	L	H	H	
Food	Taste	5	L	L	L	H	
	Healthy	1	M	L	L	M	
	Quality	4	H	L	L	H	

A customer needs map is useful when flow charting a process. The map provides a defined beginning and ending point for each process, and provides a guide so we won't get lost in the details. Customer needs mapping is a beginning, simple approach used to identify the ability of a process to meet customer needs. A more detailed methodology is explained in the section on *Quality Functional Deployment* (QFD) which "deploys" the functions necessary to meet customer needs.

Now It's Your Turn

1. *Use the rough draft shown of a beginning customer needs map for a person requesting information from Friendly Texan Insurance Company. Identify the detailed customer wants (perceptions/needs) and identify the internal processes beginning used by the insurance agency to fulfill the request. Hint: Assume most requests for information are by phone. Note the type of "wants" vary immensely between current customers and potential customers.*

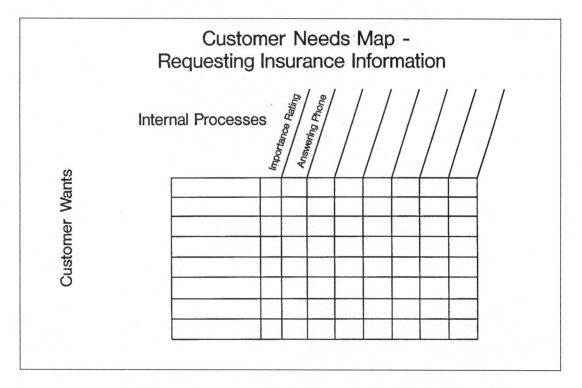

2. *Develop a customer needs map for a trade school that specializes in offering the latest computer and business training to the adult population in a metropolitan area.*

Quality Functional Deployment

Quality Functional Deployment (QFD) is an advanced form of customer needs mapping which encourages users to focus on the broader process of how results are obtained. QFD was developed by the Japanese in 1972. It is a formal process for translating customer requirements into appropriate technical requirements. QFD is used to assure that all of a company's operations are driven by the customer's needs, rather than by top management (or by design engineers).

Quality Functional Deployment

A set of matrices are used to relate consumer needs to counterpart characteristics which are expressed as technical specifications and process control requirements. The four major QFD planning documents are:

1. *Customer requirements planning matrix:* Used to translate the consumer's needs into product counterpart characteristics.

2. *Product characteristic deployment matrix:* Used to translate final product counterpart characteristics into critical component characteristics.

3. *Process plan and quality control charts:* Used to identify critical process and product parameters along with control points.

4. *Operating instructions:* Used to identify operations that must be performed to assure important parameters are achieved.

The *customer requirement planning matrix* is the major portion of the QFD concept. The structure looks like a house, hence QFD is often referred to as "The House of Quality." A six-step, detailed procedure will be used in creating our QFD "house." A bank's commercial lending department will be used as an example.

Service	Individuality	Good Rapport	
		Calls Customer by Name	
	Timeliness	Meet Customer Deadlines	
		Rapid Data Access	
	Simplicity	Single Page	
		Easy-to-understand	
		Details Highlighted	
	Courtesy	Friendliness	
		No Waiting in Line	
Economic	Types of Loans	Line of Credit	Regular
			Guidance
		Unsecured Loans	Revolving
			Term
			Demand
		Secured Loans	Equipment
			Real Estate
			Accounts Rec.
			Inventory
	Cost to Customer	Compensating Balances	
		Interest Rates	
		Fees	
		Guarantees	

Step 1: Identify Customer Needs

Customer attributes (consumer needs if you wish) are the product or service requirements stated in customer's terms. Marketing research plays an important part in identifying these needs which must be subdivided into manageable sub-needs. This is similar to what we just accomplished in customer needs mapping.

Our example of a customers of a bank's commercial service department shows two major needs: service and economic loans (i.e., low interest rates and favorable loan terms). These major categories are broken down into their major components. Service is composed of individuality, timeliness, simplicity, and courtesy. Each of these are subdivided again. In this case, courtesy is comprised of friendliness of staff and not having to wait in line before seeing a loan officer.

The resulting customer needs requirement matrix appears as shown. The remainder of the house appears as a skeleton.

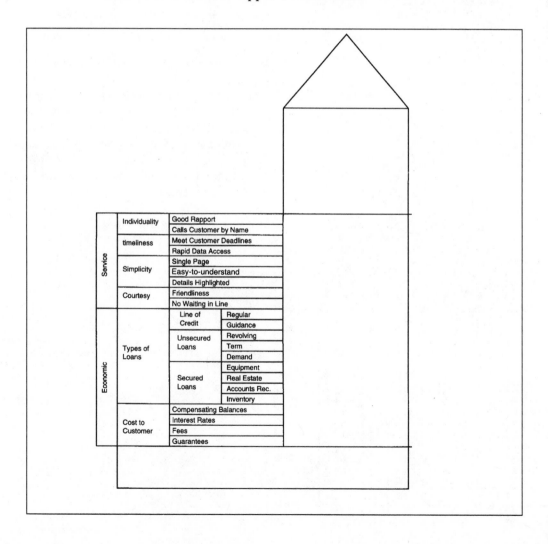

Service	Individuality	Good Rapport	
		Calls Customer by Name	
	timeliness	Meet Customer Deadlines	
		Rapid Data Access	
	Simplicity	Single Page	
		Easy-to-understand	
		Details Highlighted	
	Courtesy	Friendliness	
		No Waiting in Line	
Economic	Types of Loans	Line of Credit	Regular
			Guidance
		Unsecured Loans	Revolving
			Term
			Demand
		Secured Loans	Equipment
			Real Estate
			Accounts Rec.
			Inventory
	Cost to Customer	Compensating Balances	
		Interest Rates	
		Fees	
		Guarantees	

Step 2: List the Product/Process Characteristics That Will Meet the Customer's Needs

Product/process characteristics are the technical counterparts that must be deployed to meet consumer needs. They are stated across the top of the matrix.

Internal processes (or technical product characteristics) are often related to each other. These relationships are shown with the following symbols:

⊙   Circle with a dot in the middle denotes a very strong relationship.

○   Circle denotes a strong relationship.

△   Triangle denotes a weak relationship.

These symbols help assess trade-off characteristics between the processes. They appear as the roof in our house as shown. A very strong relationship is shown between the Credit Department and the Loan Committee. Another very strong relationship is shown between computer input and funds transfer. A strong relationship is shown between the terms of loan and the proofing of the loan (i.e., proofreading legal contract requirements). A weak relationship is shown between the loan officer's portfolio and training and development. Additional relationships also exist but are not shown in this simplified example.

Step 3: Relationship Matrix Between Customer Attributes and Counterpart Characteristics

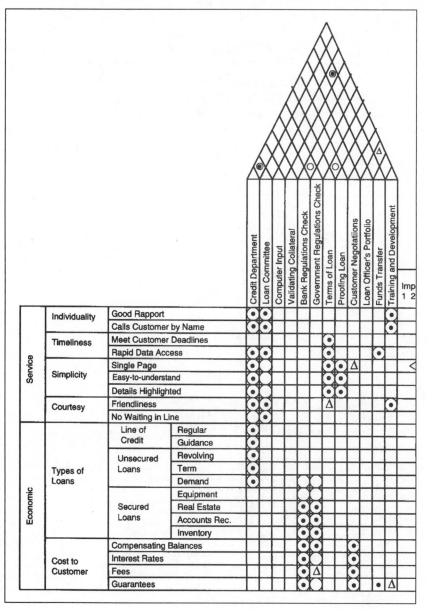

Now that we have the roof (the technical counterparts) we need to develop the basic matrix. This matrix shows the relationship between customer attributes (needs) and the counterpart characteristics. The symbols previously explained are used to show several relationships in our examples. Friendliness is very strongly related to Training and Development. Unsecured loans are very strongly related to the Credit Department and are strongly related bank regulations and government regulations check. Guarantees are weakly related to Training and Development.

Step 4: Market Evaluations

In this step, each customer attribute is rated from 1 (minor importance) to 5 (extremely important) from the viewpoint of the customer. Competitive evaluations are performed to highlight strengths and weaknesses in the ability of competitors to meet this consumer need. If products were evaluated instead of services, the strengths and weaknesses of competing products would be evaluated.

This evaluation can help set priorities in our design process and give direction for our advertising programs. In our example, the commercial loan customer felt a good rapport was necessary, but were where neutral towards being called by name. However, it was extremely important that their loan deadlines be met. Competitive evaluations of the services offered by Banks A and B showed they did an excellent job on establishing a good rapport with the customer and calling customers by name. However, both banks, are out of town banks, and do a poor job on meeting customer loan deadlines. This represents a possible selling point for our local bank.

In this example, only a couple of technical counterpart characteristics are identified as needed to meet customer needs. If this were true in actual practice, then either the process is redundant, or the QFD designers may have missed some important customer attribute.

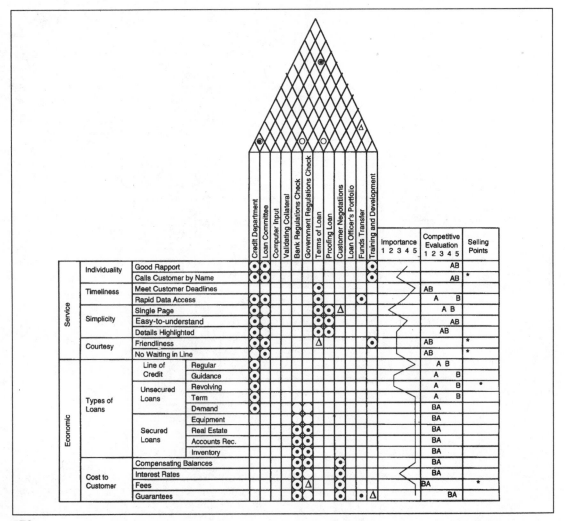

Step 5: Evaluate Counterpart Characteristics of Competitive Products and Develop Targets

This is often accomplished via in-house testing, which is then translated into measurable terms. Benchmarking also has a role at this point. If a competitive product or service satisfies a customer attribute, but the counterpart characteristics indicates otherwise, something is wrong. Either the measures used are faulty, or there is something which we don't know that is affecting customer perceptions.

It was previously mentioned that commercial loan customers need the bank to meet their deadline for loan approval. Our competitors, Banks A and B, who have their main offices located out of town, do not feel this need is important. Furthermore, an interview with our former customers who have been through our competitor's loan process indicates their technical process regarding the loan committee as 2 (poor). (More on this is found in the next section on selecting counterpart to be deployed.)

Something seems wrong with unsecured loans consisting of revolving, term, and demand loans. This was identified as very strongly effecting the credit department and a competitive evaluation showed Bank B to be very strong in this area. Yet, both A and B's Credit Department both received a ranking of 3. Either both banks are "reading this wrong" or there is something we've missed in identifying the consumer's needs.

Step 6: Select Counterpart Characteristics to Be Deployed in the Remainder of the Process

Identify the characteristics that have a strong relationship to customer needs or have poor competitive performance. These characteristics will need to be clearly identified so that proper action can be taken in the design and production process to assure that customer needs are met.

After reviewing the QFD matrix, the committee working on the process has assigned a target of 5 for deployment of our Credit Department and Loan Committee. Appropriate resources will have to be deployed to assure the customer's needs are met by these two groups. Immediate deployment must be made to the loan committee to assure their processes are designed, taking the customer's needs into consideration.

Are You a Total Quality Person?

I strive for continuous learning.

	Seldom	Sometimes	Always
	☐	☐	☐

Quality Functional Deployment

Don't take the "easy-way-out" and assign a target of 5 to all counterpart characteristics. It's expensive to deploy a redesign to a process, particularly a service process. The people performing these internal processes feel they are doing a good job, yet we are asking them to change to meet customer needs.

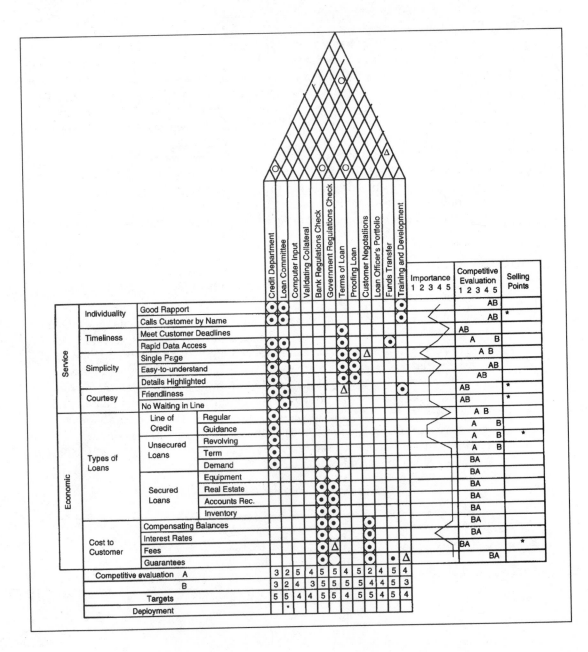

172

Confused?

Please don't be confused, you just need more practice in using QFD diagrams. For example, suppose management of a large supermarket wanted to apply the QFD concept to their store. Management would begin the process by practicing a consumer orientation, in that they would first conduct perceptual studies and brainstorm consumer thought processes to develop an orientation of the store from the consumer's viewpoint. Then they could identify the internal store functions, and list these functions on top of the grid as shown.

			MERCHANDISING DEPARTMENT	PRICING ANALYSIS	STORE SCHEDULING	PRODUCT BUYERS	TRAINING & DEVELOPMENT	STORE OPERATION SERVICES	DATA/SCANNING INPUT	PERISHABLE QUALITY ASSURANCE	STORE DESIGN & LAYOUT	ADVERTISING DEPARTMENT	STORE
SERVICE	COURTESY	FRIENDLINESS											
		SPEED OF CHECKOUT											
	EFFICIENCY	CLEAN STORE											
		SHELVES WELL STOCKED											
		PRODUCT CUSTOMER WANTS											
		EASY SHOPPING											
		ACCURATE CHECKOUT											
ECONOMIC	ADDED VALUE	ADVERTISED SPECIALS											
		STORE COUPONING											
		PRODUCT QUALITY — GROCERY											
		PRODUCE											
		MEAT											
		DELI											
		DRUG/GM											
		PHARMACY											
	PRICING	EVERYDAY LOW PRICES											
		STORE BRAND											

*Thanks are due to Mr. Jeff Hurton, Manager Store Operation Services, The Kroeger Company for sharing his ideas.

After developing the basic QFD grid, suppose management hires an independent marketing firm to interview the customers shopping at the store to find out what customers felt regarding the various department's ability to meet their needs. Remember, the symbol relationships are:

⊙ Circle with a dot in the middle denotes a very strong relationship.

○ Circle denotes a strong relationship.

△ Triangle denotes a weak relationship.

The findings from customer surveys then could be transferred to the completed QFD diagram shown. Note that this supermarket has a strong strength in produce, meat, and deli sections. They are somewhat strong in grocery items and very weak in pharmacy items. They are also very weak in the perception of "everyday low prices" and in "store couponing." Can you envision how such a diagram could be used by store management to focus their QI improvement efforts?

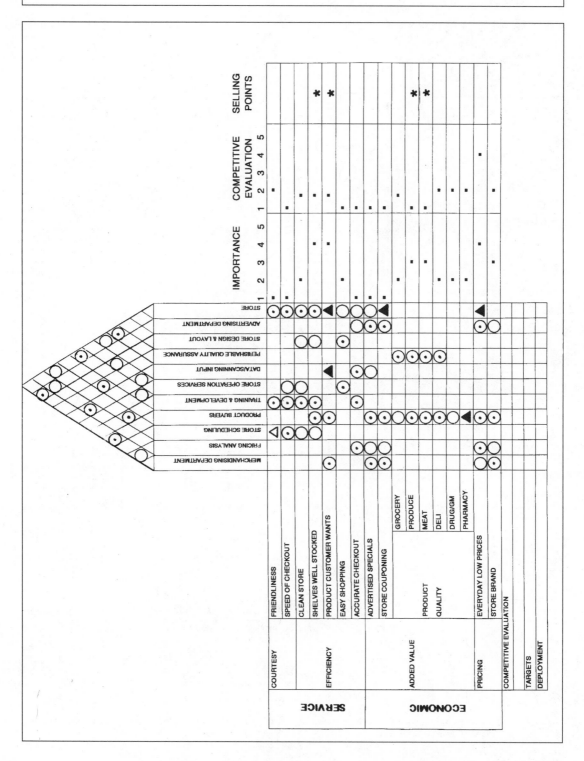

Now It's Your Turn*

1. *Get together in your assigned teams. Apply an in-depth QFD analysis to a product or a service of your choice. Then sketch the "House of Quality."*

2. *A manufacturer of household appliance irons (often called steam irons) is concerned that their current products do not meet consumer needs. A quality improvement team conducted a series of focus group discussions where people where asked to design their "ideal" clothing iron. Participants in these focus group discussions consisted of heavy iron users (10 percent), occasional iron users (60 percent), and nonusers (30 percent). The major service attributes shown on the left were identified.*

   The focus group participants were then asked: "Why do you iron clothes?" After considerable confusion on that seemingly simple question, teams merely asked participants to discuss anything that comes to mind when the issue of ironing is mentioned.*

Iron Design Requirements†

Easy to use
Light weight
Instant on/off
Spray feature
See-thru water reservoir
Self-cleaning
Internal cord storage
Teflon coated
Other**

"What comes to mind when the issue of ironing is mentioned?"‡

Time saving
For wrinkle-free clothes
For a smooth appearance
Force of habit
Drudgery
Burned fabric
Last-minute touch up
No place to keep hot iron
Can't determine correct temperature
Out of water
Dirty plate (bottom)
Difficult to control moisture

Using the above information as a guide, construct a relationship matrix identifying customer attributes and counterpart characteristics.

*The answers to Problem 2 is in the appendix.
†The first four items are ranked in order of importance.
**Other—additional requirements were identified but were lost by the secretary. Please use your own requirements.
‡Many other ideas were mentioned rather quickly and the team did not have sufficient time to record the ideas. Please expand this list to include your own ideas.

3. *A medium-sized magazine wants to understand their small advertisers and, hopefully, this understand can be used to increase advertisements. Instead of conducting focus group analysis, the manager of the advertising department has been going to trade conventions and reading articles dealing with understanding client needs. Several customer attributes were identified.*

The first attribute is good return. *Customers want to know if their advertising dollars will result in increased business. Advertisers, particularly smaller advertisers, will spend money in advertising only as long as they perceive there will be a positive return. They gauge a good return as increased sales, increased sales leads, and increased business exposure.*

The second major attribute is called total package. *Advertisers want to deal with a company that handles all their advertising needs. This includes:*

1. *A representative that knows the advertiser's business.*

2. *An advertising price in terms of an affordable plan.*

3. *Reach in terms of "reaching" an adequate number of customers with one advertising vehicle.*

4. *Meeting a market segment appropriate for their business.*

The third attribute is called ease of use *which consists of customers being able to place an ad with a minimum of problems. This includes:*

1. *Knowledgeable staff that can price the ad.*

2. *Sales representatives that are skilled in translating needs into tangible copy.*

3. *Easy access to staff.*

Finally, the advertiser is concerned with appearance *in that the ad is a status symbol as well as a business tool. This includes:*

1. *Appropriateness of graphics.*

2. *Creativity of ad.*

3. *Clear message to audience.*

The advertising manager created the beginning QFD matrix shown. Your job is to design (identify) six major organizational systems (internal processes) that could meet these customer needs without regard to any existing systems. Then identify the likely relationship that would exist between the customer needs, and the organizational systems. Be prepared to defend your logic.

Are You a Total Quality Person?

	Seldom	Sometimes	Always
I practice positive reinforcement.	☐	☐	☐

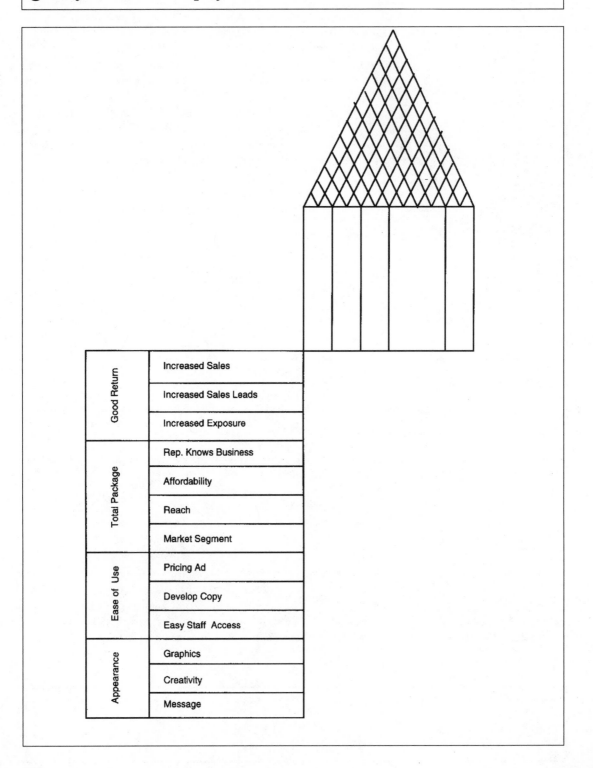

Hoshin Planning Techniques

Hoshin planning, often called the *seven management tools*, is a technique that ties quality improvement activities to long-term organizational plans. Hoshin planning* focuses on policy deployment issues including the identification of planning objectives and what actions management and employees will take. The three basic Hoshin planning processes are: general planning, immediate planning, and detailed planning. These processes and the related Hoshin planning tools are shown in the following table.

Hoshin Planning Process: Seven Management Tools

I. General Planning	1. Affinity Chart
	2. Interrelationship Diagram
II. Intermediate Planning	3. Tree Diagram
	4. Matrix Diagram
	5. Matrix Data Analysis
III. Detailed Planning	6. Process Decision Program Chart
	7. Arrow Diagram

We will first review the use and limitation of each of the Hoshin planning techniques. Then their application will be demonstrated.

Tool 1: Affinity Chart

Sort related ideas into similar groupings and label each grouping.

Useful when there are a large volume of ideas and there is a need to identify broad issues.

Limitations: None, but expect to encounter a couple of ideas that are difficult to include in any meaningful grouping.

Tool 2: Interrelationship Diagram

Identifies cause and effect links between ideas generated.

Useful when root causes need to be identified.

Limitations: Cause-and-effect linkages soon become numerous. Attempts to identify linkages between all ideas (not just major categories) can be overwhelming.

---

*For an excellent treatment of the detailed Hoshin planning process, read Bob King's book: *Hoshin Planning: The Developmental Approach*, Methuen, MA: Goal/QPC Publishers, 1969.

Tool 3: Tree Diagram

Maps out detailed groupings of tasks that need to be accomplished.

Useful when broad tasks or general objectives need to be clearly divided into subtasks.

Limitations: No major limitations provided there are a limited number of levels (sub-groups, sub-subgroups, etc.)

Tool 4: Matrix Diagram

Shows relationships between activities such as people and tasks; consumer wants and system capabilities.

Useful when relationships must be clearly shown, or when impact of demands have to be identified on system capabilities and priorities developed.

Limitations: No real limitations.

Tool 5: Matrix Data Analysis

Shows relationships between two variables.

Useful when strengths of relationships must be visually shown.

Limitations: Only two relationships can be compared at a time (i.e., display limited to x and y axes.)

Tool 6: Process Decision Program Chart (PDPC)

Maps out contingencies that can occur, along with countermeasures.

Useful when countermeasures need to be "thought through" when implementing a new plan that has potential problem areas.

Limitations: Contingencies and countermeasures quickly explode into hundreds of combinations.

Tool 7: Arrow Diagram (Activity Networks)

Detailed planning and scheduling tool that identifies time requirements and activity relationships.

Useful when detailed planning and control is needed on complex tasks with numerous interrelationships.

Limitations: Planning accuracy is greatly influenced by accuracy of estimates. Diagrams can become complex on large tasks.

Now, let's go through a Hoshin planning process for Friendly Texan Insurance Company.

I. General Planning

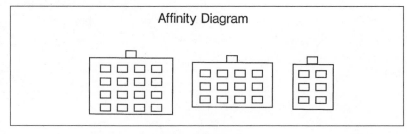

Affinity Diagram

Tool 1. Affinity chart

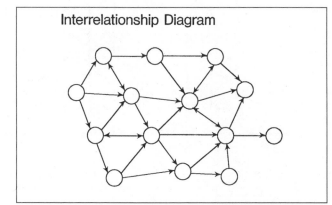

Interrelationship Diagram

Tool 2. Interrelationship diagram

General planning starts with a study of consumers so that the organization can be focused on meeting their needs. Affinity charts and interrelationship diagrams can assist in identifying the concerns people have regarding insurance, security, and health in our medium-sized town so that our firm, Friendly Texan Insurance Company, can develop plans to meet those needs.

Friendly Texan Insurance might begin the process of acquiring data by reading trade magazines and newspaper articles dealing with insurance needs, conducting brainstorming sessions, holding focus groups with consumers, and conducting services. This would result in a lot of data about insurance needs. Then what?

Friendly Texan Insurance could start the process of general planning by constructing an *affinity chart*. This is accomplished by brainstorming a topic and placing that topic on a 3-by-5-in. card. The cards are taped on a board as ideas are generated. After brainstorming is completed, identify the major categories (larger, general grouping of ideas). Arrange the cards under these larger categories, until all related cards are grouped together.

For example, after brainstorming the general topic of our customers' insurance concerns—concerns regarding jewelry, stereo sets, televisions, and cameras—might have a general heading of "theft insurance." Once a grouping emerges, make out a header card and place it above the group of data items.

The affinity chart is particularly useful when issues are complex because it provides a method of "mapping" that is easy to understand. Discussion of the chart also helps achieve a breakthrough in traditional thinking by looking at data in a new manner.

Next, an *interrelationship diagram* (often called a *relations diagram*) is another general planning technique. An interrelationship diagram uses the header cards developed in an affinity chart and asks: "Which one influences another?" For example, one of the header cards in our affinity chart might be labeled "prosperous neighborhood concerns" which might influence concerns regarding the nature of jewelry security/insurance. An arrow would then be drawn to indicate the influence. Critical items are those items that have the most arrows going in or out.

181

Interrelationship diagrams also help focus on cause and effect. That is, it tries to remove "personalities" and vested interests from the discussion by concentrating on what effects (influences) what. Team members must possess a detailed knowledge of the interrelationships in order to contribute to the process.

II. Intermediate Planning

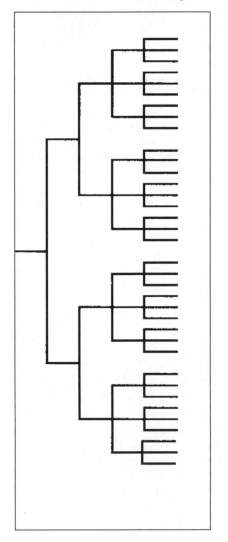

Tool 3: Tree diagram

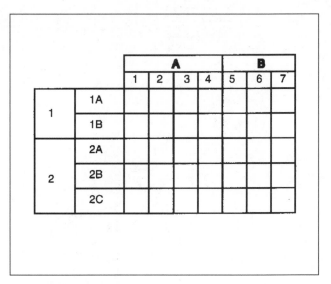

Tool 4: Matrix diagram

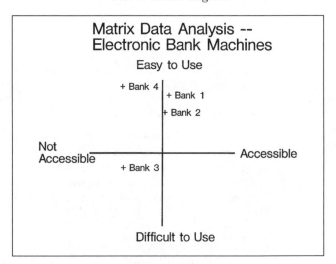

Tool 5: Matrix data analysis

Intermediate planning occurs after general planning and is used to breakdown the general planning premises into segments that can be individually addressed. A *tree diagram* is constructed by using the header cards from the affinity chart and asking: How can we address these concerns?

A form of a tree diagram was previously developed in the section on Quality Functional Deployment (QFD) when identifying customer needs for users of a bank's commercial services departments. A tree diagram version of the bank's customer needs matrix is shown.

Service	Individuality	Good Rapport	
		Calls Customer by Name	
	timeliness	Meet Customer Deadlines	
		Rapid Data Access	
	Simplicity	Single Page	
		East-to-Understand	
		Details Highlighted	
	Courtesy	Friendliness	
		No Waiting in Line	
Economic	Types of Loans	Line of Credit	Regular
			Guidance
		Unsecured Loans	Revolving
			Term
			Demand
		Secured Loans	Equipment
			Real Estate
			Accounts Rec.
			Inventory
	Cost to Customer	Compensating Balances	
		Interest Rates	
		Fees	
		Guarantees	

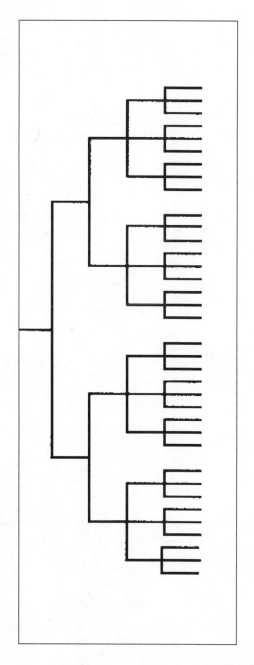

Hoshin Planning Techniques

A completed tree diagram of commercial banking needs is shown. Some readers find this tree diagram easier to understand than the QFD matrix. Which do you prefer?

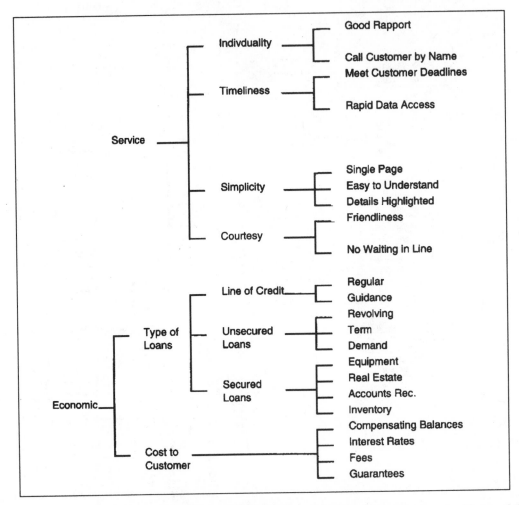

The matrix diagram used in intermediate planning is a duplicate of the QFD matrix that was previously shown and will be explained. The customer needs are stated on the left of the matrix, and the top of the matrix identifies who in the organization is responsible for meeting those needs (i.e., the departments). The same QFD relationship symbols are used where:

⊙ Circle with a dot in the middle denotes a very strong relationship.

○ Circle denotes a strong relationship.

△ Triangle denotes a weak relationship.

The matrix diagram for commercial banking customer needs is shown below. Note the blank columns in this matrix. A relationship has not been identified between customer needs and the internal functions of computer input, validating capital, and the loan officer's portfolio. Perhaps these functions could be eliminated.

			Credit Department	Loan Committee	Computer Input	Validating Collateral	Bank Regulations Check	Government Regulations Check	Terms of Loan	Proofing Loan	Customer Negotiations	Loan Officer's Portfolio	Funds Transfer	Training and Development
Service	Individuality	Good Rapport	◎	◎										◎
		Calls Customer by Name	◎	◎										○
	Timeliness	Meet Customer Deadlines							●					
		Rapid Data Access	◎	◎					●				●	
	Simplicity	Single Page	●							◎	●	△		
		Easy-to-understand	●							◎	●			
		Details Highlighted	●							◎	●			
	Courtesy	Friendliness	◎	◎				△						●
		No Waiting in Line	○	●										
Economic	Types of Loans — Line of Credit	Regular	●											
		Guidance	●											
	Unsecured Loans	Revolving	●											
		Term	●											
		Demand	●				○	○						
	Secured Loans	Equipment					○	○						
		Real Estate					◎	●						
		Accounts Rec.					◎	●						
		Inventory					◎	●						
	Cost to Customer	Compensating Balances					◎	●				●		
		Interest Rates					●					●		
		Fees					●	△				◎		
		Guarantees					◎	●				◎	●	△

Matrix data analysis (often called *market segmentation*) is used to compare your products and services to competitive products and services. Textbooks in market segmentation have been written that explain mathematical methods for developing this relationship which are beyond the scope of this book. For our uses, identify two features from the consumer's prospective, then plot the existing products on the grid. If a "gap" exists, then this is an area where a new or revised product or service would have a competitive edge.

In the matrix data analysis previously shown for electronic bank machines, a machine which is both easy to use and accessible to consumers would have a competitive edge. Note that these are service features.

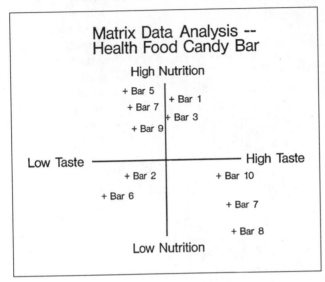

Matrix Data Analysis -- Health Food Candy Bar

A matrix data analysis is shown for product features, in this case, health food candy bars. Note there is a "gap" in the high taste and high nutrition segment of the chart. If a new product could be developed that would meet this market gap, the product would have a definite competitive edge.

III. Detailed Planning

Another Hoshin planning tool, the *Process Decision Program Chart* or PDPC, maps out the events that may occur along with needed countermeasures when moving from a problem statement to possible solutions. An example of the possible "things" than can go wrong if we attempt to introduce an improved health candy bar is shown below. Countermeasures are identified for possible negative

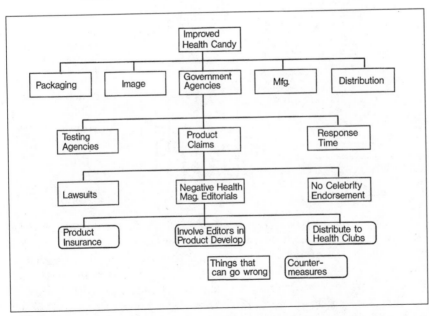

Tool 6: Process Decision Program Chart

health magazine editorials. A word of caution when using a PDPC. The chart tends to "explode" with numerous alternatives. Break the chart into various bite-sized subportions to prevent it from becoming unmanageable.

The *arrow diagram* is a simplified version of two techniques: Program Evaluation and Review Technique or PERT and Critical Path Method or CPM. Although PERT and CPM were developed in the United States and can be found in numerous management texts, the Japanese simplified these planning tools so that more people would use them. This technique is particularly useful in construction projects and in developing plans for marketing and plant expansion. Basically, the arrow diagram is the same as PERT/CPM without the math.

Let's walk through a PERT example to see how the technique is used as a planning tool. The example shown is a plan of the activities required to open a small medical facility (Note: An actual detail plan for such an activity would be comprised of hundreds of elements.) The medical facility project has the following activities, precedence relationships, and time estimates in weeks:

	Activity	Predecessor activity	Times a	m	b
A	Construct facility.	None	20	23	30
B	Inspect it.	A	3	4	5
C	Install equipment.	A	6	12	14
D	Hire staff.	None	3	4	5
E	Train staff.	D	4	5	6
F	Make minor adjustments.	B	1	2	2
G	Run "trial" patients.	E, C, F	2	3	4

Preliminary PERT Network

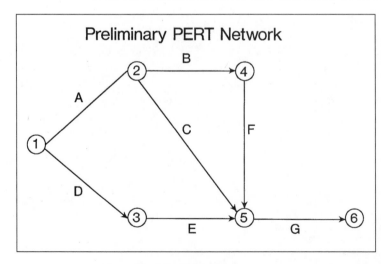

Tool 7: Arrow Diagram

Taking this information into consideration, a preliminary PERT network could be constructed as shown.

Estimates of activity completion time are obtained from the supervisor responsible for each activities. Three time completion estimates are requested. An optimistic estimate is based on activity completion time, assuming the steps in the activity could be completed without encountering significant problems. Next, a pessimistic time estimate is requested which assumes that numerous problems will be encountered when completing the activity. Finally, a most likely time for completion of the activity is requested.

Completion times can be in any time units (minutes, hours, weeks, months), but typically weeks are used. Once the optimistic (a), most likely (m), and pessimistic (b) times are known, activity completion times can be calculated using the formula:

$$\text{Time} = \frac{\text{Optimistic time} + 4 * \text{Most likely time} + \text{Pessimistic time}}{6}$$

Often abbreviated to:

$$T_e = \frac{a + 4(m) + b}{6}$$

The calculated T_e values for our medical facility are shown.

| | Times | | | Calculated |
Activity	a	m	b	T_e
A Construct facility.	20	23	30	23.7
B Inspect it.	3	4	5	4.0
C Install equipment.	6	12	14	11.3
D Hire staff.	3	4	5	4.0
E Train staff.	4	5	6	5.0
F Make minor adjustments.	1	2	2	1.8
G Run "trial" patients.	2	3	4	3.0

The critical path is the longest path through the network. The final PERT network, including the critical path, is shown.

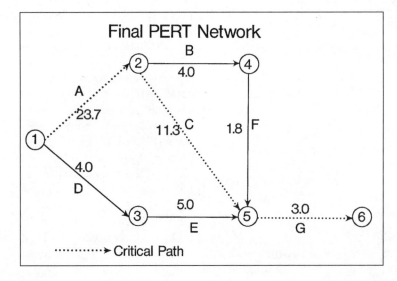

Final PERT Network

Critical Path

Another detailed planning tool similar to the arrow diagram is the *Gantt chart*, developed by Henry Gantt in 1910. This chart was a forerunner of PERT and CPM. It shows time on the horizontal axis and activities on the vertical axis. An arrow diagram is shown along with a Gantt chart for comparison. Note that deployment charts can also be used for planning and control purposes but are limited to smaller applications.

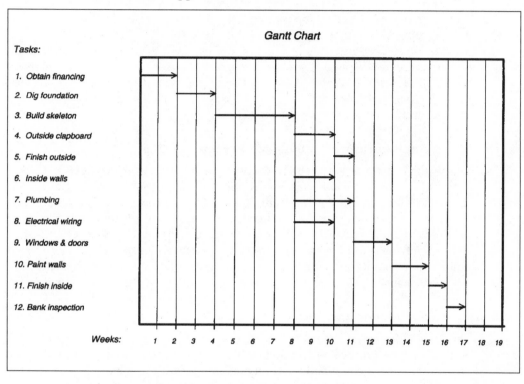

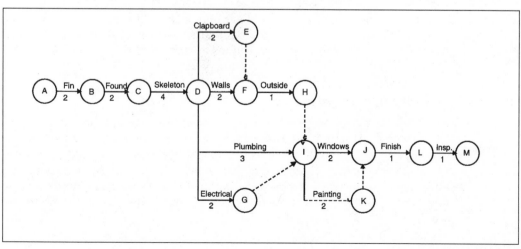

Now It's Your Turn

Apply the Hoshin planning process to the Friendly Texan Insurance Company.

Gap Analysis

Gap analysis is used to develop an understanding of services offered from different viewpoints. Five major gaps are evaluated so that when differences are identified between perceptions (gaps), action can be taken to close the gap. Examples will be presented using a fast-food restaurant that services a walk-in luncheon trade. At this restaurant, the customers place their food order at a service counter, the bill is paid, the order is filled, and placed on a tray. The customer then takes the tray and locates a table where they can eat their lunch.

Gap 1. Consumer Expectation: Management Perception Gap

This is the difference between consumers' expectations and management's perception of consumers' expectations. Service management often does not understand what service features imply high quality to the consumer. The consumer's major expectation when eating at this fast-food restaurant is they will be able to begin eating their food quickly. Management's perception of consumers' expectations might stress fast counter service. A gap exists when a customer is serviced quickly, but cannot find a place to sit down to eat their meal because tables have not been cleaned.

Gap 2. Management Perceptions: Service Quality Specifications Gap

This is the difference between management perceptions of consumer expectations and the service quality specifications which are developed. That is, management does not always include all the quality attributes that the customer wants in the service specifications. Suppose restaurant management perceives the need to fill orders quickly. However, in actual delivery (service specifications) this might be possible only if a standard, precooked hamburger is ordered without any special requests. That is, management's perceptions are accurate, but the service quality specifications only deal with a subset of the perceptions.

Gap 3. Service Quality Specifications: Service Delivery Gap

This is the difference between service quality specifications and the actual service that is delivered. Although the correct specifications may exist, they may not be followed, particularly in rush periods. For example, the service quality specifications might be to open another cash register when there are more than six people waiting in line. However, during a busy luncheon trade, there might not be enough employees available to open another register, hence customers are forced to wait.

Gap 4. Service Delivery: External Communications Gap

This is the difference between actual service delivery and what is communicated about the service to consumers. Suppose management prides themselves on serving hamburgers within one minute of being ordered and advertises a policy of "service within a minute." Also, assume our restaurant offers pizza as a menu item, and does a reasonable job of filling these orders quickly. However, the preparation time is about five minutes.

Unless management can deliver every product every time within a minute as promised, a service delivery gap will exist. It's better to under promise and over deliver to prevent this gap from occurring.

Gap 5. Expected Service: Perceived Service Gap

This is the difference between consumer expectations of the services and their perceptions of the actual service received. The key to creating a high quality perception in the minds of the consumers, is to exceed their expectations. Suppose our fast-food restaurant customers expect to receive fast service. However, if they perceive the service is rapid, but is delivered by a grumpy worker who bangs things around, then a gap exists. A competitor who not only meets customer expectations for rapid service, but who is also successful in establishing an enjoyable dining environment, might exceed customer expectations. Such a firm would soon develop repeat customers.

Summary of Five Service Gaps

Gap 1. Customers' expectations and management's perceptions.

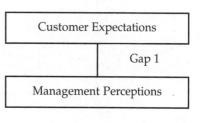

Gap 2. Management's perceptions of customers' expectations and service quality.

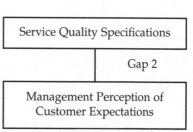

Gap 3. Service quality specifications and service delivery.

Gap 4. Service delivery and external communications.

Gap 5. Customer expectations of service offered and services received.

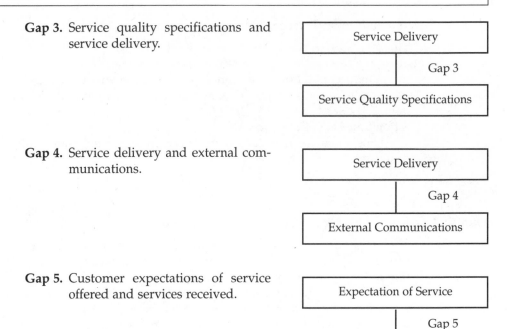

Measuring Gaps

Let's walk through an example of how a gap can be measured. By nature, measurements of quality are difficult, particularly in service organizations. One service organization where customer dissatisfaction is often prevalent can be found in health care. Attention will be directed to a group of physicians serving patients in a medical office. The purpose of this example is not to question the competence of physicians, but rather to identify differences in thinking (gaps) between physicians and patients.

We will measure the first gap, which is concerned with the difference between customers' expectations (the patients) and management perceptions (the physicians). A list of variables that are of primary importance to the patients would have to be generated, perhaps by conducting focus groups and identifying the six most common patient concerns. These concerns would then form the basis for two questionnaires: one questionnaire for the patient and a second using parallel reasoning for the physicians. Both questionnaires would be phrased differently to communicate to two different groups. A sample questionnaire for patients and physicians is shown using a seven-point Likert scale.

Sample Questionnaire for Patients, Using a 7-Point Likert Scale

This questionnaire asks your opinion about issues regarding services received at American Health Systems. Please choose the one number that best matches how you feel about the statement. The further away from the middle (4), the stronger is your feeling about the statement.

For example, if you felt that the parking at our facilities was adequate, but could be better, you might cross through the number "6" as shown.

	Strongly Disagree						Strongly Agree	Unknown
There is ample parking at our facilities.	1	2	3	4	5	~~6~~	7	0

In My Opinion:	Strongly Disagree						Strongly Agree	Unknown
1. The office is attractive and clean.	1	2	3	4	5	6	7	0
2. The staff was professional.	1	2	3	4	5	6	7	0
3. The amount of time spent waiting to see the doctor was reasonable.	1	2	3	4	5	6	7	0
4. I was satisfied with the services provided by the doctor.	1	2	3	4	5	6	7	0
5. There was a high level of concern for my health problem expressed by the staff.	1	2	3	4	5	6	7	0
6. The prices were reasonable.	1	2	3	4	5	6	7	0

Note: If a preliminary survey indicates that several people answer "Unknown" for a question, then eliminate that question. A brief, well-focused questionnaire produces the best responses.

Ideas for Consideration When Checking an Out of Control Process

✓ Are new or untrained people involved?
✓ Does operator fatigue occur?
✓ Are different methods used by different employees?
✓ Are operators consistently reporting all data, good as well as bad?
✓ Do the samples come from different operators on different machines, on different shifts?
✓ Has there been a change in raw materials?
✓ Have tools become worn?
✓ Has there been a change in maintenance procedures?
✓ Has there been a change in the environment (e.g., temperature, humidity)?

Sample Questionnaire for Physicians, Using a 7-Point Likert Scale

This questionnaire asks your opinion about issues regarding services provided at American Health Systems. Please choose the one number that best matches how you feel about the statement. The further away from the middle (4), the stronger is your feeling about the statement.

For example, if you felt that the parking at our facilities was adequate, but could be better, you might cross through the number "6" as shown.

	Strongly Disagree						Strongly Agree	Unknown
There is ample patient parking at our facilities.	1	2	3	4	5	~~6~~	7	0

In My Opinion:	Strongly Disagree						Strongly Agree	Unknown
1. The office is attractive and clean.	1	2	3	4	5	6	7	0
2. Your staff is productive and helpful to your patients.	1	2	3	4	5	6	7	0
3. The rate at which you see patients is fast enough to prevent patient dissatisfaction.	1	2	3	4	5	6	7	0
4. Patient services are both professional and productive.	1	2	3	4	5	6	7	0
5. You and your staff are concerned about the welfare of your patients.	1	2	3	4	5	6	7	0
6. Patient charges are reasonable.	1	2	3	4	5	6	7	0

Note: The use of an "Unknown" column might be perceived as an insult.

After administering the questionnaires to the patients and the physicians, the results would be tabulated in the format shown.

Patient–Physician Gap Analysis Summary			
Question	Patient scores	Physician scores	Difference in scores
1. Clean office			
2. Professional staff			
3. Patient waiting			
4. Services provided			
5. Patient concern			
6. Reasonable charges			

The patient and physician summary scores would then be reviewed, with particular attention paid to major differences (gaps) between the groups. This then helps us to focus on potential troublesome areas.

Now It's Your Turn

1. *A small firm decided to apply the concept of gap analysis to the three areas shown. Identify what gaps exist and identify what can be done to close each gap. How can we be assured the gap will remain closed?*

Accounting Department:

> *Accounting Management:* We provide all departments with accurate and timely reports.

> *Internal Departments:* We don't see reports. But, we don't have much use for accounting reports.

Facilities Management:

> *Facilities Manager:* We keep the firm as clean as possible considering the low budget we receive.

> *Employees:* Our offices are rather dirty and somewhat "dingy." But that's OK, it's a nice place to work.

Customer Service Department:

> *Management:* We provide high quality services at a low cost that customers could not get locally.

> *Customers:* I have to wait weeks for repairs, and they charge a fortune.

2. *The Friendly House* is a 1400 room convention hotel located in Savanna, Georgia. It is the largest hotel in the area. Sixty percent of their business comes from conventions, including trade shows and technical associations. In the convention business, a buyer will "purchase" rooms after discussion with the Sales Department at Friendly House. The Sales Department reports to the hotel manager. Services are actually delivered to customers (people attending the convention) via the Convention Department which reports to the food and beverage director.*

   Several large convention groups have recently complained that they did not receive the facilities they were expecting. Management suspects the problem may be due to the way they are organized, and that a gap has developed between service delivery by the Convention Department and external communications from the Sales Department.

   Develop two questionnaires. The first to be administered to convention room "buyers" and the second to be administered to people attending the convention. Develop a means by which the questionnaire results can be compared to highlight perceived service gaps.

3. *Develop a brief questionnaire that will measure a gap in fast-food services. (Clearly state which of the gaps you are measuring.)†*

Taguchi Methods

Quality control activities have traditionally been concerned with control charts and process control. This orientation is called *on-line quality control*. Dr. Genichi Taguchi, a Deming Prize winner, and a Japanese statistician, has extended quality improvement activities to include product design and process design. Dr. Taguchi calls this *off-line quality control*. His methods include a system to develop specifications, design specifications into a product (or process), and a system to produce products that continuously surpass specifications.

As shown in the table on the following page, there are seven aspects to Dr. Taguchi's off-line quality control.

1. The Quality of a Manufactured Product Is Measured by the Total Loss Created by That Product to Society as a Whole

Taguchi suggests that instead of measuring quality by how good a product is, take a look at the loss or negative aspects of the product on society. There are two costs to quality: the production cost to produce the product and the inferior quality cost to the consumer. These two costs should be added together to identify the total cost of the product. When management is deciding what parameters to use, look at the effect of changing a parameter on the total cost.

---

*The answer to this problem is in the appendix.
†For a complete discussion of gap analysis, see Zeithamal, Valarie A., Parasuraman, A., and Berry, Leonard L. *Delivering Quality Services*, New York: The Free Press, 1990.

Taguchi's Off-Line Quality Control

1. The quality of a manufactured product is measured by the total loss created by that product to society as a whole.
2. Continuous quality improvement and cost reduction are necessary to have a healthy organization in a competitive economy.
3. Quality improvement requires the neverending reduction of variation in product and/or process performance around nominal values.
4. Society's loss due to performance variation is frequently proportional to the square of the deviation of the performance characteristic from its nominal value.
5. Product and process design can have a significant impact on a product's quality and cost.
6. Performance variation can be reduced by exploiting the nonlinear effects between a product's and/or process's parameters and the product's desired performance characteristics.
7. Product and/or process parameter settings that reduce performance variation can be identified with statistically designed experiments.

In other words, if the product is made cheaply, and results in a high cost for repairs, it might be better to increase the quality of the produced product. That is, management should consider increasing the cost of production if that brings about a more than equal lowering of repair cost, so that the total cost to society is minimized.

2. Continuous Quality Improvement and Cost Reduction Are Necessary to Have a Healthy Organization in a Competitive Economy

The process of quality improvement is continuous and must never stop. High quality and low costs are necessary for corporate health. Products and processes must be constantly, and relentlessly improved in a neverending manner.

3. Quality Improvement Requires the Neverending Reduction of Variation in Product and/or Process Performance Around Nominal Values

Unit-to-unit performance variation should be reduced, even if the product is within specification limit. For example, suppose a luxury car manufacturer had specifications of + or − 3 mm for the gap between the car's front doors and the front panels. Suppose quality engineers measured the gaps in the cars produced, and found the actual gaps varied from 1.4 mm to 4.1 mm. This variation from the nominal gap measured (3 mm) caused increased wind noise at high speeds.

Engineers need to reduce this loss by designing the door hinge so it is more sturdy, reducing the variation in the gap between the door and front panel when the door is closed. That is, variation of any sort will tend to have an adverse impact and must be reduced.

4. Society's Loss Due to Performance Variation Is Frequently Proportional to the Square of the Deviation of the Performance Characteristic from Its Nominal Value

Taguchi introduces a loss function for performance characteristics outside specification limits. This loss function is very costly, and the loss is minimized only when the standard deviation of the product approaches zero. That is, it pays to make products with a minimum deviation from specifications.

5. Product and Process Design Can Have a Significant Impact on a Product's Quality and Cost

The design of a product plays a large role in the number of manufacturing imperfections. Given the same levels of process control, a better design will always result in few manufacturing problems.

6. Performance Variation Can Be Reduced by Exploiting the Nonlinear Effects Between a Product's and/or Process's Parameters and the Product's Desired Performance Characteristics

Taguchi suggests a three-part procedure for developing products that surpass customer needs. This procedure includes system design, parameter design, and allowance design.

System design consists of establishing prototype specifications based on quality-of-performance studies that considers both the needs of customers and the requirements of manufacturability. Parameter design involves determining the specifications for product and process parameters so that the final product produced will be less sensitive to variation. Sensitivity to variation consists of environmental factors, product deterioration, and manufacturing variations. *Environmental factors* reflect the environment in which the product will be used, including operator variations. *Product deterioration* consists of wear and tear that will occur over the product's life cycle. *Manufacturing variations* are the manufacturing conditions that cause the product to deviate from its specifications.

In allowance design, the acceptable variation limits are determined, assuming that some variability has to be tolerated. It is less expensive to reduce performance variation through parameter design if feasible.

7. Product and/or Process Parameter Settings That Reduce Performance Variation Can Be Identified with Statistically Designed Experiments

Taguchi uses statistical tests to identify interactions between parameter design and noise variables. Design parameter variables are assigned mathematical variables, such as low = 0, medium = 1, and high = 2. Noise variables are the factors that cause changes in the product's performance characteristics. The experimenter then systematically varies the levels of the major noise variables to determine their effect on the product's performance characteristics.

Conclusion

Implementation of Taguchi's methods for product and process design improvements can be very beneficial. Reducing errors in the design process helps to reduce the number of imperfections in the manufacturing processes. All levels of process control then become easier to manage.*

---

*See Taguchi, G., and Wu, Y. *Introduction to Off-Line Quality Control*, Nagoya, Japan: Central Japan Quality Control Association, 1980.

Quality Improvement Systems

The *quality improvement systems* discussed in this section require a considerable commitment of organizational resources to install. A brief overview follows. Refer to the appropriate section for more details.

Technique: Quality Cost Systems

Provides the cost of poor quality so that the organization's quality improvement effort can be directed.

Useful when there are hidden costs to poor quality, and those costs are not taken into consideration in improvement efforts.

Limitations: It is very difficult to develop a system to capture and report all factors involved in the cost of poor quality.

Technique: The Learning Organization

If an organization can learn how to learn, it can continuously improve itself, and soon outdistance the competition.

Useful when trying to achieve breakthrough thinking about developing a future organizational structure.

Limitations: Although desirable, the concepts involved in achieving a learning organizational are somewhat abstract, and difficult to operationalize.

Technique: Customer/Supplier Agreements

States the customer's requirements on products or services delivered by a supplier.

Useful when a written understand is needed of the quality requirements, particularly regarding services delivered by internal suppliers (other departments).

Limitations: It is difficult to state all the quality requirements regarding a service performed. It is very difficult to enforce such requirements on internal departments.

Quality Improvement Systems

Technique: Shojinka

A flexible production system under which workers can be altered to meet changes in production demand.

Useful when production must change rapidly to meet rapid changes in demand. Frequently used in a just-in-time environment.

Limitations: Requires a flexible machine layout and cross-trained employees.

Technique: Just-in-Time

A philosophy that believes inventory should be used, and items should be manufacture as they are needed. Holding inventory is wrong and costly.

Useful when a quick response is needed to customer requests, particularly production requests.

Limitations: Requires flexible equipment utilizing cellular manufacturing and cross-trained workers who have been given the authority to make production decisions.

Technique: Quality Teams

Employees groups ranging in authority from task teams with virtually no authority, to design teams that are empowered to make significant organizational changes.

Useful when decisions must be quickly made by a group of employees, without waiting for other approval.

Limitations: Requires well trained employees, and managers committed to operating as a "coach."

Technique: Quality Council

An executive committee that is dedicated to maintaining the organization's TQM focus.

Useful when coordinating TQM teams, when their activities and suggestions cut across functional lines.

Limitations: Requires a meaningful commitment from the top CEO to be effective. Also required is an executive committee that operates as an organizational team. Some executives tend to simply "represent" their functional areas and stifle cross-functional improvements.

Technique: ISO Standards

A series of standards describing the elements for maintaining a quality management system.

Useful when either required by a customer or when a focused method is used to document and improve the delivery of quality products.

Limitations: Care should be taken to obtain employee involvement in developing the necessary procedures to get people to "buy into" the system of making high quality products. There is a tendency in an ISO system to create procedures to satisfy ISO requirements when such procedures are not use (followed) by employees.

Technique: Baldrige Award

A framework for installing TQM with a high customer focus throughout an organization. Award contains seven major categories that can be used to identify strengths and areas for improvement.

Useful when you do not know what to look at to improve organizational quality.

Limitations: Although the award provides an excellent framework for improving quality, reporting requirements can become complex.

Quality Cost System

TQM is a continuous process encompassing all aspects of an organization—from design of the product or service through production and use of the product or service. A major element missing from many quality improvement programs involves the quantative measurement of cost of quality in terms of dollars and cents. A *quality cost system* is needed so that resources can be intelligently allocated to sustain the quality improvement process.

Cost estimates of poor quality in "typical" firms range from 15 to 40 percent of sales, with 30 percent of sales being a commonly quoted figure.* However, well managed firms have been able to reduce their quality costs to as little of 3 percent of sales. Thus, bringing quality costs under control represents an untapped area where substantial savings can be achieved.

A Quality Cost System (QCS) is an information system that identifies, measures, and controls quality costs. If properly implemented, a QCS supports the TQM effort as well as provides an opportunity for profit improvement.

A QCS measures all costs associated with nonconformance (i.e., the cost of doing things wrong). This is accomplished by focusing on measuring costs of not doing things right the first time in terms of what it costs to "do things over."

QCS elements are of four major types: *prevention, appraisal, internal failure,* and *external failure* costs. Prevention and appraisal costs are often combined and called *controlled costs,* while internal and external failures are called *failure costs* (i.e., the

---

*See P.B. Crosby's books: *Quality Is Free*, New York: McGraw-Hill, 1979 and *Quality Without Tears*, New York: McGraw-Hill, 1989.

costs expended as a result of discrepancies in the process). Controlled costs occur because a lack of conformance can exist whereas failure costs occur because a lack of conformance does exist. Total quality cost is the sum of control costs and failure costs. Spending more money in product design (an increase in prevention costs) can result in a decrease in external failure costs, thereby reducing the total quality costs to a minimum, while maintaining required quality levels.

Categorizing Quality Costs	
Controlled costs	Prevention
	Appraisal
Failure costs	Internal
	External

The basic concept of spending more in controlled costs to reduce failure costs has been intuitively practiced my many organizations. An increase in prevention costs (such as a quality training program) should result in a larger decrease in the cost of failure, thereby reducing total quality costs.

Implementing a Quality Cost System

The first step in implementing a QCS is to determine if there is a need for such a system. This can be undertaken by a review and analysis of financial data to determine general cost levels. Select a pilot area known for quality problems and present these costs to top management to show the potential savings. Once top management is sold on the potential value of a QCS, a coordinator should be appointed to develop an implementation plan.

Unfortunately, most organizations do not have a cost accounting system capable of categorizing quality costs in a usable manner. A system of quality cost codes will have to be developed in a way that the costs of prevention, appraisal, internal, and external failures can be distinguished and traced. Then considerable modification will be required to the existing cost accounting system. This, in turn, will require training so that personnel will collect and record data on a uniform basis. If necessary, the present system may have to be supplemented by separate forms designed especially to capture quality costs.

Use of Quality Cost Data

Use of Quality Cost Information
Identify relative importance of various quality problems.
Indicate the financial significance of quality costs.
Establish goals and budgets for quality costs.
Evaluate the performance of quality improvement activities.

Once a quality cost system is installed, the system will measure the value of the quality effort, identify the strong and weak points of the quality program, indicate how quality improvement investments can be effectively made, and provide information regarding cost reduction.

Conclusion

A quality cost system does not solve quality problems. It is merely a tool to point quality improvement efforts in the right direction. However, given the high hidden cost of quality, a good quality cost system will be an invaluable management tool.

The Learning Organization

TQM programs often fail because organizations have failed to deal with a current truth: continuous improvement requires continuous learning. Without learning, companies repeat old practices and meaningful changes do not occur. Dr. Peter Senge coined the phrase "The Learning Organization" in his book, *The Fifth Discipline**. An exact definition of a *learning organization* is difficult but a generally accepted definition is:

> A learning organization is an organization skilled at creating, acquiring, and transferring knowledge, and at modifying its behavior to reflect new knowledge.[†]

The learning organization is characterized by moving from adaptive learning towards generative learning. Adaptive learning concerns itself with reacting to the changing business environment and coping with current situations. Generative learning expands an organization's capabilities and creates new opportunities. Generative learning requires new ways of looking at the world. Generative learning sees the systems that control events and focuses on the systems rather than on the results or the event itself. Senge identifies five major disciplines needed to create a learning organization. These are personal mastery, mental models, shared vision, team learning, and system thinking.

The Five Disciplines of a Learning Organization

1. Personal mastery
2. Mental models
3. Shared vision
4. Team learning
5. System thinking

Personal Mastery

Personal mastery involves the discipline to continually expand your ability to create the results you truly seek. It is a quest for continual improvement and the deepening of a personal vision. The energy needed for this continual improvement is derived from creative tension.

Creative tension comes from clearly seeing what we want to be, and the realistic evaluation of what we now have. If our vision is realistic and attainable, we will have enthusiasm and energy to work towards it.

---

*Senge, Peter M. *The Fifth Discipline*, New York: Doubleday, 1990.
[†]Garvin, David A. "Building a Learning Organization." *Harvard Business Review*, July–August, 1993, pp. 78–91.

The Learning Organization

Mental Models

Mental models are pictures we have of how the world works. This is powerful because people with different mental models observing the same activity, will perceive the activity differently. Expanding our mental models results in bringing multiple perspectives to focus on a problem.

Mental models are based on assumptions we hold. To "see" reality objectively, we must be able to identify our assumptions, and scrutinize them. We must also be able to restructure our assumptions to carry our understanding beyond events, and more towards the system that caused the events.

Shared Vision

A *shared vision* uplifts aspirations and results in people working together to achieve a common goal. A shared vision is more than trying to convince others through inspirational speeches: It involves transferring ideas so that others will want the same thing to happen. Leaders must be willing to share their personal vision in order to develop a shared vision to which followers will want to commit.

The shared vision must be important enough and visible in order to gain acceptance. Every problem solved by the leader should be solved in the context of the shared vision.

Team Learning

Team learning involves creating the climate so that the team can achieve the results members desire. Team members must feel free to resolve the difficult issues that are essential to the team working together and to participate in meaningful dialogue. The transfer of knowledge must occur between teams as well as within teams. In this way the organization learns along with the individual and team learning which takes place.

System Thinking

In *system thinking*, there is no one to blame for the problems which occur, because the problem in of itself is contained within the system. Leaders engaged in systems thinking feel part of a larger purpose that goes beyond their organization. Senge lists some of the skills system thinkers will have to learn how to acquire.[†] These skills include seeing interrelationships not snapshots, distinguishing detail complexity from dynamic complexity, focusing on areas of high leverage; and avoiding systematic solutions.

[†]Senge, Peter M. "The Leadership Work: Building Learning Organizations," *Sloan Management Review*, Fall, 1990, pp. 7–23.

In the past, most of us have concentrated on focusing on events that have occurred. We have not looked deeper to focus on the process. We tend to view activities in terms of "snapshots" rather than interrelationships. We must learn to focus more on the interrelationships, and less on the events themselves so that more meaningful adjustments can be made to the system.

Senge's concept of detailed complexity has many variables. Dynamic complexity arises when causes and effects are separated from one another by long periods of time. We must strive to view situations over a longer time period if we are to continually improve our understanding of dynamic complexity.

System thinking can produce a dramatic improvement if properly focused. The first and obvious solution is not the one that can create high leveraged improvements. Leadership must continue to search for solutions in highly leveraged areas to create dynamic improvements.

Short-term thinking is one of the culprits which promotes symptomatic solutions, only to have worse problems emerge at a later time. We must concentrate on the identifying the underlying causes of problems so that we can deal with root causes. An organization's ability to learn is its primary competitive advance. System thinking is the integrative element that unites the other four disciplines together. This thinking must be learned and practiced in all other disciplines before the organization can aspire to become a learning organization.

Customer/Supplier Agreements

A *customer/supplier agreement* (CSA) is a written agreement stating the customer's requirements on products or services delivered by a supplier. If this agreement can be correctly negotiated and agreed to by both parties, the customer is partnered with the supplier, encouraging both parties to find ways to become successful. Some extensive contractual arrangement with external suppliers can be considered CSA agreements. However, as TQM advocates have long recognized, an organization has both internal and external suppliers.* Our attention is directed to the use of written CSA to heighten the importance of efforts conducted by internal departments.

Few internal departments have attempted to write a CSA for a good reason: Why commit yourself to performance specifications, particularly if you do not have to do so. That is, it is often not in the departments best "interest" to produce documents that highlight service and performance gaps. Perhaps complaints will initially increase when a CSA is installed, when progress is slower than expected on several performance factors. However, the mere act or specifying key service/product factors, along with a ranking of the importance of the factors, will result in improved communications. This, in turn, should decrease complaints.

*For an excellent treatment of the total scope of CSA, read the article by Peter Dentre, "Customer/Supplier Agreements: Taking the Mystery Out of Relationships." *Journal for Quality and Participation*, July–August 1993, pp. 68–71.

Customer/Supplier Agreements

CSA can cover any aspect of service and are often found in progressive data management centers. Such data centers traditionally have attempted to develop service specifications which can serve as a model for many departments.

<table>
<tr><td>Data Management Centers:
Typical Service Specifications</td></tr>
<tr><td>On-line availability
Report processing cycles
Job turn-around time
Program modifications time
System response time
Data entry time
Repair time, by machine category
Time to answer an incoming call
Type of user training provided
Effectiveness of user training</td></tr>
</table>

This is an excellent starting point, but what is proposed in a CSA agreement is closer to an ISO* standard. There is often a need to identify critical issues involving design and implementation, testing, validation, and maintenance of software and systems for user departments. Standards will have to be developed on critical issues and an agreement reached on how audits will be conducted for conformance to the standards.

CSA on service functions, particularly skilled functions provided by internal auditing departments and human resource departments, must deal with "difficult" issues. These include issues of courtesy, ability to communicate, concern, providing timely information, and providing up-to-date information.

CSAs vary enormously, but even an internal CSA should be viewed as a formal document comprised of at least the sections shown.

Introduction Section

The introduction in a CSA should identify the parties involved and what they hope to accomplish. If a process is used, a description of the process is necessary. (Placing a flow chart in the appendix will help outsiders understand the major processing steps involved.) If a service relationship exists, then key attributes of the service should be described.

General Responsibility Section

In this section, specify who will do what. For example, the supplier might agree to notify the customer of all changes prior to implementation. In turn, the customer agrees to notify the supplier of issues that may effect the supplier, well before the issues become a formal policy.

Performance Section

This section involves performance measurements, reporting, and corrective action. Specify the performance factors to be measured, the frequency of the measurement, how they will be reported, and the time frame for taking corrective action.

---

*See discussion on ISO standards for more details. ISO 9000-3:1991(E) contains guidelines for the application of ISO 9001 to the development, supply, and maintenance of software. This is an excellent standard to generate "ideas" for an CSA. Of course, the ultimate CSA is to apply the ISO standard itself.

Priority Section

This section specifies priority of the product/services provided, particularly priority of performance measurements. In order to have a meaningful CSA, the customer must not dictate that all performance measurements are "top priority." A frank admission of what is "top" and what "would be nice to have" permits the supplying department more flexibility.

Conclusion

CSAs are in their infancy and their major reason for use is to highlight the internal department's effort and contribution to an organizational TQM effort. All internal departments should have the same reporting requirements as departments directly involved in servicing the customer if the organization is to improve their quality processes.

Shojinka

In a Japanese production system, *Shojinka* means that flexibility has been attained so that the number of workers can be altered to meet changes in production demand.* That is, Shojinka meets demand changes through flexibility by increasing or decreasing workers to meet an increase or decrease in demand. Three factors are needed to realize the Shojinka concept: (1) a flexible machine layout; (2) a cross-trained employee; and (3) continuous improvement of operations.

The basic machine layout consists of a U-shaped format whereby the entrance and exit of the line is from the same direction (read the just-in-time, cellular manufacturing discusswion). The number of workers can be added or reduced in the inner area of the U-shaped work place to meet changing demands. To accomplish this, employees must be trained to perform the multiple functions that are required in the work cell.

U-Shaped Production Cell

*For a complete description of a Shojinka system, see Yasuhiro Monden's book *Toyota Production System*, Norcross, GA: Institute of Industrial Engineers.

A typical employee must be trained in working positions 1, 2, and 3 in the U-shaped production cell shown. In addition to flexibility of working multiple tasks within the work cell, large changes in demand will require that workers exit the work cell for work in other locations. That is, if a work cell is designed to produce 10 units per time period with five employees, if the demand decreases to four units (a 60 percent decrease in demand), only three employees (a 60 percent decrease in employees) will be required. This places a premium on training as the two extra employees must have skills in other production areas so they can be efficiently utilized.

Frequently, a demand-pull condition in a just-in-time environment is utilized. When an input of one unit of work arrives at the U-entrance to the production cell, there should be an output of one unit of work from the cell. The time required to perform various operations within the U-shaped cell will undoubtedly vary. By keeping a standard inventory at each work place, unbalanced operations will be visualized, so that areas needing process improvements will be highlighted.

Of course, a Shojinka system always employs a jidoka approach to production line control. *Jidoka* is the Japanese term for the practice of allowing an employee to stop the production line when defective parts are being made.

Just-in-Time

Just-in-time (JIT) manufacturing is a philosophy that says we use inventory and manufacture items as they are needed or just-in-time. Holding inventories is wrong and producing long manufacturing runs and storing items in finished goods inventory is wasteful, and prevents firms from adopting to changing customer needs.

JIT Characteristics and Tools	
Characteristics	JIT Tools
Small lot sizes	Kanban
Small inventories	Self-directed teams
Frequent deliveries	Manufacturing cells
Fast setups	Good housekeeping
Flexible labor	Visible information systems
Participative management	
Close vendor relations	

To install a successful JIT system, a number of different characteristics must be considered. These characteristics appear as shown.

JIT is more than an alternative management approach: It is a philosophy that believes inventories must be avoided at all costs. Traditional manufacturing management would agree with JIT advocates that inventories should be avoided. However, they feel that inventories are a necessary "evil" that permits long production runs. With long production runs comes economies of scale by minimizing setup and training time.

Furthermore, traditional management feels that inventories serve a useful purpose by providing a "buffer" between production and variations in consumer demand. When demand is slow, inventories permit production to continue "economical production" levels by producing to inventory. Besides, advertising can always be used to encourage sales when inventories become too large. On the other hand, when demand is higher than the current production, products can be shipped from inventories. Thus inventories help stabilize production so manufacturing management can closely plan product and work force requirements.

Traditional Process View Versus JIT Processes

Traditional Processes	JIT Processes
Economies of scale	Economy of scope
Learning curve	Truncated product life cycle
Task specialization	Multimission facilities
Separable variable costs	Joint costs
Standardization	Variety
Expensive flexibility	Profitable flexibility
Leading to:	Leading to:
Centralization	Decentralization
Large plants	Disaggregated capacity
Balanced lines	Flexibility
Smooth flows	Inexpensive surge
Standard product design	Many custom products
Low rate of change	Responsiveness
Inventory used as a buffer	Production tied to demand
"Focused factory"	Repeated minor reorganization

Management holding a JIT philosophy views inventories as a major liability without merit. Inventories are expensive in that they increase work-in-process (WIP), and worse, large inventories mean that a firm cannot quickly adapt to changes in consumer demand. With inventories, particularly large inventories, we will want to sell off the existing stock before making changes to the existing product to meet revised customer needs. That is, inventories paralyze a firm because sales will be lost to competitors capable of rapidly meeting changing customer needs. In fact, if there is no inventories, minor changes can be immediately implemented with no increase in cost to the consumer.

Just-in-Time

Advantages of a Just-in-Time System

Reduces inventory investment.

Reduces paperwork.

Increases product quality.

Reduces manufacturing lead times.

Reduces space requirements.

Encourages work force participation.

Increases equipment utilization.

JIT advocates point out that large inventories hide manufacturing deficiencies in that management never makes "real" demands on the system. You just assume it takes two months to produce a specialty order because it has always taken two months. Marketing never is allowed to make minor product changes without extensive engineering drawings first being created, then coordinated with production. Traditional management could not conceive of an employee team changing over a production process to meet an immediate demand, without first being told to do so by supervision. It is a "given" that all production process changes have to be designed by engineering, planned by production control, coordinated by administration, then executed by skilled maintenance personnel under managerial supervision.

Under JIT, there is no inventory so demand "pulls" the product from production. Customers love JIT. It permits them to change purchasing volume and gives them the flexibility of making product changes on a timely basis. Firms of all sizes using a JIT system can have a competitive edge by providing a high level of customer service.

However, the impact of a JIT system on supervision is severe because under JIT, employees meet the needs of the Kanban system without seeking administrative approval. This means that less direct supervision will be needed of the specific production and scheduling task. Instead, supervisory talent is needed in training, developing empowered work teams, and in assisting in quality improving efforts.

The impact of JIT on employees varies. Some employees won't like the system because they prefer the traditional, structured working environment. Others employees appreciate a less boring and less structured environment where they can work on different jobs as needed to meet varying production requirements.

Difficulties in Using a Just-in-Time System

Requires workers to take responsibility for production control.

Requires a supporting management atmosphere.

Cannot respond rapidly to major changes in product design.

Not well-suited for specialty ordered products.

Requires a large number of production setups.

Requires frequent shipments from reliable suppliers. and frequent delivery to customers.

JIT in Service

Service applications of JIT are everywhere. Salad bars provide a good example of a JIT system. Instead of prestocking thousands of combinations of salads, customized salads are created, often by the customer, to meet exacting customer specifications. The firm assures the availability of relatively standardized components.

Modularized menu items, which can be mixed and matched to customer specifications are becoming common in restaurants. Tax accountants often use computers for income tax preparation and provide clients with standard breakdowns and reporting systems to improve turnaround time. Specialty automobile service firms have emerged such as quick change oil lubrication shops that have refined their production process to an extent where reserving time slots is not necessary: Just show up and they will quickly process your car.

How to Install a JIT System

Installing JIT is difficult because it is more than an "inventory system." It is a philosophy embracing three major technologies—hardware, software, and humanware technologies.

Cellular Manufacturing

A small group of equipment arranged in a repetitive production layout to produce similar items.

Not Common

Common

Common

Common

Economies Due To :

* Dedicated Equipment   * Fast Set Up

* Reduced WIP   * Shorter Throughput

* Reduced Material Handling

The Hardware Technology. Traditional "line" manufacturing is not well suited for a JIT approach because flexibility is needed to meet rapid demand changes. One such flexible system is known as *cellular manufacturing*. Machines are arranged in a flexible manner known as production cells. What makes this unique is that the arrangement of the machines can be changed by employees as required to adapt to the production of different products. Major cellular manufacturing forms are shown.

A JIT system requires manufacturing equipment that can be rapidly changed over to produce different products. That is, machines that take an hour to change over from one production set up to another cannot be used in a JIT environment. Machines have been developed to meet the need for quick, flexible change-over, and attention has been paid to Single Minute Exchange of Dies (SMED). The ultimate JIT now seems within reach: a single unit flow. That is, make a unit, modify the production machine to meet the needs of the next production unit, then make the next unit.

213

To assist in changing over machines, a new generation of flexible equipment has been designed. Such equipment does not have to wait for overhead lifting devices, instead swing-out or rotating devices are integrated into the equipment so that portions of the machinery can be rapidly changed. Support equipment has been designed so that heavy machine sections can be slid in and out as required. Instead of changing drills, drills are enclosed on spindles that automatically index to the size needed.

Equipment and product quality is maintained through operator involvement. The operator must have the authority to shut down the equipment if correct parts are not being produced. Additionally, the operator must accept responsibility for preventative maintenance. Under a JIT system, there is no one to "blame." The operator "owns" that section of the production process and it is management's job to assure the operator has the necessary tools to produce high quality work.

The Software Technology. JIT is a demand pull system that is different from the master scheduling methods found in traditional Material Requirements Planning (MRP) systems. A Kanban system can be used to implement JIT (see Kanban explanation). In a Kanban system, customer orders go directly to the actual group of employees that will manufacture the product in the form of an empty container. The empty container is the "authority" employees need to produce the amount that fills the container. Thus the demand "pulls" the product from production.

One way of accomplishing a JIT system is to have the master schedule specify the product ship date which is sent to the final assembly area. The master schedule also calculates lead times, which are given to component suppliers and to material suppliers. There is a constant flow of information to all areas, but the actual products are "pulled" by final assembly via a Kanban system from the subassembly area, which in turn pulls from component fabrication. The master schedule has "alerted" the material supplier that they can expect a "pull" from fabrication and to have enough material available to meet the "pull" order when it arrives. Thus inventories are held to an absolute minimum throughout the system.

Different sections of production have to respond virtually immediately to changes, particularly employee requests for materials and assistance in production changeovers. Many firms install visual signals, such as lights to indicate status of critical machines and processes. That is, an infrastructure will have to be developed so that employees can monitor progress in production from the floor.

The Master Schedule and J-I-T

```
Products                     Master
Shipped                      Schedule
   ↑                            ┆
   │                            ┆
Final           ◄───────────────┘
Assembly        ◄──────────┐
   ↑                       │
   │                  Component
Subassembly       ◄─── Supplier  ◄┈┈┈
Area                              
   ↑                 ┈┈┈┈┈► Information Flow
   │
Component
Fabrication          ─────► Material Flow
   ↑
   │
Material        ◄┈┈┈┈┈┈┈┈┈┈┈┈┈┈┘
Supplier
```

The Humanware Technology. Skilled employees are needed who are willing and able to take on the additional responsibilities of changing production to meet customer orders without management approval. Empowered work teams are mandatory, which means that management practices will have to changes. Management must practice open lines of communication, and remove the barrier traditionally found between management and labor. An atmosphere of mutual trust and respect is vital for this to succeed.

The "humanware technology" is the most difficult aspect of JIT. Employees will need training and assistance to succeed in such an open, flexible system. Each employee will have to be committed to producing high quality goods and services, and be willing to take on the function of inspecting the product themselves. That is, there is no end-of-the-line inspector to check their work. When it is completed, it goes onto the customer (who may be the next section in the plant, but is often the external customer).

Implementing a JIT system places severe demands on management. Management must learn how to share power, not exercise power. Proactive management is needed to works with empowered work teams as a "facilitator" rather than looking for something to go wrong. Empowered teams must be given many of the functions typically performed by supervision. This may result in reducing a need for an entire layer of management.*

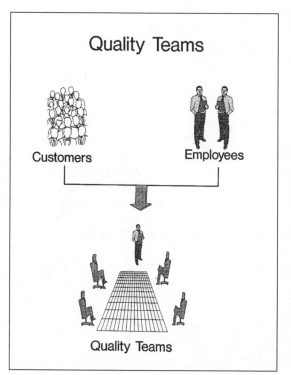

Quality Teams

There are four major types of QI teams: *task teams*, *project teams*, *functional teams*, and *self-directed teams*. A fifth team type, called *designed teams*, will be added to this list. Entire books have been devoted to discussing different teams types and how their effectiveness can be improved. The purpose of this summary is not to duplicate the discussions found in such books, but rather to highlight a few major factors that can be used to improve team effectiveness.

The purpose of any team is to bring together a group of people to concentrate on solving a common problem. Teams can also provide a method by which consumer and employee viewpoints can be identified and discussed. Particular concern will be paid to identifying the conditions under which QI team type is effective.

*Thanks are due to Mr. Mark J. Mahoney, Production Manager of Ambrake Corporation for sharing his ideas and Ambrake's JIT system.

Characteristics of an Effective Team

Effective teams do not occur by chance. You have to work at understanding group interactions and in improving interactions between team members. A good beginning point is to have everyone on a team review the characteristics of an effective team in the following list. Then ask all members to work together to try to improve their teams' effectiveness.

Characteristics of an Effective Team

1. The "atmosphere" tends to be informal and relaxed, without obvious tensions. People are involved and interested without signs of boredom.

2. There is a lot of discussion in which virtually everyone participates, but discussions remain pertinent to the team's major task. If the discussion gets off the subject, someone will bring it back in short order.

3. The team's task is understood and accepted by the members. There will have been free discussion of the objective at some point, until it was formulated in such a way that the members of the group could commit themselves to it.

4. Members listen to each other! The discussion does not jump from one idea to another unrelated idea. Every idea is given a hearing.

5. The team is comfortable with disagreement and shows no sign of avoiding conflict simply to keep everything in agreement. Disagreements are not suppressed or overridden by premature action, nor is there a "tyranny of the minority." Disagreements are discussed so that solutions can be found.

6. Most decisions are reached by a consensus in which it is clear that everybody is in general agreement and willing to go along.

7. Criticism is frequent, frank, and relatively comfortable. There is little personal attack, either openly or hidden. Criticism is constructive and oriented toward removing obstacles facing the team.

8. People are free to express their feelings and ideas on the team's problems and operations.

9. When action is taken; clear assignments are made and accepted.

10. The team's chairman does not dominate, nor does the team defer unduly to him or her. Different members, because of their knowledge or experience, act as "resources" (leaders) without power struggles. The issue is not who controls the team, but on how to get the job done.

11. The team is self-conscious about how it functions, and will examine how it is performing.

Task Teams

This is the simplest form of team structure. Membership is either elected or appointed to the team which is assigned a well-defined task. *Task teams* are temporary in nature, work-related, and membership is comprised of people from the same department.

Advantage: It is quick and easy to form a task team. Since everyone reports to the same administrative structure, minimal coordination is required.

Disadvantage: Most meaningful changes or ideas cut across functional lines. Since membership is from within one function (department), approval must be obtained by going up the hierarchy. This limits the teams effectiveness to develop and/or implement meaningful changes.

Project Teams

Project teams are comprised of members from different departments that are assigned an important, but relatively well-defined task. Issues are discussed in project teams, but the team members typically must obtain department approval on issues before committing departmental resources.

Advantages: Existing management feels more comfortable with project teams than with functional teams because the exact nature of the project is known and approval cycles are well-defined.

Disadvantages: Because project team members are "bound" to their departments, there is little the team can do without obtaining approval. This tends to restrict the creativity of the team.

Functional Teams

Functional teams are assigned tasks that cut across functional lines (i.e., cut across departmental or other authoritative lines). Functional teams are comprised of representatives from different departments. The team is given a charge by top management to develop proposals and revise work systems without obtaining departmental approval. They are more permanent than task teams and are given higher level and more important assignments. Functional teams need to be coordinated by a facilitator reporting to a quality council. The facilitator, working with multiple functional groups, will help assure the groups are progressing towards a conclusion of their assignment and that they are exercising power consistent with their assignment.

Functional teams are frequently given assignments that require power and authority of different functional units be changed so that customer needs can be better meet. (See the just-in-time discussion where a QI team proposed that on prototype parts, marketing should deal directly with the production work force, thus eliminating engineering, production control, procurement and quality control from the "approval" cycle to speed customer delivery.) Care must be taken to assure functional teams concentrate on doing the job better, and that they do not get bogged down with political considerations that are inevitable in "organizational reality."

Advantages: Functional teams are useful in reducing the time to introduce new products by bringing together otherwise diverse groups such as manufacturing, marketing, and engineering.

Disadvantages: They are given decision-making authority, but frequently feel they still have to "obtain approval" from their "home department" which may be counterproductive.

Self-Directed Teams

Self-directed teams, also called *empowered teams*, are responsible for completing a broad, ill-defined scope of work. The teams are given an assignment of a broad unit of work to be accomplished. Team members then identify the specific steps to be completed. Self-directed teams are capable of organizing themselves, requesting support from the necessary functional units, and accomplishing the task without seeking departmental or higher administrative approval.

Self-directed teams are not required to "conform" to departmental approval/regulations. For example, a self-directed work team might be formed by an automobile manufacturer to develop a new sports car. The team will be comprised of representatives from the major departments. If the team finds they can react quickly by working cross-functions then they are expected to do so without seeking approval.

Advantages: Self-directed teams can adapt to and meet the needs of a rapidly changing environment.

Disadvantages: Existing management often feels threatened by these teams because they have the authority to take action without obtaining approval. Employees often feel there is a lack of mutual trust between other employees and between themselves. This may prevent self-directed teams from operating at maximum effectiveness.

The Design Team

A special purpose team, called a *design team*, is often used to provide leadership in developing ideas for organizational improvement. This team is similar to a self-directed team but concentrates on developing ideas, not in implementing production assignments.

A design team of six to ten employees is appointed by the *quality council*. The team often evaluates what other organizations are doing and then engages internal groups in discussions of ways to respond to customer demands. (See discussion on benchmarking.)

Steps in Developing Design Teams

✓ Organization is committed to finding a better way
✓ Quality council/teams investigate what others are doing
✓ Executive group clarifies mission
✓ Quality council appoints a design team
✓ Read about similar groups and visit sites
✓ Analyze environment, technology, and jobs
✓ Discuss draft plan with involved groups
✓ Recommendations to quality council
✓ Implement design and evaluate

The design team should concentrate on the elements of good service quality. Although the exact elements of good service quality will vary between organizations, the following characteristics are generally found in high quality organizations: existence of a service bible; demonstrated customer concern; flipped pyramid; friendly communications; and leadership that is genuinely concerned with the employee and the customer. The design team should address each of these elements.

Service Bible

Everyone in the firm, both top management and all employees, must have a clear definition of how high quality service is provided to the customer. If this definition isn't clearly written and understood by all employees, then each employee will have his/her own interpretation of service quality and will treat customers differently.

One technique that can be used to improve service quality is to develop a *service bible*. This bible sets forth the "dos and don'ts" for all employees. The real value in a service bible lies in involving employee teams in its creation. Each group should discuss what should/should not be in the service bible (use employee teams). Then engage all front-line employees in regular meetings so that everyone understands the policies. Identify each market segment and customer requirements. You are trying to find common "feelings/needs" among customers. Develop a service bible and define all important points.

Demonstrated Customer Concern

Customer concern can be *demonstrated concern* by obtaining the customer's point of view with regular surveys to determine their level of satisfaction. But don't stop there. Circulate the findings to internal QI teams and react to them. Always try to make the customer the "star of the show." Perhaps customers to the firm or certain days can be designated "special customer days." When discussing proposals that have a potential effect the customer, a good technique is to ask: "What would our customers think of...." Of course, always respond to customer complaints and try to give the customer more than they asked for when solving a problem.

Flipped Pyramid

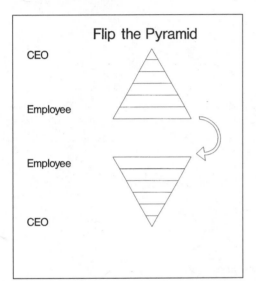

Flip the Pyramid

CEO

Employee

Employee

CEO

If front-line employees feel they are not important, service care will deteriorate as employees become indifferent to customer's feelings. Organizations have a pyramid-type structure where the CEO is on top, the employee is at the bottom, and there are various managerial ranks separating them.

Directives and policies typically come from the CEO using a "top down" approach. You need to flip the pyramid by having ideas, particularly customer service ideas, come from the bottom up. That is, develop procedures, and open up lines of communication to encourage a flow of ideas from the front-line employee to the CEO.

How to "Flip the Pyramid"

✓ Collect information from front-line employees.

✓ Give them the tools to do their jobs. Often employees do not have the information they need to do the job they want.

✓ Develop a mentor program where experienced people teach newcomers to help them integrate into the organization quickly.

✓ Require all staff to engage in front-line customer sales, at least for one day every six months. This will reinforce the importance of front-line people, and it will help staff understand customer needs.

✓ Reward extraordinary performance: have an employee of the month, and share information in the company's newsletter.

✓ Delegate authority to front-line employees to solve problems. Why can't you trust your employees to accept returns and rectify must customer complaints, on the spot?

Friendly Communications

Review all internal and external communications to assure wording is consistently positive. Use friendly language in all bills, brochures, and policies. Eliminate "legal wording" and documents that are intimidating. Remember "how" you say something in writing and verbally is as important as "what" you say. Does your team really know how employees answer the telephone? Have you every phoned your firm and evaluated how the call was processed. Do employees answer calls and questions in a positive, warm manner even at the end of the day when they are busy and tired? One way of overcoming deficiencies and increasing the importance of reacting positively to the customer's request is to ask employees to participate in discussion groups to improve customer service.

Concerned Leadership

A relationship should be developed between the design team and the organization's key managers that would permit the team to offer suggestions regarding how leadership can increase its effectiveness in improving quality. Service bibles are not enough. The CEO must demonstrate a personal commitment to improving quality, which is easier said then done. Perhaps the most important way this can be demonstrated is for the CEO to "walk the talk" and be highly visible and accessible by front-line employees.

Quality Council

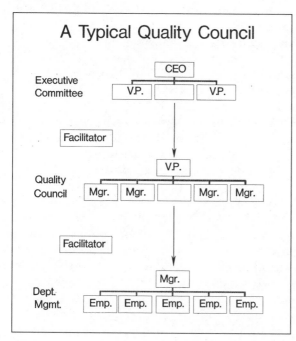

A Typical Quality Council

A *quality council*, often called a *steering committee*, is needed to focus an organization's QI efforts. The council is composed of senior management who oversee the various cross-functional task teams and assist in keeping the organization focused on continuous quality improvement. This council provides the structure needed to choose projects, assign and assist QI teams, and to follow up on implementation. Without a formalized structure such as a council, quality ideas are typically discussed then put on the "back burner" because most good ideas cut across functional lines.

A typical quality council is shown. A senior member of the executive committee (such as the executive vice president) should chair the council which is normally composed of department management. As the the executive vice president has numer-

221

ous other duties, a facilitator is often assigned to coordinate with the various quality teams. Conferring with teams on a regular basis to assure they stay on track and assuring teams do not become "bogged down" is a time-consuming process. Hence the role of a facilitator quickly grows into a full-time job. Ideally, the facilitator should possess both technical QI skills and human relations/team building skills so that assistance can be given to teams when needed.

The problem most organizations face is not in getting employees to offer improvement ideas, but rather in providing assistance in implementing ideas. After the council becomes established, employee membership can help others understand the role of the council. One way of doing this is to start a two-month rotating position held by an employee who received recognition for outstanding contributions to the organization's QI effort.

Successful Quality Councils

It is not unusual to find organizations that have a quality council, but what is unusual is to find a council that is successful in implementing and directing their TQM program. There are many reasons for this lack of success, the primary reason being that quality councils are often composed of a group of executives who are used to operating autonomously.

A successful quality council must be an executive team dedicated to improving quality. The council is not a get-together of strong willed people to "hammer out" agreements. The council must have a clearly defined function, the personal commitment of the CEO, should be chaired by senior management, and be comprised of management from the major departments in an organization.

An effective quality council is one whose members have helped in establishing the organization's mission and vision statement, and they have a shared vision of the organization's future. Council members *must* be willing to change and not take the attitude of "defending" their home turf or of "representing" particular vested interests. Employees will quickly recognize political alliances and if a certain group, say the engineering division, repeatedly exercises inflexibility, enthusiasm will be lost.

For example, suppose Ajax Manufacturing Company specializes in high volume production, produced to exacting customer specification. Ajax is profitable and sales are satisfactory, but a QI team felt there was a better way of doing business. Senior marketing people (technically competent in the products Ajax is producing) call on key accounts on a routine basis. When these key accounts are engaged in prototyping (creating a new product) Ajax salespeople integrate themselves closely with the firms buyers and design people.

A QI team came up with a recommendation that minor customer changes could be noted by Ajax senior sales representatives on engineering documentation which they carry. The team recognized that the changes would have to be limited in scope and could not be substituted for permanent engineering. The QI team found qualified and willing manufacturing hourly employees that could produce this documentation (which was faxed to them), without sacrificing quality, and then send the revised parts back to the customer by small package air delivery.

That is, changes are not first sent to engineering to upgrade their engineering document. Nor are the revised engineering documents sent to manufacturing engineering for tool and machine specification. Nor does production control schedule the changes. Nor does material control order the needed material (for one thing, there is no updated bill of material). Nor does quality control inspect the material or finished product. Nor is the part sent via inside transportation to shipping to be routed out in a standardized manner.

What happens is that the skilled, senior level machinist calls a local steel supply house for immediate delivery of the material needed, produces the prototype, then calls a local overnight shipper to pick up the part as soon as it is available. The payoff for key customers during prototyping prior to volume production is a reduction in turnaround time from three weeks to three days.

How would typical directors of engineering react to the QI team's proposal that virtually removes them from the design loop? Would he/she put obstacles in the path of such innovation? When it actually was time to implement the proposal, would the director of manufacturing and the director of quality really permit such empowerment? Would production control allow a machinist to "bump" schedules, even if for a few hours? Would purchasing permit an hourly employee to order material without first going through purchasing?

The effectiveness of a quality council is determined by how they handle suggestions that cross functional lines. A moment's thought on this example can identify dozens of valid reasons why such a change cannot be accomplished, but only one reason why we should install the proposal: The customer wants it.

Membership on a quality council must be seen as an opportunity for members to contribute. The importance of the tone established by the senior chair of the committee cannot be overemphasized. A council that works together as a team and adopts a positive "we can make this new idea work" sends a message to all members of the organization: Your ideas really count.

Sustaining the TQM Movement

The questions confronting a quality council that is trying to sustain a TQM movement are formidable. For example, how should rewards be given? Personally, I recommend "showering" groups with dinner for two at local restaurants. It's a gentle way for an organization to say "thanks," and it is further reinforced when the person dines with a "significant other."

Initially, indicators of quality should be considered in some manner in annual performance reviews. These indicators may be relatively loose, consisting of factors such as number of ideas submitted, work on QI teams, and the like. However, sooner or later, organizations should consider Juran's approach to sustaining a TQM program. Specific QI goals should be set, plans established to meet the goals, and progress should be measured. Progress towards meeting QI goals should be evaluated and incorporated into a formal annual performance review process.*

*For an excellent discussion of how to increase the effectiveness of a quality council, read "Planning for Successful Steering Committees," by Mr. Dan Ciampa, *Journal for Quality and Participation*, December, 1992, pp. 22–34.

ISO Standards

What Are the ISO Standards?

ISO 9000	Overview of standard series
ISO 9001	Includes design and after-sale servicing
ISO 9002	Model for production and installation
ISO 9003	Requirements assured solely at final inspection and test (retailers, distributors)
ISO 9004	Quality system elements

The Geneva-based *International Organization for Standardization* (IOS) first published a series of standards in 1987. These standards became known as the *ISO* (meaning equal) *standards* that provide a basis by which a registered company would assure buyers of their capability of producing quality goods.

A series of five ISO manuals are used to describe the elements for establishing and maintaining a quality management system. A company registered as complying with ISO standards has demonstrated to an accredited third party (an approved outside auditor) that its processes have been documented and that the company is systematically auditing and being audited that they are following the policies and procedures necessary to produce high quality products.

The term *ISO* describes the series of international standards dealing with product design, production, delivery, service, and testing. A summary of the five ISO standards is shown. ISO registration is achieved by compliance with one or more of the following standards: ISO 9001, 9002, or 9003.

Overview of ISO Standards

Standard number	Title	Function
9000	Quality management and quality assurance standards: guidelines for selection and use.	Provides an overview of the quality concepts and the models which can be used to implement them.
9001	Quality systems: model for quality assurance in design, development, production, installation, and servicing.	Used when conformance to specification requirements during design, development, production, installation, and servicing is required.
9002	Quality systems: model for quality assurance in production and installation.	Used when conformance to specification requirements is limited to production and installation.
9003	Quality systems: model for quality assurance in final inspection and test.	Used when conformance to specification requirements is to be assured by the supplier solely at final inspection and test.
9004	Quality systems: model for quality management and quality systems— guidelines.	Used for developing and implementing an internal quality system for design and manufacturing.

ISO Registration Process

RAB → Certifies

RAB —Accredits→ Registrar —Employs→ Auditors

Registrar —Registers→ Suppliers

Suppliers ←Audits— Auditors

Suppliers —Assures Quality→ Purchasers

RAB   Registration Accreditation Board
ASQC American Society for Quality Control
ANSI American National Standards Institute

The Registration Process

The *Registration Accreditation Board* (RAB) are groups of accredited registrars to whom firms apply to have their processes registered. There are about 75 registrars in the United States specializing in various industries. These registrars employ auditors (certified by the RAB) to audit the processes of suppliers that have achieved registration. These audits assure that the suppliers are continuing to confirm to the ISO requirements.

ISO registration provides a framework for ensuring that a firm's quality will be maintained in all phases of the business. ISO standards assess the effectiveness of management in providing high quality, consistent goods and delivery to customers. ISO registration will also provide a set of requirements which are accepted worldwide, although there are currently problems with European recognition of some registrars.

ISO and TQM

ISO standards are directed towards improving a firm's production processes. A TQM system is the big picture and is concerned with customer satisfaction and all activities conducted by a firm. Although one could correctly argue that leadership is required for a successful ISO program, the leadership role as described in the TQM model provided by the Baldrige Award structure is far more encompassing. Thus, a good way of viewing ISO is that the emphasis in the ISO registration process is on the management of process quality. This is not meant to minimize the role of ISO in a TQM system. The ISO standards provide an excellent beginning point for a firm starting a TQM program.

TQM and ISO

The TQM system shown is the Malcolm Baldrige National Quality Award System.

TQM System

| Driver | System | Measure of Progress | Goal |

Leadership   Information and Analysis   Quality and Operational Results   Customer Focus and Satisfaction

Strategic Quality Planning

Human Resources

ISO -> Mgt. of Process Quality

Becoming ISO Registered

A firm must first decide which of three levels of certification to obtain: ISO 9001, 9002, or 9003. (ISO 9000 is an overview and ISO 9004 is used for internal quality, not for outside certification.) There are a couple of critical questions that can be asked to determine which registration to seek. If a firm is engaged in design efforts and or after-sale servicing, the firm typically seeks ISO 9001 registration. ISO 9002 registration is for firms involved in production and installation, but who produce to other firm's specifications (that is, they do not have a design function). Thus, ISO 9002 registration is less demanding than ISO 9001. ISO 9003 is typically sought by distributors and retailers.

Implementing ISO

The process of implementing ISO begins with the executive committee developing a brief, meaningful quality policy. This general policy, forms the "thrust" for the firm, and must be posted and knows to all employees and customers.

The quality manual is usually a statement of the key quality policies and provisions for the firm. To keep the paperwork to manageable size, procedures are normally referenced, but are not included in the manual. However, the procedures are available on-site where they are to be referred to and followed by the employees. Detailed job instructions on critical processes are referenced in the procedures and kept on site. Adequate records and documentation must be kept that demonstrate that quality products are being produced.

All ISO policies, procedures, and pertinent data must be documented and be ready for inspection at any time. It is the responsibility of the employees to follow the instructions laid out by the quality procedures and keep accurate documentation of their work. A member of the management team is assigned the role of internal auditor to assure all employees are correctly trained and are following the procedures. A typical internal ISO audit sheet is shown.

Implementation Responsibility

Quality Policy	Top Management
Quality Manual	Middle Management
Procedures	Industrial Engineer
Job Instructions	Supervisor and Employees
Records and Documentation	Employees

ISO Audit by Paragraph

Paragraph/Audit Score	#1	#2	#3	#4	#5
4.1 Management responsibility					
4.2 Quality system					
4.3 Contract review					
4.4 Design control					
4.5 Document and data control					
4.6 Purchasing					
4.7 Control of customer-supplied product					
4.8 Product identification and traceability					
4.9 Process control					
4.10 Inspection and testing					
4.11 Control of inspection, measuring, and test equipment					
4.12 Inspection and test status					
4.13 Control of nonconforming product					
4.14 Corrective and preventive action					
4.15 Handling, storage, packing, preservation, and delivery					
4.16 Control of quality records					
4.17 Internal quality audits					
4.18 Training					
4.19 Servicing					
4.20 Statistical techniques					

Audit Findings

#1 No system

#2 Verbal system, no documents

#3 Documentation incomplete and not organized

#4 Documentation complete but not being followed

#5 Documentation and compliance with ISO standard

Suggestions on ISO Registration

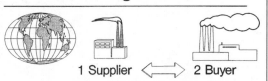

ISO Registration

1 Supplier ⟷ 2 Buyer
3 Third party audit

Key to registration is third party audits

Ask your key customer for an
assessor specializing in your industry

Registration generally good for three years

You will be audited twice per year. First
question: Let me see your internal audits

External costs - Initial registration and audits

Most of what is needed for ISO registration
exists, but is not documented

Use ISO to get people involved in thinking
about improving your process quality

The key to registration is the *third-party audit*. This is the audit the registrar will conduct on the firm approximately twice per year. Firms should use a registrar that is familiar with their industry, and understands standard industrial practices.

A good beginning point for firms seeking an ISO registrar is to ask the key customers in your industry who they recommend. The cost of ISO registration is very reasonable and often the internal evaluation of policies and procedures will result in savings that offset that cost. If you use a registrar that is familiar with the practices employed in your industry, costs will be held to a minimum. If your firm is selling in the European market, then use a registrar that is recognized and accepted by the primary nation you will be selling with.*

---

*A complete description of ISO standards is contained in the author's article along with Jeff Waring titled: "An ISO 9000 Certified Pizza Isn't All That Far-Fetched." Published in *The Journal for Quality and Participation*, Oct/Nov 1993 pp. 20–23.

TQM Contributors

The major TQM contributors are Deming, Crosby, and Juran. When you read over the summaries of their contributions, think through how each contributor would evaluate:

1. An organization's use of its human resources.

2. The role of management.

3. The concept of reduction of variation in the processes that produce goods and services.

4. The methods used by an organization to continuously improve the quality of their goods and services.

Deming's Guide to Quality

Dr. W. Edwards Deming has strong views on how quality can be improved. He believes that the key to quality improvement lies in the use of statistics and in management accepting the fact that they are responsible for poor quality because they own the process. Dr. Deming believes that the purpose of statistics is to study and understand process and product variations. Statistics should be used to help identify these variations and to reduce variations.

Management's job is to lead an organization in a neverending, continuous improvement of quality. Neverending improvement is achieved by a continual reduction of variation in the processes that produce a product or a service. That is, Dr. Deming believes that variation itself is wrong. Whatever contributes to product and process variation should be identified and eliminated so that the right product and service is produced the right way every time.

Dr. Deming believes we know we are working in organizations that are not producing high quality goods and services. This results in stress because we know we could be doing better. Stress leads to problems on the job and personal problems (drugs, alcohol abuse, family strife). Consequently, the effect of poor management is creeping into our lives and is pervasive in our culture.

Deming's Guide to Quality

General Quality Questions

How many managers has your firm had in the last 10 years?

Does your firm have a long-term orientation? Do they develop and communicate plans for the future and work toward a better life?

Does your firm have a mission statement that is known and lived by all your employees?

Does your mission statement reinforce your firm as something you should identify with?

Does your firm deserve admiration?

What is your firm doing to drive out fear and to break down barriers between departments?

Do employees have pride in their work?

Deming identifies three major types of quality.

Types of Quality

1. *Quality of design.* Consumer research: Why do customers come to your firm? Did you ever conduct a consumer attitude survey?
2. *Quality of conformance.* Extent to which a firm and its suppliers are able to surpass the design specifications required to meet customer needs.
3. *Quality of performance.* Evaluate how well the product performs, then redesign the product to perform even better.

Deming's 14 Points

1. Create Consistency of Purpose Toward Improvement of Services.
Combine this with a plan to improve your competitive position. Deming uses the term "mission statement" to include both a vision and the mission statement. He believes that quality improvement begins with a meaningful mission statement that employees and investors can "buy into." A mission statement should address:

Investors	Customers
Employees	Citizenship (community)
Quality philosophy	Distribution of profits
Plans for growth	Fields of interest
Direction (long term)	Corporate objectives (long term)

A mission statement is a living document created with two-way communication. Without a clear, well-understood mission statement that everyone "buys into," the organization is floundering without a sense of direction. Unfortunately, most mission statements are not known and understood by employees. For example, could you write your interpretation of the mission statement of either the current or former firm you worked for?

Sample Topics in a Mission Statement

People: Employees are an asset. Training is a continuous process for all. Teamwork is emphasized. Responsibility, authority, and accountability are delegated as closely as possible to those performing the work. Vacancies filled from within; job security.

Customers: Their satisfaction will determine our future existence. Long-term relationships; employees are encouraged to become involved with customers' needs.

Suppliers: Long-term/single source if appropriate.

Community: Do we conduct business ethically? Are we a positive influence? Is the community really aware of what we do?

Vendors: Are we purchasing the best?

---

2. Adopt the New Philosophy.   We can no longer live with accepted levels of defects, delays, or mistakes. Defects are not free. Someone gets paid for making them.

Quality is defined as surpassing customer needs and expectations throughout the life of the product or service. We create an arm's length relationship with our vendors so it is easier to lay blame on them. (We should manage for success, not for failure.)

The attitude by management and employees must be that quality is built in. You do not "inspect defects out." Everyone should be alert as to why workmanship is less than perfect and they should work together to correct the problems. Quality and cost effectiveness are not opposite goals.

Check the Effectiveness of Your Organization's Quality

How do you define customer quality?

Do your employees know what constitutes high customer quality?

How do you know you are pursuing high quality?

What do your customers think of your quality compared with other firms in the industry?

Management cannot possibly define customer quality without survey information about the customer's needs and expectations.

3. Cease Dependence on Mass Inspection.   Require statistical evidence that quality is built in. Deming stresses the need for statistical controls on all processes. Inspection neither improves nor guarantees quality. It does not make goods better nor does inspection improve the process. Teamwork is needed between the firm and its suppliers for process improvement.

4. End Practice of Awarding Business on the Basis of the Price Tag. Develop detailed measures of quality along with price. Often firms concentrate on developing technical specifications and ignore performance specifications (which include customer satisfaction). This are not equivalent. For example, in serving a steak at a restaurant, the important measurement is customer satisfaction not the technical specifications (serving an 8 oz. steak). We take the "easy way out" because performance specifications are difficult. They include many variables in addition to the technical specification of the steak's size.

Procurement people must learn statistical methods to assess quality and to make decisions. Communicating back to the vendor is a key element in improving quality. Only in a single-source relationship will a vendor be willing to modify his process to meet revised quality of design specs at a reasonable price. Besides, there is a hidden cost when a firm uses multiple vendors. These costs include variations among different vendors and a higher cost, in general, because each vendor is just beginning the learning curve cycle (i.e., high production hours are spent on each smaller production runs.)

There should be a constant application of statistical SQC on all processes and and all vendor supplied items to prove a satisfactory level evidence of quality. Lawyers need to be trained in the Deming philosophy so contracts can be created that encourage the pursuit of quality rather than "a sue for breach of contract" attitude.

5. Find Problems.   It is management's job to work on continually improving the system. This point is the key to understanding Deming's philosophy. Deming stresses that any process or product variation is bad. There are two types of variations: *special variations* that are under the control of the operator and *common variations* that are "common" to the system and beyond the ability of the operator to control.

Statistics can assist in pointing out the causes of this variation which must be sought out and eliminated. Business schools must teach statistical methods for quality control in which everyone in the firm participates under the direction of a competent statistician.

Are You a Total Quality Person?

I treat others fairly.

	Seldom	Sometimes	Always
	☐	☐	☐

Sources of Process (System) Variation

Special: These variations are due to an assignable or specific cause. (Deming believes only 6 percent of all variations are caused by this). Train the operator to find these variations and make the necessary adjustments, such as readjusting the machine under the operator's control. After all special variations are eliminated, the process is considered to be stable. However, the process may still have too many rejects due to common variation.

Common: Cause of 94 percent of all variation. These are system problems and management owns the system. *Employees just work within the system and cannot change this.*

Deming constantly reinforces an important point: *A process is in control only when it can be controlled by the worker.* Management must eliminate all common variation so that the worker can concentrate on and adjust for special variation that is under their control.

Common Variation (Management's Problem) Is Caused by

Hasty designs, quick answers to customers

Inadequate testing of incoming materials and waiving specifications

Failure to know the capabilities of the process that are in a state of statistical control

Failure to provide workers with statistical signals that will tell them how they are doing and when to make changes

Smoke, noise, unnecessary dirt, poor light, humidity, confusion

Control charts can help the operator separate common variations (which the operator should call to the attention of management) and special variations (which the operator should be trained to control). Upper Control Limit (UCL) and Lower Control Limit (LCL) charts are useful to assist in the separation of common and special variations. A process is stable if it exhibits only common variation (due to limitations in process).

Advantage of a Stable Process

Management knows the process capability and can predict its performance, cost, and quality levels.

Production is at a maximum and costs are minimum.

Management has data to back up its argument if they want to change specifications.

A stable process that produces too many defects will do so as long as the system remains the same. Since only management can change the system, the process cannot be improved until management bring the process into statistical control. Tools to accomplish this include:

- Flow charts
- Check sheets
- Pareto analysis
- Brainstorming
- Fishbone (cause-and-effect) diagrams
- Histograms
- Scatter diagrams
- Control charts

Most poor quality is created by common causes inherent in the production system. Poorly designed services, inadequately trained workers, and poor working conditions are under management, not employee, control. Management is at fault and must develop a stable process. Then, after a stable process is developed, employees can be held accountable for isolated special causes (i.e., employees can only reduce those variations that are under their control).

6. Institute Modern Methods of Training

When Developing a Training Program

Identify the objectives of the firm.

Identify goals that will be met through training.

A possible goal could be for everyone to understand and meet the mission statement.

Orient new employees.

Train supervisors in statistical thinking.

Develop/instigate team building.

Analyze what needs to be taught.

Only after carefully analyzing what needs to be taught, develop training programs.

---

7. Institute Modern Methods of Supervision. Employees are frequently penalized for problems in the system. They are being blamed for things beyond their control. Management must provide customer feedback to employees and they must develop an open, supportive atmosphere where there is mutual trust and where employees do not fear management.

Questions for Consideration

Does management feel they must police employees or else employees will slack off and productivity will decrease?

Do employees fear management because interactions are generally blaming sessions?

Are employees aware of how their job fits into the extended process?

Are awards/punishment based on common variation (i.e., system variations over which the employee has no control)?

Supervision should be the link between management and the work force. They should instigate teamwork by serving as coaches, not policemen.

8. Drive Out Fear So Everyone May Work Effectively. Most people find work unpleasant, not because they don't like what they do, but because of the climate in which they do it. Fear comes from a feeling of being powerless because a boss has control over important aspects of your life.

9. Break Down Barriers Between Departments: Everyone Must Work as a Team. The structure of a firm creates barriers between departments and barriers between areas within departments. These barriers must be removed. There are too many restrictions on communication, too many administrative levels, too much fear of performance appraisals, numerous quotas, and, as a result, employees often have a negative attitude.

10. Eliminate Numerical Goals, Posters and Slogans That Seek New Levels of Productivity Without Improving Methods. Management must make changes to the production system for people to meet the goal of improving the quality of the products and services they produce. As long as the process continues to be stable, the same amount of defects will be produced. "Zero defects" are hollow words.

Horrible Posters That Hold Employees Accountable for Meeting Vague Goals

Do it right the first time.
Our job is quality.
Increase sales 10 percent.
Increase profits.
Safety is job one.
Be careful.

11. Eliminate Work Standards That Prescribe Numeric Quotas. Quotas do not provide a road map for improvement, but instead prohibit good supervision and training. Workers are encouraged to produce goods that may contain defects just to meet quotas. Quotas do not take common and special variation into consideration as a basis for taking action to improve the process.

Get rid of MBO (Management By Objectives). MBO is just a method to legitimize arbitrary numerical goals. Using MBO, management typically breaks down the "grand plan" into smaller subsections which are then assigned to an individual. Note that the employees are not given any new tools; they must scavenge from the existing system to meet goals. Increases that are "negotiated" are arbitrary.

12. Remove Barriers That Rob Employees of Pride of Workmanship. The United States is an underdeveloped nation. We are not using workers to their fullest potential because we rob them of their right to have pride in their work. Because management is not responsive and does not work with the employee to improve the process, employees often feel that loyalty to a firm is misplaced and that their energies should be devoted to their families and personal priorities.

If employees do not understand the firm's mission and what is expected of them, they will be confused and unable to identify with the firm. Although the system is at fault, the employee often receives a below average performance appraisal. This results in anger, disloyalty, and loss of pride.

Barriers That Rob Employees of Their Pride of Workmanship

Managerial ignorance concerning common and special variation.

Performance appraisal systems that destroy teamwork by encouraging people to focus on individual goals, rather than on organizational goals.

Daily production reports that focus on yesterday's production without any acknowledgement of variation.

Failure to identify the cost of quality in terms of visible and hidden costs.

Get rid of performance appraisals. Employees and most managers do not like performance appraisals and view them as a necessary evil. Employees become concerned with obtaining a good performance rating instead of being concerned with what is best for the organization.

Forced performance appraisal systems are the worst! These evaluation procedures state that only 10 percent of the employees can be evaluated top, only 25 percent in next category, and so on. This process is absurd and must be stopped.

Performance appraisal systems do not distinguish between the performance of the people and the influence of the system on the people. Employees are often held responsible for outcomes of the process they cannot change. Employees react to a performance evaluation and change their behavior to earn a better rating for the next rating period. If variation was understood, the employee is probably reacting to a common variation which is beyond their ability to control. By adjusting their behavior, they are actually creating more variation in the system.

Employee promotion should be based on the employee's ability to work as a team. Statistical distributions will highlight that only 2 people out of 1000 are truly superior or truly inferior. Performance evaluation systems damage the motivation and commitment of the majority of a firm's employees because of this feeling of helplessness brought about by being held accountable for activities over which they have no control.

13. Institute a Vigorous Program of Education and Training. Statistical training, communications, and future-oriented education are key. This reinforces Deming's concern with a educated work force. This point, point 13, refers to a continuous, broad education for self-development. His point 6 (previously discussed), refers to training in specific job skills.

14. Create a Program That Will Push the Prior 13 Points Each Day for Neverending Improvement. Create a cycle of successes with a strong management backing for quality. A statistical leader is needed to encourage management to use statistical thinking in their decision making.

Now It's Your Turn

1. *Select one of the following organizations and pretend you are Deming. Conduct a quality audit of that organization. Do NOT simply go over his 14 points. Pretend you are Deming and that you are speaking to the president of the organization. What would Deming say were the organizations' three weakest points? What are their three strongest points? Why?*

Typical Organizations

Any local firm
Local gas station
Local dry cleaner
Local grocery store

Crosby's Guide to Quality

> **Profile of a Problem Firm**
>
> Employees grumble and complain about poor services and poor food.
>
> Support staff is grumpy about "everything."
>
> There has been an increase in customer complaints.
>
> Management does not provide a clear definition of quality.
>
> Mentality: Schedule first, cost second, quality third.
>
> Management does not know the price of nonconformance: lost customers, poor customer satisfaction, changing staff.
>
> Management denies that it is the cause of the problem. They make speeches, send everyone to management development programs, but do not make meaningful changes.

Do you talk about a need for a meaningful, ongoing quality program at your firm? Do you agree there is a problem but put off doing anything? Then you have identified the problem with quality. It is something everyone talks about, but no one is willing to fully commit to the improvement process?

For example, what does a person do with a serious overweight problem? They rationalize the seriousness of the problem and postpone taking action. The only time some people will take action is when you can prove to them they are confronting likely death.

Crosby is the "father of the *zero defects* (ZD) approach" to quality. If an overweight person wants to gain control, then no fatty foods can be tolerated. Likewise, an alcoholic attempting to change must take a ZD approach to booze (i.e., not one drink is permitted).

Organizations are no different. They must develop the attitude that they will not tolerate defects. Anything less than a ZD approach will not result in an organization's total commitment to improving their quality. Without this total commitment, improvements are unlikely.

Employee "demotivation" is common, prompting management to become "worried" about motivation and getting people "turned on." What really happened? Didn't we hire motivated people? Why did they become demotivated after working for us? Employees become turned off with a firm and its management through the normal irritating, unconcerned ways they are dealt with.

> **Poor Management Practices That Make Employees Irate**
>
> Performance that reviews are a one-way street; dishonest evaluations show people that the firm has no integrity.
>
> Excessive expense account rules: edicts an eternal battle with the Accounting Department.
>
> Meetings where the boss rules (i.e., be a faithful listener).
>
> Bosses who do not really listen to their employees.

Hassled People Do Not Produce Quality Work!

Sometimes employees who feel hurt or unappreciated do little work at all. This hassle results in many employees spending more time "protecting themselves" than they do making something happen. You do NOT want a program to eliminate hassle. Eating a sandwich is a program; raising children is a process. You never finish a process.

Many firms do not succeed with quality programs because they are not determined enough. Typical symptoms include the following:

Symptoms of an Unsuccessful Quality Program

The effort is called a program rather than a process (this encourages people to just go through the motions).

Effort is aimed at the lower employees in the firm.

People are cynical when the concept of quality is discussed.

Management is impatient for results.

Crosby defines *quality* as conformance to requirements. Establish the highest possible standards, then conform to these standards. Management must assure that requirements are developed and clearly understood by everyone. Then management must remove procedures and other obstacles that get in the employee's way. *DIRFT* stands for Do It Right the First Time! This is compatible with the ZD approach of simply not tolerating errors.

The system of quality is prevention. Look at the process and identify opportunities for error. Use Statistical Quality Control (SQC) to identify critical process variables. Measure these variables and adjust the process as required. Management in the United States has difficulty allowing employees to accept control. They can not stand to let employees adjust the process and because of this, SQC has not been fully accepted in the United States.

The Performance Standard Must Be Zero Defects

There is *no* acceptable level of defects. A typical Payroll Department does not make mistakes because people will not tolerate errors in their paychecks. Look at the confusion that would occur if an employee were consistently underpaid and he/she had to ask for the money that was rightfully due them. The damage to moral would be enormous.

Even if an organization's processes are 99 percent effective, that is not good enough! Suppose a process consists of two parts, and each part works correctly 99 percent of the time. Therefore, the total process will work correctly 98 percent of the time (99 percent times 99 percent). This doesn't sound like much of a problem, but if the process consists of 100 parts, the process is capable of making a good product only 34 percent of the time. (Multiplying .99 times itself 100 times yields .34.)

Of course, there is a problem getting people to commit to making zero defects. People have been conditioned throughout their lives to accept the fact that human beings are not perfect and, therefore, will make mistakes. We accept errors as a way of life and as a way of doing business. This acceptance of errors is the reason we do not produce high quality goods and services. Mistakes are caused by lack of knowledge and lack of attention.

The Measurement of Quality Is the Price of Nonconformance

The *price of nonconformance* includes all expenses involved in doing things wrong. This can be 35 percent of our costs. Crosby identifies numerous items including possible customer loss to highlight the high hidden cost of poor quality.

Steps in Quality Improvement

1. Appoint a management committee.
2. Establish a quality improvement team.
3. Set up measurements.
4. Identify the cost of poor quality.
5. Develop quality awareness.
6. Undertake corrective action programs.
7. Zero defects planning.
8. Employee education.
9. Implement a zero defects kick-off day.
10. Begin quality goal setting.
11. Practice error-cause removal.
12. Give recognition to accomplishments.
13. Develop a quality council.
14. Do it over again.

Now It's Your Turn

1. *Select an organization of your choice and audit that organization, pretending you are Crosby. (If you previously selected an organization in the Deming section, use the same organization.) What would Crosby say were their three weakest points? Their three strongest points? Where would Crosby likely differ from Deming?**

*See Crosby, Philip B., *Quality Without Tears: The Art of Hassle-Free Management*, New York: New American Library, 1984, for additional ideas.

Juran: Leadership for Quality

Dr. Joseph Juran takes the position that no one is against quality. The issue is "how do we do it?" His answer is that *management must learn how to manage for quality.* The way to manage for quality is to approach quality as if it was as important as a major financial problem confronting an organization.

If an organization had a financial problem, management would install a three-step process:

1. *Financial planning:* Set business financial goals, develop the actions and resources needed to meet goals, translate goals into money, and summarize them into the financial plan or budget.

2. *Financial controls:* Evaluate actual performance, compare actual to goals, and take action on differences. Actions such as cost control or expense control would be used.

3. *Financial improvement:* Do better than the past. Strive for cost reduction, purchase facilities to raise productivity, access acquisitions, etc.

Middle management has formal goals, budgets, and review processes (including merit ratings) on dollars received and spent. This accounting type of controls should be applied to quality on an ongoing basis.

Management often does not realize how long implementation will take. They tend to "start up" a program (not an ongoing process) then delegate their portion of the process. Quality is not simply a "monthly" team meeting, but an activity that is fully integrated into everyone's job.

Managing for Quality: Trilogy Overview

1. Quality Planning. Set business quality goals and develop the means for meeting those goals. Poor planning is the source for poor quality. Planning improvements can occur only with feedback such as design reviews and mortality tables (i.e., lessons learned).

Quality is defined as meeting customer expectations. Therefore:

Identify customers

Determine customer needs

Develop product features to meet customer needs

Establish product goals

Develop processes to meet the product goals

Provide feedback

2. Quality Control. Run the process that meets the product/service goals. In most firms, people do not have the means for improvement. The best they can do is meet what is planned in the process. The key to quality control is self-control. Self-control occurs when people have a system that lets them: know their quality goals; know their performance against those goals; and have a means for adjusting the process (see the "Group Empowerment" section).

3. Quality Improvement. Improve competitiveness and reduce quality deficiencies. There must be clear responsibility for improvement. Top management must be fully involved through personal participation on project teams. Statements of "intent" are not enough. Management must do everything possible to avoid "here comes another drive" syndrome.

The improvement process includes a few basic steps. Quality improvement occurs on an incremental, project-by-project basis. Those organizations that wait for a "massive" breakthrough will be overtaken by an organization that has hundreds of small improvement processes with full employee involvement. Everyone must become involved in discovering causes, identifying specific improvement projects, and working to improve quality. Remember, the quality council is comprised of upper management membership. The main job for these key managers is to establish an infrastructure for continuous improvement:

Essential Leadership Tasks

Include quality goals in the business plan.

Serve on quality council.

Serve on project teams.

Develop procedures for selecting improvement projects.

Approve strategic quality goals.

Allocate resources for teams and for improvement efforts.

Publish results.

Newsletters.

Give recognition.

Revise merit system.

Managing for Quality: Details

Quality management is the way by which we achieve quality (quality planning, control, and improvement). The role of upper management is to serve on the quality council, establish goals, provide resources, review progress, give recognition, revise the reward system, serve on project teams, and recognize and deal with employee apprehensions.

If employees feel their jobs might be eliminated, reduce this conflict by stating that "no employee will lose employment as a direct result of his/her involvement in a quality improvement effort."

The quality council is the key element in the organization's infrastructure. Quality improvement occurs on a project-by-project basis, so organize project teams for specific quality improvement projects. This council should meet on a regular basis and:

- Approve department quality goals;
- Develop plan for meeting quality goals; and
- Evaluate quality performance.

Quality planning is the activity of determining customer needs and developing the processes to meet those needs. Quality planning should determine what features are of major importance to the customer and how key product features compare with those of competitors. Market research is needed to track changing expectations.

Statements such as: "Quality has top priority" are meaningless unless accompanied by an action plan. No one, including top management, takes these statements seriously. Several years are required to establish quality improvement as a continuing, integral part of the organization's operation.

Timetable for Installing TQM

Activity	Months
Study of alternatives and decision to commit to annual quality improvement.	6
Selection of test site, conducting pilot test (including training).	12
Evaluation of test site results; revision of approach, decision to scale up.	6
Scaling up across firm and merging into business plan.	24

Quality control is the managerial process consisting of evaluating actual performance, comparing to goals, and taking action on the differences. The feedback loop works by having sensors (market surveys) monitor attitudes and report back to an umpire. At the worker level, use technological type sensors where controls are aimed at the product and process features set out in procedures manuals. At the managerial level, broad market feedback is needed dealing with broad issues of competitiveness and customer needs.

Self-control of quality is a form of ownership that responds to basic human instinct. Self-control is absolutely necessary for motivation. To have self-control, a person must have a means of:

Knowing what goals are (published standards).

Measuring and interpreting performance.

Changing process to bring it into conformance.

It's risky for management to hold workers "responsible" for quality. What is required is the recognition of the concept of *controllability*. Each feature of a product or process becomes a control subject—a center around which the feedback loop is built based on a sensor.

Effective Quality Measurement Requires

A unit of measure—quality feature that permits evaluation.

A sensor (a measuring instrument) that carries out the evaluation. If a sensor does not exist to monitor a quality feature, then a project improvement team should be assigned the responsibility of developing a sensor.

Planners must develop a means so that employees can adjust the process to bring it in conformance with goals. To do this:

- Key product/process features must be known.
- A means for adjusting the process setting msut be provided for.
- A predictable relationship between amount of change in process setting and amount of effect on product feature must be identified.
- Planners must understand natural process variability.

Planners must acquire an in-depth knowledge of the relationship between process variables and the organization results. They must provide employees with reasonable performance goals and with process adjustment capability. Although SPC (Statistical Process Control) charts can be used, the statistical tool is *not* an end in itself. The important thing is a project team to identify which projects to tackle, assign clear responsibility, and provide needed resources.

Topics to Consider When Implementing Self-Control

System for employees to communicate their views to management.

System for management to keep employees informed of possible changes to the process they "own" before the changes are made.

Training that explains the why as well as the how of doing something.

Stress quality in the employment interview.

Supervision that practices quality management.

Supervision that merges employees into the planning process.

An organization's products and services must provide customer satisfaction. A list of general quality goals is only a wish-list. Subdivide the goals into specific, detailed goals for bite-sized projects.

Mini Quality Audit

Does your president stress high quality?

Who are your key customers?

What are their needs?

How well are those needs being serviced?

How do your services compare with your competition?

Vested Interests That Often Prevent Implementing Self-Control

Managers lose their "prerogatives" about the time employees spend on projects versus time spent producing.

Staff specialists face competition in planning and analysis.

Employees concerned with the impact of quality improvements on job security. Concerned about rewards for extra work.

Juran summarizes several perceptual errors made by management regarding quality.*

Errors in the Perception of Quality

The work force is mainly responsible for the firm's quality problems.

Workers could do good quality work but lack the motivation.

They are not in a state of self-control and cannot produce good work.

Quality will get top priority if upper management so decrees. This isn't true. Fundamental changes are needed in the way management conducts business. For example, all organizations should be involved in: goal setting; planning to meet goals; resource allocation; measures of quality; progress reviews; and rewards based on meeting/exceeding quality goals.

To change people's behavior, it is first necessary to change their attitudes. Actually, change behavior, then attitudes will change. For example, managers who have been required to serve on quality improvement teams exhibit greater receptivity to quality improvements.

---

*See Juran, Joseph M., *Juran on Leadership for Quality: An Executive Handbook,* New York: The Free Press (Macmillan Inc.), 1989, 376 pages.

Now It's Your Turn

1. *Select an organization of your choice and audit that organization, pretending you are Juran. (If you previously selected an organization, use the same organization.) What would Juran say were their three weakest points? Their three strongest points? Where would Crosby likely differ from Deming?*

   Suppose Deming, Crosby, and Juran were addressing the executive board of the organization you selected. (This board is comprised of the president, chief executive officer, and three executive vice-presidents.) Which of the philosophies of these contributors would be easiest for the executive board to embrace? Which philosophy would be most difficult for them to embrace? Support your selection with specific underlying philosophies. Do not simply restate the points previously summarized.

Selected Readings on TQM, Baldrige Award, and ISO Standards

How to Stop Talking About and Begin Progress Toward TQM Now!*

How many quality programs has your firm tried in the past 10 years? Do any of these programs sound familiar?

Quality Circles

Work Teams

Employee Suggestion Programs

Participative Management

Labor-Management Teams

SQC (Statistical Quality Control)

Job Enrichment

Task Forces

Flattened Organizations

Strategic Business Units

Gain Sharing/Profit Sharing

ESOP (Employee Stock Ownership Plan)

If you have undertaken, and subsequently abandoned, two or more of these programs, it's time you got a handle on the quality issue. Stop approaching the

*Based on the author's article appearing in *Business Horizons,* June 1993.

quality problem with a passionate longing: Attack the problem head-on by installing a total quality management (TQM) system in your firm.

TQM has a universal appeal because it is an ongoing, long-term system to achieve customer satisfaction through continuous quality improvement of a firm's goods and services. Perhaps the most important point to consider when beginning progress towards total quality management is to avoid creating the impression of "Here comes another program." To prevent this from occurring, a two-step approach is needed. First, involve all departments in the process of identifying customer needs. Then create a quality council to provide a structure for quality improvements.

The Employee as a Customer

Examples of poor customer services are all too prevalent and seem to be everywhere. Rather than rehashing traditional problems in achieving customer satisfaction, perhaps the problem is that it is simply easy to forget the importance of satisfaction when handling everyday problems. Training programs can undoubtedly help fill this void, but you need an on-going system to reinforce the training.

You can reinforce the importance of providing quality services by involving the entire firm in the process. This is accomplished by expanding the definition of a customer to include internal as well as external users of services. Employees are internal customers of support departments, yet few support departments systematically attempt to identify their user's needs. That is, customer satisfaction is something management preaches, not practices.

The functions performed by support departments frequently remove them from direct external customer interaction. This situation in itself is not bad, but many support groups compound the problem by isolating themselves through procedures that require administrative approval before processing user requests. For example, if facilities should be updated to improve customer services, numerous, lengthy justifications will be required to satisfy payback periods and return-on-investment criteria. The requesting department has to furnish the data, not the support department which assumes the historical role of "evaluating" the request.

All these hurdles take their toll by slowing down the process of adapting to meet customer needs. The point is not that requests for funds shouldn't be reviewed, but rather that support departments must move from being reactive to being proactive in the drive to improve quality. Support groups should develop an understanding of customer needs so that recommendations come *from* them, not *to* them.

In addition, support departments should systematically survey their users and then modify services as needed. Although this sounds simple, it rarely occurs in practice. Frequently, you are left with the impression that support departments are not really concerned about providing high quality services.

For example, when was the last time:

- The Accounting Department surveyed users to determine if their reports are useful?

- Facilities Management asked if their janitorial services meet expectations?

- Inventory Control asked if their service is prompt?

- The Computer Department asked if you can understand their instruction manuals?

A positive environment for quality improvement is created when all departments adapt their services to meet customer needs. However, as shown in Fig. 1, various departments interact differently with their external and internal customers, which means that a multitude of methods will be needed to identify customer needs.

Consumer-oriented departments such as Sales and Customer Services have a high frequency of external customer interaction. A friendly, positive attitude coupled with a smile may go a long way to enhancing the customer's satisfaction with the product or service. Short surveys can help finetune the process.

Support departments such as Shipping interact with external customers and with internal departments such as Inventory Control, Accounting, and Sales. In addition to using surveys to identify areas for possible improvements, "coffee breaks" or luncheons with internal users can be used to open up lines of communication.

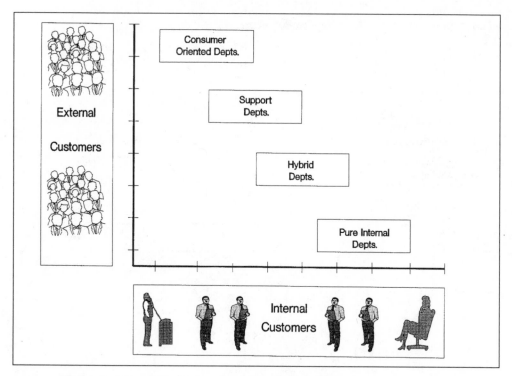

Figure 1. External and internal customer interactions.

Hybrid departments (Accounting, Transportation) have a more complex quality mission. Sections within these departments, such as Billing, "react" to external customers in terms of responding to a problem brought to them. Surveys tend to measure the efficiency in which the department provided the desired information, and the degree to which the customer was satisfied with the services. Hybrid departments need to become "proactive" by categorizing problems and modifying services to prevent the problem from emerging in the first place.

Pure internal departments (Legal, Auditing, etc.) seldom interact with external consumers and devote most of their attention to internal interactions. The role of such departments is often to develop policies for other departments to follow. For example, the Legal Department may advise Human Resources regarding hiring/promotion procedures. Consequently, the information flow tends to be filtered before it reaches the internal departments. Because of this "filtering," some of the potential impact of the information may be lost.

Instead of relying on other departments for information regarding policies, internal departments should make every effort to open up lines of communication with all users to obtain the information firsthand. Working with the appropriate departments to identify specific customer segments is important. Surveys and focus groups can provide feedback as to the appropriateness of policies. An example of this organization is shown in Fig. 2.

Creating a Structure for Quality Improvement

A new employee comes to work enthused, wanting to make a contribution. Suggestions are frequently offered and although some ideas may lack practicality,

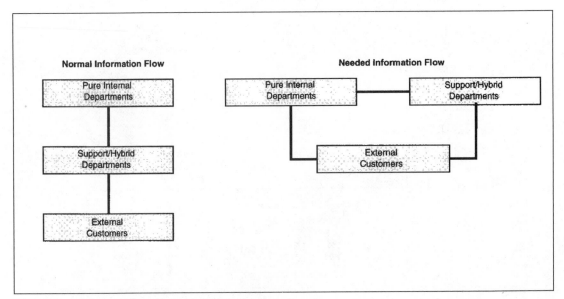

Figure 2. Information flow from external customers.

a refusal given with a logical explanation is part of the learning process and is not viewed negatively. The problem occurs when a good suggestion is placed on the "backburner" because its implementation would cut across functional lines. In other words, "it's a good idea but it is too much trouble to install it." Employees soon recognize that life is easier if they simply keep quiet and just do their job.

This presents a hidden problem when top management stresses the importance of quality. Many employees feel they have tried to make improvements, but the system restricts their efforts. Motivational speeches accomplish little, if anything. What is needed is an ongoing process to focus a firm's quality efforts.

A quality council should be established to place worthwhile suggestions on an authoritative agenda, coordinate cross-functional teams, and oversee schedules. The council also provides a mechanism to continuously reinforce the need for high quality. The council should be comprised of key management and chaired by a powerful vice-president who is also a member of the executive committee. Reporting relationships for the quality council are shown in Fig. 3.

Many CEOs are aware that a quality council alone cannot bring about the attitude changes necessary to sustain continuous quality improvements. Top management support is definitely needed, and while there is nothing wrong with the CEO personally chairing the quality council, practicality suggests there is a limit on this person's time. Hence, the council should be chaired by a senior VP and the

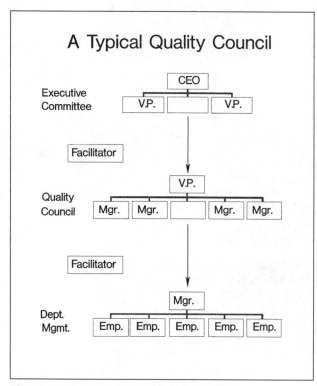

Figure 3. Structure for quality improvement.

CEO's time should be used for reinforcement and recognition programs after the council becomes operational.

Quality council planning guidelines are shown in Table 1. A multi-phase implementation is suggested because of the large, complex task facing the council. Allow at least six months to get started and to make management aware of fundamental TQM concepts. Keep all employees informed via internal communications of what TQM is about and what is happening in the firm.

In Phase II, department managers will have to implement TQM concepts. This is a critical phase of the process because without middle management support, TQM is doomed to failure. Therefore, all managers should participate in improvement projects to gain firsthand experience.

In Phase III, select a test department for implementation. Employees in the test department should be trained in TQM concepts and self-empowered teams should be formed. A good beginning point for employee teams is to define what constitutes high quality. This is undoubtedly difficult to do, but improvements in quality can occur only if the process is understood. Topics such as how a customer should be greeted (including the importance of eye contact, a friendly smile, and referring to the customer by name), should be discussed.

During this time, the council should refine its procedures and develop skills working with employee groups. Thus, the council is changing from a planning role to an interactive role as shown in Table 2.

Ultimately, the quality council may want to consider monthly quality awards for outstanding achievements. If this is the case, then award winners should sit on the council, perhaps on a two-month rotational basis.

Table 1. Quality Council: Planning Guidelines

Develop a Phased Implementation Plan

Phase I:	Start Up—6 months
	Educate management in TQM concepts
	Develop council procedures
Phase II:	Department Managers practice TQM concepts—4 months
	Make formal proposals to council
	Get recognition and award programs operational
Phase III:	Test Department—3 months
	Create self-control groups
	Implement and revise council procedures
Phase IV:	Scale up across firm—1 year
	Concentrate on employee involvement

Table 2. Quality Council: Interactive Role

I. Oversee implementation of TQM.

II. Assist in forming teams:

- Study teams assigned tasks such as identifying and surveying customer needs.

- Task teams with specific objectives and completion dates such as establishing a supplier plan.

- Self-managed team. Small groups of employees accepting responsibility for their work.

III. Assist in designing teams:

- Appoint vertical membership (study/task teams).

- Review horizontal membership (self-managed teams).

IV. Develop and implement recognition programs.

V. Revise merit system to reflect participation and accomplishments.

Conclusions

A two-step approach is needed to install total quality management. First, involve all departments in the process of identifying and adapting to customer needs. Then install a quality council to add a focus to your quality improvement efforts. The council will develop empowered task teams, coordinate groups in the task of improving quality, and develop mechanisms for reinforcing the importance of high quality. Once this is accomplished, you will have started the process of continuous quality improvement.

The Baldrige Award: A Questionnaire to Improve Organizational Quality*

Have you heard of the Baldrige Award but thought it was basically for large firms such as Xerox, IBM, or Motorola? Well, think again. The award provides an excellent framework by which both manufacturing and service firms can improve their quality systems.

Quality services are often the distinctive niche of a firm. The issue confronting management of these companies is not merely to want to provide high quality services. Rather the issue is how to achieve high quality services that will assure the firm's survival.

The Malcolm Baldrige National Quality Award has been presented by the U.S. Commerce Department since 1987 to recognize American companies which excel in quality achievement. As shown in Fig. 4, the award is divided into four

*Based on a paper presented by the author to the 1993 Kentuckiana Quality Conference.

Figure 4.

major sections: the driver, the system, the measure of progress, and the final goal. The *driver* is the leadership process which must develop the system and "drive" all of the processes. The *system* is the detailed quality system composed of the following categories: information and analysis, strategic quality planning, human resources, and quality and operational results. The *measure of progress* is the quality results achieved. Finally, the *goal* of a quality system is customer satisfaction; the ultimate test of a firm's success.

There are two *quality output* categories: quality results and consumer satisfaction. This reflects the dual nature of quality: a firm must actually provide high quality goods and services, and the firm must be *perceived* as providing high quality. That is, it is not enough to simply produce high quality unless this quality is reflected in terms of consumer satisfaction. On the other hand, if the consumer is initially satisfied, but the service received does not live up to expectations, then the consumer will quickly become dissatisfied.

Not all the categories in the Baldrige Award count equally. As shown in Table 3, customer satisfaction is weighed the heaviest because it is the most important category.

Table 3. Baldrige Award Categories

	Categories	Weights (%)
1	Leadership	9.5
2	Information and Analysis	7.5
3	Strategic Quality Planning	6.0
4	Human Resource Development and Management	15.0
5	Management of Process Quality	14.0
6	Quality and Operational Results	18.0
7	Customer Focus and Satisfaction	30.0

The objective of each award category will be briefly explained. A questionnaire will then be presented to guide management in identifying where attention should be directed when attempting to refine their quality systems.

Baldrige Award Categories

The *leadership* category examines the degree to which senior management creates and sustains visible quality values. The emphasis is on action taken, not simply what management says they are doing. If management's involvement is limited to making speeches, then little will be accomplished. The president and executive group must be personally committed and be willing to meet with TQM teams to provide leadership and support. Mission statements are not enough: Management must "walk the talk" by putting into practice what they preach about the need for high quality.

The *information and analysis* category examines the use and management of data that support the TQM system. The critical factors influencing service and product quality should be identified for all major functions performed by the firm. It is important that quality services are offered where quality is defined by the customer. A "management by fact" approach is taken, requiring that hard data regarding customer satisfaction be used in decision making.

In order to have an effective information and analysis system, or for that matter, an effective TQM system, all departments must have a clear definition of their customer and the customer's needs. This is particularly true of internal departments. The customers of a support department are the other departments which use their services. Quality data collected by, and reported by support departments, must reflect key quality factors in the delivery of services.

Strategic quality planning examines the planning process for achieving quality improvement. Emphasis must be placed on quality objectives and given the same priority as financial objectives. Firms can begin the process of strategic quality planning by scheduling quarterly management workshops to discuss two points: How specific quality improvement goals fit into overall business goals, and how current levels of performance on specific quality goals are gauged against a competitor.

The *human resource development and management* category examines the effectiveness of the company's efforts to develop the full potential of the work force. Hassled people do not produce quality work. Measurements of morale must be taken on a regular basis and acted upon. In addition, employees must be informed of quality goals, trained in the use of quality techniques, evaluated on quality-based criteria, and given recognition/rewards for quality accomplishments.

A matrix of the firm's human resources goals and their impact on quality goals will add a focus to this category. An example of this matrix is shown in Table 4 which relates human resource goals to quality goals for retail and commercial customers.

The *management of process quality* category examines the approach used to assure that high quality services are created and maintained. Many firms have

Table 4. Human Resource Goals and Quality Goals

Human resource goals	Quality goal— retail	Quality goal— commercial
Hire receptionist from construction industry		x
Train employees in TQM	x	x
Revise annual evaluations to include TQM goals	x	x

excellent accounting procedures to assure cash is managed correctly and that inventories are correctly stored. Audits are routinely conducted to assure these procedures are followed and that corrections are made if there are problems.

Traditional audits, even quality audits, are not good enough for service firms dealing with factors affecting customer satisfaction. Audits are reactive in nature in that they catch errors after they are made. Proactive quality systems, not reactive systems, are needed for gathering information about customer requirements and translating that information into service standards.

One proactive system is called *quality function deployment* (QFD). (See Hauser & Clausing's article.) The QFD process begins by gathering information on the customer's specific requirements. After a dozen or so characteristics are identified, these characteristics are prioritized by the customers. This prioritized list of customer requirements is given to engineers (or management system designers) who design the new product or service to meet the specified needs.

The *quality and operational results* category examines quality levels of the business operations based on an objective measure of inputs, processes, and outputs. This category documents the internal success of the firm's quality improvement efforts. (Customer satisfaction will be discussed later as a separate category.) Quality measurement should be installed on the factors shown in Table 5.

Table 5. Key Measurement Factors

Quality measurement	Key factors for measurement
Input	People, raw materials, components, customer requirements
Process	Design of services Production of services Technical performance Delivery of services
Output	Services provided Documentation Results

Outputs are not always products, but can be in terms of the number of customers served, deliveries made, or questions answered. This criteria becomes clearer by comparing quality results (performance) to yearly goals along key quality performance factors (– indicates improvement is necessary). (See Table 6.)

Table 6. Comparison of Quality Results to Goals

Key factors	Quality results	Yearly goal	Difference	Comments
Stock outage on sale item (rain checks) issued	240	150	–90	Must notify purchasing before running out of stock
Returns	40	50	+10	Tell sales to keep up the good work!
Next-day delivery	92%	100%	8%	Pull item from inventory quicker

The *customer focus and satisfaction* category is the final and most important category of the Baldrige Award. The emphasis of the category is to be able to prove customer satisfaction with services. Most managers have long recognized the importance of human interactions in service representatives who come in direct contact with customers. However, as previously pointed out, a TQM approach expands the definition of a customer to include internal groups such as accounting and maintenance. These groups must be able to prove customer satisfaction (i.e., using department's satisfaction) with their services.

A focus of all departments is needed to continually improve quality, but if your customers still think your firm is average or inferior compared with the competition, all the quality improvement effort is wasted. For that reason, systematic efforts must be made to monitor and report both internal and external customer satisfaction.

Firms should analyze potential markets for their services by stating customer requirements for each segment, and then developing specific satisfaction goals. For example, a matrix shown in Table 7 was established by a service firm for two groups of customers: Retail and commercial accounts. Customer requirements are listed along the left side. The plus (+) sign indicates the degree of importance, double plus (++) indicates high customer importance.

This matrix is used to direct the gathering of customer satisfaction data and the interpretation of its relative importance. Service firms must gather data not only on their own customers, but on the satisfaction of customers of competitive firms. This information, coupled with an analysis of customer complaints, may identify customer requirements not otherwise apparent.

Table 7. Customer Requirements by Group

Customer requirements	Retail	Commercial
Deliveries		
Courteous drivers	+	+
Appearance	++	+
Reliability	+	++
Timeliness	+	++
Knowledge		
Customer name	+	+
Basic industry terms		++
Buyer relationship	+	++

The Baldrige Questionnaire

A questionnaire has been designed to identify what is needed for an effective TQM system within each of the Award's categories. By necessity, this is a general questionnaire and a low score in a category may not indicate a deficiency. The reader should feel free to revise the questionnaire to incorporate their own questions on key quality indicators for their firm.

Conclusion

The criteria used in the Baldrige Award subdivides a quality system into controllable categories so that specific topics for improvement can be identified. Second, the criteria encourages management and employees to think through the fundamental functions performed by the firm. Each business segment must be clearly identified so that the quality variables needed to create high quality services can be specified.

If a firm is just starting to systematically evaluate their quality systems, they will undoubtedly have a negative response to many questions. Avoid overreacting by trying to tackle all the items that need improvement at the same time. Prioritize your needs, and gradually build your quality system.

It is a long-term process to improve an organization's quality systems. Attitudes and basic management styles will have to change in order to incorporate employees into the decision making process. The process of continuous quality improvement has indeed emerged as the management challenge of the 1990s.

Using the Baldrige Award to Identify Areas for Quality Improvement

This questionnaire asks your opinion about issues regarding quality at your firm. Please choose the one number that best matches how you feel about the statement.

LEADERSHIP

In My Opinion:	Strongly Disagree						Strongly Agree	Unknown
1. Our firm has a known quality policy statement.	1	2	3	4	5	6	7	0
2. Our employees know our long-term quality goals.	1	2	3	4	5	6	7	0
3. Management is visibly involved in the development of a quality culture.	1	2	3	4	5	6	7	0
4. Our management has received adequate training on quality concepts.	1	2	3	4	5	6	7	0
5. Management practices what they preach.	1	2	3	4	5	6	7	0
6. Our quality policy emphasizes the need for continuous improvements.	1	2	3	4	5	6	7	0
7. Quality improvement responsibilities have been clearly communicated to all employees.	1	2	3	4	5	6	7	0
8. Our quality committees coordinate between deptartments	1	2	3	4	5	6	7	0
9. The community knows of our quality goals.	1	2	3	4	5	6	7	0
10. Management provides adequate resources for quality improvement.	1	2	3	4	5	6	7	0

INFORMATION AND ANALYSIS

In My Opinion:	Strongly Disagree						Strongly Agree	Unknown
11. Our firm reports data on all important dimensions of customer quality.	1	2	3	4	5	6	7	0
12. Our firm reports data on all important service dimensions.	1	2	3	4	5	6	7	0

13. Quality data is reported in all departments.	1	2	3	4	5	6	7		0
14. Data is collected on TQM training completed by our employees.	1	2	3	4	5	6	7		0
15. We analyze data on our supplier's view of our quality.	1	2	3	4	5	6	7		0
16. We track our scrap costs.	1	2	3	4	5	6	7		0
17. We identify the causes of poor quality.	1	2	3	4	5	6	7		0

STRATEGIC QUALITY PLANNING

In My Opinion:	Strongly Disagree						Strongly Agree		Unknown
18. We use competitive data from other firms when developing quality goals.	1	2	3	4	5	6	7		0
19. We have an operational plan (1-2 year) that describes our quality goals.	1	2	3	4	5	6	7		0
20. Our employees are involved in quality planning	1	2	3	4	5	6	7		0
21. Department management has challenging quality goals.	1	2	3	4	5	6	7		0
22. The quality function is a part of our business plan.	1	2	3	4	5	6	7		0
23. We have specific methods for monitoring progress towards improved quality.	1	2	3	4	5	6	7		0
24. There are quality plans in effect for all departments.	1	2	3	4	5	6	7		0
25. We have quality plans for our suppliers.	1	2	3	4	5	6	7		0

HUMAN RESOURCE DEVELOPMENT

In My Opinion:	Strongly Disagree						Strongly Agree		Unknown
26. We have a known plan for the utilization of employees in quality improvement.	1	2	3	4	5	6	7		0
27. Quality criteria are used in employee performance evaluations.	1	2	3	4	5	6	7		0

HUMAN RESOURCE DEVELOPMENT (cont.)

In My Opinion:	Strongly Disagree						Strongly Agree	Unknown
28. Quality goals are communicated to all employees.	1	2	3	4	5	6	7	0
29. Our employees believe in the seriousness of providing top quality services.	1	2	3	4	5	6	7	0
30. All employees are trained in quality improvement concepts.	1	2	3	4	5	6	7	0
31. Our firm rewards employees for their quality improvement efforts.	1	2	3	4	5	6	7	0
32. Our firm collects data on employee morale.	1	2	3	4	5	6	7	0

MANAGEMENT OF PROCESS QUALITY

In My Opinion:	Strongly Disagree						Strongly Agree	Unknown
33. Customer quality expectations are defined.	1	2	3	4	5	6	7	0
34. Customer requirements are transferred into the planning process for improvements.	1	2	3	4	5	6	7	0
35. There is an effective system for processing information on customer expectations.	1	2	3	4	5	6	7	0
36. We audit our quality management system.	1	2	3	4	5	6	7	0
37. We work with suppliers to improve quality.	1	2	3	4	5	6	7	0
38. Support departments have defined quality goals.	1	2	3	4	5	6	7	0
39. Documents showing our quality are kept up to date.	1	2	3	4	5	6	7	0
40. We have an effective system for communicating quality ideas to top management.	1	2	3	4	5	6	7	0

QUALITY AND OPERATIONAL RESULTS

In My Opinion:	Strongly Disagree						Strongly Agree	Unknown
41. Our firm is one of the top three firms in the area in terms of customer satisfaction.	1	2	3	4	5	6	7	0
42. We have shown steady improvement in quality over the last three years.	1	2	3	4	5	6	7	0
43. We can demonstrate improvements in quality by our support departments.	1	2	3	4	5	6	7	0
44. We can demonstrate improvements in quality by our suppliers.	1	2	3	4	5	6	7	0
45. There has been a steady decrease in customer complaints in the last three years.	1	2	3	4	5	6	7	0
46. We have developed several new products and services in the last three years.	1	2	3	4	5	6	7	0

CUSTOMER SATISFACTION

In My Opinion:	Strongly Disagree						Strongly Agree	Unknown
47. Our customers like the quality of our services.	1	2	3	4	5	6	7	0
48. Customer satisfaction data is reported.	1	2	3	4	5	6	7	0
49. Customer satisfaction has been improving over the past three years.	1	2	3	4	5	6	7	0
50. We can prove we have higher levels of customer satisfaction than our competitors.	1	2	3	4	5	6	7	0
51. We have an effective process for handling customer complaints.	1	2	3	4	5	6	7	0
52. Our job definitions encourage our employees to quickly resolve customer complaints.	1	2	3	4	5	6	7	0
53. We use innovative approaches to assessing customer satisfaction.	1	2	3	4	5	6	7	0

The ISO Pizza: A Commonsense Approach to Installing ISO Standards*

The Geneva-based International Organization for Standardization first published the ISO standards in 1987. The series consists of five manuals that describe the elements for establishing and maintaining a quality management system. A company registered as complying with ISO standards has demonstrated to an accredited third-party that its systems (processes) have been documented and that the company is systematically verifying the results of its systems.

ISO 9000 is a series of international standards dealing with product design, production, delivery, service, and testing. A summary of the five ISO standards is shown in Table 8. ISO registration is achieved by compliance with one or more of the following standards: ISO 9001, 9002, or 9003.

Table 8. Overview of ISO Standards

Standard number	Title	Function
9000	Quality management and quality assurance standards: guidelines for selection and use.	Provides an overview of the quality concepts and the models which can be used to implement them.
9001	Quality systems: model for quality assurance in design, development, production, installation, and servicing.	Used when conformance to specification requirements during design, development, production, installation, and servicing is required.
9002	Quality systems: model for quality assurance in production and installation.	Used when conformance to specification requirements is limited to production and installation.
9003	Quality systems: model for quality assurance in final inspection and test.	Used when conformance to specification requirements is to be assured by the supplier solely at final inspection and test.
9004	Quality systems: model for quality management and quality systems— guidelines.	Used for developing and implementing an internal quality system for design and manufacturing.

*Based on an article by the author and Jeff Waring appearing in *The Journal of Quality and Participation*, January 1994.

It is easier to understand the ISO process if a universal product is used to explain what would be involved in achieving ISO certification. At the time of this writing, we do not know of a pizza firm seeking ISO certification, but the idea is not as far-fetched as it might sound. Our hypothetical firm will be called PizzaMan.

Why Seek ISO Certification?

The ISO certification will provide a framework for ensuring that PizzaMan's quality will be maintained in all phases of the business. The ISO standards assess the effectiveness of PizzaMan's management in providing high quality, consistent pizza and good delivery to its customers. This provides a foundation upon which PizzaMan can improve their quality systems.

ISO certification will also provide a set of requirements which are accepted worldwide. This will help PizzaMan cope with some external forces which effect the business, such as the European demand for pizza. So far, a Euro-Pizza has not been developed, which would provide PizzaMan with a competitive edge over pizza makers. Besides, the publicity from local newspaper food critic might enhance sales.

Becoming ISO Certified

PizzaMan must first decide which of three levels of certification to obtain: ISO 9001, 9002, or 9003. (ISO 9000 is an overview and ISO 9004 is used for internal quality, not for outside certification.) PizzaMan will seek ISO 9002 certification of their production and delivery systems, which is a common certification for many firms.

PizzaMan must now develop a policy statement and a policy manual containing the specific policies and procedures that will make ISO-Pizza a reality. Before PizzaMan starts implementing their procedures, they should hire a certified ISO auditing firm to perform a preassessment audit. After the certification agency has approve PizzaMan's procedures, and the procedures are implemented, the agency will conduct an on-site audit. If PizzaMan passes the audit, it will be certified. Otherwise, they will have to resolve any problems identified and retry for certification.

Setting Up an ISO System

The basic elements of an ISO system which must in place before ISO certification can be awarded are shown in Fig. 5. Each element must have proper documentation which can be examined at a moment's notice by anyone wanting information on PizzaMan's ISO process.

The process of achieving ISO 9002 certification begins by developing an overall quality policy. The highest level at which PizzaMan should take the lead in this

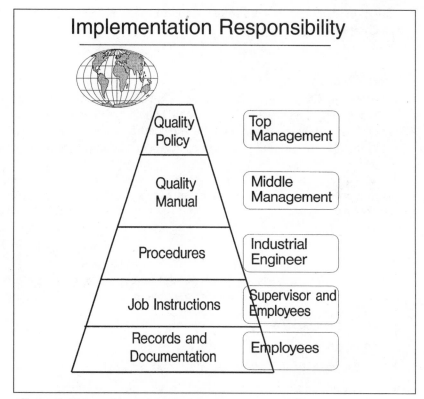

Figure 5. ISO quality system documentation.

activity is the owner. The policy should be brief, simple, easy-to-read, and developed after input from the customers, management, and employees. This quality policy lays the ground work for the rest of the ISO elements. An example of a quality policy is shown in Fig. 6.

The quality policy identifies long-term goals and objectives. This policy should be discussed with management and employees, and prominently dis-

---

PizzaMan's Quality Policy

PizzaMan is dedicated to providing its customers with a superior pizza and quick friendly service. It will accomplish this by:

- Carefully controlling the pizza making ingredients and processes to provide consistency and good taste.
- Delivering the pizza in the promised amount of time or giving the pizza to the customer for free.
- Training all employees in the requirements of production and delivery of a quality pizza.

Figure 6.

played in all stores. It is not unusual for an ISO certifier to ask an employee about the company's quality policy.

The Quality Manual

After the quality policy is developed, a quality manual will have to be created. This manual addresses the 18 specific ISO 9002 quality elements as they pertain to PizzaMan. Management must take the lead in developing the quality manual which also identifies the procedures necessary to implement the major ISO elements.

A sample quality manual is shown in Table 9. Only procedures 14.1 and 14.2 dealing with offering a free pizza are shown in detail to conserve space. Other procedures will have to be developed and referenced in the quality manual.

Management Responsibility

The ISO requirements clearly put most of the responsibility for quality systems on management. Along those lines, the PizzaMan managers will be responsible for:

- Defining policies, methods and plans
- Defining roles and responsibilities
- Defining specifications on incoming food products
- Preventing inadvertent use of unapproved food products
- Ensuring that all personnel are trained and qualified
- Keeping up-to-date procedures and instructions
- Being aware of customer needs and attitudes
- Ensuring shipment of only quality ISO pizzas
- Auditing performance and making corrections when necessary
- Keeping records pertaining to quality

Procedures

Procedures will have to be written to specify how the ISO elements are to be carried out. These procedures must include specific job instructions. Typically, the job instructions are developed by the foreman with employee input. Sample ISO procedures dealing with when to offer a free pizza are shown in Table 10. These procedures are tied into PizzaMan's quality manual.

Table 9. PizzaMan's Quality Manual

ISO element	PizzaMan quality system policy	PizzaMan procedures
4.1 Management Responsibility	*Quality Policy:* PizzaMan is dedicated to quality pizza making and fast delivery. The policy outlining our commitment to quality will be explained to all employees. The Quality Policy will be displayed prominently in each store.	1.1 Management quality system review
	Quality Objectives: PizzaMan strives to deliver the finest tasting ISO-Pizza, as determined by the customer, and will control the quality, taste, consistency, and delivery of these pizzas by following the procedures outlined in the quality manual.	
	Organization: The PizzaMan store is run by full time managers who guide shifts of workers in the preparation and delivery of pizzas. Store managers are fully trained in the ISO systems as set forth by this quality manual and will follow its procedures and practices. Shift employees will will be trained and experienced in conducting the ISO procedures as set forth by this manual.	
	Management Reviews: PizzaMan will conduct biannual management reviews which will be used to asses the effectiveness of the managers in implementing the ISO quality systems and seek improvement in managers' performance where necessary.	
4.2 Quality systems	*Quality Systems Policy Manual:* PizzaMan will maintain concise descriptions of all of the ISO quality elements and procedures in a controlled manual located in the PizzaMan store. This manual shall be made available to all PizzaMan employees.	2.1 Policy manual distribution
4.3 Contract review	The Purchasing Manager is responsible for approving all contracts both from suppliers, and from purchasers of our products. We will only engage in contracts where we can deliver the highest quality product.	3.1 Contract review procedure
4.4 Design control	Does not apply to PizzaMan	4.1 Not required

The ISO Pizza

ISO element	PizzaMan quality system policy	PizzaMan procedures
4.5 Document control	The PizzaMan specified ISO quality policies and procedures manual shall be maintained by the store manager. The master copy is maintained by the PizzaMan's owner who personally updates the store copy and explains the revised procedure to the store manager. There shall be only one copy of the manual per store. Copies of policies or procedures shall be made by a store manager. All copies shall be stamped "Uncontrolled Copy" for identification.	5.1 Document copying
4.6 Purchasing	The quality and freshness of the food items used to produce the pizza are crucial to the quality control of the final product. At least two reputable suppliers shall be identified for each food product which goes into the pizza. These suppliers shall be selected on their ability to provide quality products on a timely basis. Each individual food item and its characteristics (including freshness, color, texture, packaging, etc.) shall be described on a "Perishable Food Item" sheet which is be part of the ISO documentation package. Each qualified supplier shall be required to review and sign a copy of the food specification for that particular item. This specification shall be kept on file by the store manager as a part of its ISO documentation. Suppliers of nonperishable items (boxes, napkins, etc.) will coordinate with PizzaMan to ensure timely delivery.	6.1 Supplier qualification for perishable food products 6.2 Supplier qualification for nonperishable food
4.7 Customer supplied products	Does not apply to PizzaMan.[1]	7.1 Not required
4.8 Product ID and traceability	Purchase receipts for all food items shall be kept on file for at least 30 days. These receipts shall be used in identifying the source and delivery time of any faulty food items.	8.1 Product identification

Note [1]: This category is for products or packing supplied by the customer for use in filling their order. If PizzaMan later decides to refill customer mugs previously purchased, a policy will have to be developed.

ISO element	PizzaMan quality system policy	PizzaMan procedures
4.9 Process control	All procedures for producing intermediate food products (crust, sauce, etc.), as well as the assembly of a final pizza, shall be determined by the owner of PizzaMan and documented in the procedures manual.	9.1 Pizza sauce prepatation 9.2 Pizza crust preparation 9.3 Pizza toppings 9.4 Pizza cooking
	Critical spice mixtures shall be identified for the pizza sauce. There shall be special monitoring of these spices to ensure freshness and therefore consistent taste.	
	Final assembly procedures shall be identified for each type of pizza. These procedures shall include specific quantities and assembly orders necessary to obtain a consistent pizza.	
	All pizzas will be cooked in an oven having a single specified temperature. This temperature shall be ensured by the manager as described in the quality procedures.	
4.10 Inspection and testing	Every batch of intermediate food products shall be tested by the store manager.	10.1 Crust testing 10.2 Sauce testing 10.3 Pizza inspection
	Every store manager will be required to perform at least three spot checks of completed pizza per hour.	
4.11 Inspection, measurement & test equipment	The pizza oven shall contain a third party temperature measurement device to serve as a check for the oven's operating temperature.	11.1 Oven temperature and cooking procedure
4.12 Inspection and teststatus	All pizza and food products will bear the signature on the container of the product that reflects who tested the item, and if the item is acceptable.	12.1 Inspection status of food products 12.2 Inspection status of nonfood products
4.13 Nonconforming product	Nonconforming intermediate products or pizzas, as identified by the inspections and tests, shall NOT be reworked. They will be held for analysis by the manager and discarded after being analyzed.	13.1 Nonconforming products
4.14 Corrective action	Each product which fails inspection or testing, shall be immediately diagnosed and documented by the on-duty manager.	14.1 Correction action procedure for managers
	The employee responsible for making the failing product shall be informed immediately of the problem and advised how to avoid the problem in the future.	
	Product failure trends shall be recorded by the store manager and brought to the attention of all employees.	

The ISO Pizza

ISO element	PizzaMan quality system policy	PizzaMan procedures
4.15 Handling, storage, packaging, and delivery	All finished pizzas shall be immediately boxed and tagged with the original purchase order and set out as ready to deliver. All purchase orders shall be stamped by a time clock to record when the order was received. Delivery personnel shall carry watches synchronized with the store clock and offer the pizza free if it is not delivered in the allowed time to the customer. Delivery personnel are empowered to handle complaints, including awarding free pizzas. All complaints should be handled in a friendly, professional manner.	15.1 Free pizza due to slow delivery 15.2 Free pizza due to complaints other than delivery
4.16 Quality records	Store managers shall maintain purchased food item receipts and product failure reports for one month from the date of the receipt.	16.1 Maintenance of quality records
4.17 Internal quality audits	The PizzaMan store owner is responsible for conducting monthly quality audits of both the ISO procedures and of the food preparation process in all stores.	17.1 Audit procedure
4.18 Training	All PizzaMan employees shall be trained using the food preparation procedures outlined above. A record shall be maintained on each employee listing when the employee was first trained and when periodic reviews were undertaken.	18.1 Employee training and certification procedure
4.19 Servicing	Does not apply to PizzaMan unless they deliver in bulk to large offices, and provide reheating facilities for their pizzas (i.e., they would then have to monitor the reheating facilities).	19.1 Not required
4.20 Statistical techniques	Documented procedures for statistically controlling the product and processes used by PizzaMan shall be maintained in all stores.	20.1 Statistical control of products and processes

---

Are You a Total Quality Person?

	Seldom	Sometimes	Always
I actively listen to others.	☐	☐	☐

Table 10. Sample ISO Pizza Procedure 15.1: Free Pizza Due to Slow Delivery

Purpose: To establish how PizzaMan will determine when a customer is entitled to a free pizza due to slow delivery.

Key Personnel:

The Order Taker Involved

The Delivery Person

The Shift Manager

Note: See procedure 15.2 for complaints other than delivery

Steps

1. All delivery personnel will wear watches provided by PizzaMan and synchronized to the PizzaMan time punch.

2. When an order for a pizza is take, the customer will be informed of the delivery time (30 min for nonpeak hours, 40 min for peak). This time will be circled on the delivery form.

3. When the pizza order is taken, the person taking the order will put the time on the form using the punch clock. The order person will also initial the ticket at this time.

4. When the delivery person arrives at the door of the customer, he/she will check the current time as well as the time on the order ticket. If more than the promised delivery time has passed, the customer will be given the pizza free of charge. The customer, as well as the delivery person, will sign the ticket.

5. When the delivery person returns to the store, he/she will turn over any free pizza order slips to the manager on duty. The manager will determine actions needed to improve delivery.

Written by: J. G. Waring Approved by: P. M. Mears

Issued: 9-19-94 Last Revised: 9-19-94

Page 1 of 1

Employee Responsibility

When developing the quality manual, PizzaMan managers should outline their expectations for their employees. Typical expectations are as follows:

- Be aware of PizzaMan's quality policy and support its procedures and instructions

- Follow all pizza making procedures

- Take appropriate action when a quality problem is identified

- Fill out all quality records and forms accurately

All ISO policies, procedures, and pertinent data must be documented and be ready for inspection at any time. It is the responsibility of the employees to follow the job instructions laid out by the quality procedures and keep accurate documentation of their work.

The first two portions of the documentation system—the overall quality policy and the quality manual—are strategic in nature and remain relatively fixed over the long term. The procedures, job instructions, and data records are more fluid documents and are changed as necessary to maintain an effective system.

Conclusion

Once ISO certification has been obtained, PizzaMan must be prepared to maintain the system. This includes updating the quality procedures as needed, continuing employee training, conducting meaningful quality audits, and passing periodic audits from the ISO certification agency.

PizzaMan is now evaluating the use of handheld cellular phones to phone-in express orders (particularly order corrections) while the delivery person is standing at the customer's door. The quest for higher quality is neverending and those who don't move forward are destined to lose out to competitive forces.

Appendix A
Using the Companion Software

Using the SPC EXpert Software

The SPC EXpert software that is an optional companion to this book is a powerful statistical tool. We are barely tapping the potential of this software as we use it to assist us in analyzing data.*

Installing the SPC System

If the SPC system is already installed on a hard drive computer, skip this portion. To run this software, you will need:

An IBM-PC or compatible

A hard drive with 2 MBytes available

MS-DOS 3.21 or higher

375K RAM

VGA (or EGA) monitor

With the 3-1/2" SPC disk in drive A: Type the following, pressing Enter at the end of each line:

```
C:
MD\SPC
CD\SPC
COPY A:*.*
INSTALL    [After installation is complete, you can execute the program.]
SPCEX      [Executes the program.]
```

*SPC Expert © Copyright 1993 by Quality Software Designs is a ShareWare product and if used beyond the educational scope of this book (for commercial applications) you are required to pay a licensing fee. Upon paying this relatively small fee directly to Quality Software Designs, you will receive a printed manual explaining the full potential of this powerful tool. Academic and government users must register, but there is no licensing fee.

Executing the SPC EXpert Program

If the program is already installed on a hard drive (normally drive C:), the typical way of executing this program is to type the following after the DOS prompt C:>. Press Enter at the end of each line typed.

CD\SPC   ["Gets" you to the subdirectory.]
SPCEX   [Executes the SPC EXpert program.]

Several messages will appear. After reading them, press any key until the main menu appears as shown.

```
                        SPC EXpert : MAIN MENU


              CURRENT STATUS                  ┌──────────────────────────┐
              ─ ─ ─ ─ ─ ─ ─ ─ ─ ─ ─          │ A.   Select Data File    │
                                              ├──────────────────────────┤
    Raw Data File :                           │ B.   Select Graphic Type │
                        <Not Selected>        │   ☐ View Graphic         │
    Chart Type :                              │   ☐ Control Chart Analysis│
                        <Not Selected>        │   ☐ View Chart Patterns  │
                                              │   ☐ Expert Consultation  │
                        INVALID!              │ G.   On-Line Documentation│
                        No File & Type        │ H.   Print/Export        │
                                              │ I.   Options             │
                                              │ J.   Editor & File Manager│
    Analysis            N/A                   │ K.   Shell to Dos        │
    # Patterns          N/A                   │ Quit                     │
                                              └──────────────────────────┘

    ☐ Prev (Esc)   ☐ Save To File (F3)   ☐ Exit (F2)   ☐ Help (F1)
```

The first option, "A. Select Data File" appears in inverse and is activated by pressing Enter. After Enter is pressed, an overlay will appear on the screen as shown.

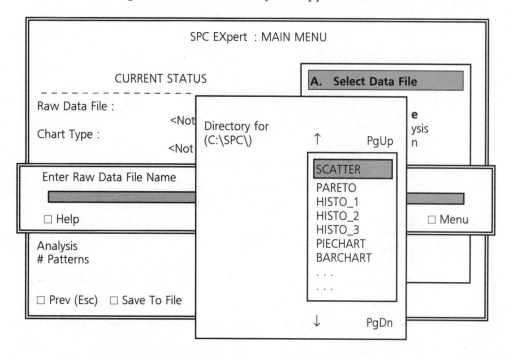

Press Enter again and another overlay will appear on the screen as shown.

Files will not appear in the order shown in this book, due to the addition of various files. Let's locate the PIECHART file. Press the down arrow until the PIECHART file is highlighted as shown.

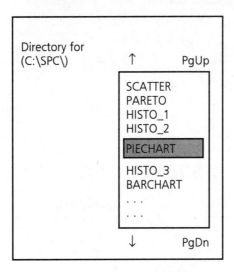

```
Directory for
(C:\SPC\)              ↑           PgUp

                   ┌─────────────────┐
                   │ SCATTER         │
                   │ PARETO          │
                   │ HISTO_1         │
                   │ HISTO_2         │
                   │ ▓PIECHART▓      │
                   │ HISTO_3         │
                   │ BARCHART        │
                   │ . . .           │
                   │ . . .           │
                   └─────────────────┘
                        ↓           PgDn
```

Press Enter again and the PIECHART file is loaded into memory. The Main Menu screen appears as shown with the "Raw Data File" selection indicating PIECHART.

```
                    SPC EXpert  : MAIN MENU

              CURRENT STATUS                 ┌──────────────────────────────┐
         − − − − − − − − − − − − −          │ A.  Select Data File         │
Raw Data File :                              └──────────────────────────────┘
                 C:\SPC\PIECHART               B.  Select Graphic Type
Chart Type :                                      □ View Graphic
                 <Not Selected>                   □ Control Chart Analysis
                                                  □ View Chart Patterns
                        INVALID!                  □ Expert Consultation
                  No        Type               G.  On-Line Documentation
                                               H.  Print/Export
Analysis            N/A                         I.  Options
# Patterns          N/A                         J.  Editor & File Manager
                                                K.  Shell to Dos
                                               Quit

  □ Prev (Esc)   □ Save To File (F3)   □ Exit (F2)   □ Help (F1)
```

With the Main Menu screen shown, we now have to select the graphic type matching the PIECHART raw data file. Press the down arrow to highlight "B. Select Graphic Type." Then press Enter and the overlay will appear as shown.

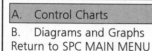

A.   Control Charts
B.   Diagrams and Graphs
Return to SPC MAIN MENU

Control charts will be discussed later. For now, press the down arrow and highlight "B. Diagrams and Graphs." Then press Enter and the overlay will appear as shown.

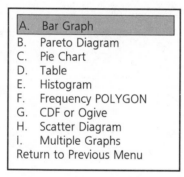

A.   Bar Graph
B.   Pareto Diagram
C.   Pie Chart
D.   Table
E.   Histogram
F.   Frequency POLYGON
G.   CDF or Ogive
H.   Scatter Diagram
I.   Multiple Graphs
Return to Previous Menu

Now let's load the chart type that matches the raw data file. Press the down arrow and highlight "C. Pie Chart." Press Enter and the overlay shown will appear.

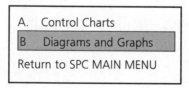

A.   Control Charts
B   Diagrams and Graphs
Return to SPC MAIN MENU

Press the down arrow to highlight "Return to SPC MAIN MENU" and press Enter. The Main Menu screen will appear as shown. Several things are now different on this screen. The Raw Data File is shown as "C:\SPC\PIECHART" which matches the chart type "PIE" just selected. This is noted as a "Valid" condition.

```
                    SPC EXpert : MAIN MENU


            CURRENT STATUS              A.   Select Data File
        - - - - - - - - - - - - -       B.   Select Graphic Type
Raw Data File :                         C..  View Graphic
                 C:\SPC\PIECHART             □ View Graphic
Chart Type :                                 □ Control Chart Analysis
                           PIE               □ View Chart Patterns
Valid Chart ? :                              □ Expert Consultation
                         Valid          G.   On-Line Documentation
                                        H.   Print/Export
                                        I.   Options
Analysis              N/A               J.   Editor & File Manager
# Patterns            N/A               K.   Shell to Dos
                                        Quit


 □ Prev (Esc)   □ Save To File (F3)   □ Exit (F2)   □ Help (F1)
```

Also notice that a new option appeared, "C. View Graphic." Press the down arrow to highlight this option, then press Enter. A pie chart will appear as shown.

This powerful SPC program is easy-to-use once you become familiar with it.

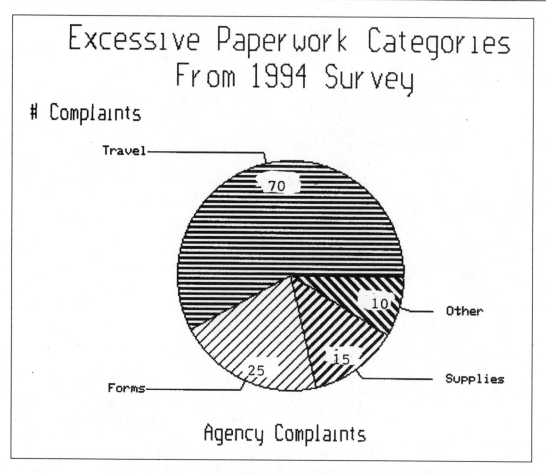

Press any key and the Main Menu screen will appear again. Now, let's take a look at the PIECHART raw data file. Press the down arrow to highlight option "J. Editor & File Manager." Then press Enter and the overlay shown will appear.

A.	Edit Current Data File
B.	Create/Edit A File
C.	View A File
D.	Copy A File
E.	Rename A File
F.	Delete A File
Return to MAIN MENU	

Note that option "A. Edit Current Data File" is highlighted. As this is the option we wish, press Enter and the contents of the PIECHART file that produced the pie chart are shown. This file can be edited to produce your own PIECHART graphs.

```
Excessive Paperwork Categories
From 1994 Survey
Agency Complaints
# Complaints
70  Travel
25  Forms
15  Supplies
10  Other
```

After viewing or editing the file, press the F2 function key to save and exit. The overlay screen will appear as previously shown.

```
A.   Edit Current Data File
B.   Create/Edit A File
C.   View A File
D.   Copy A File
E.   Rename A File
F.   Delete A File
Return to MAIN MENU
```

Press Esc (the Escape key) to return to the Main Menu as it is easier than selecting the option "Return to MAIN MENU." The now familiar Main Menu screen will appear.

Do you remember that our pie chart was frequencies, not percentages? Let's take a look at some of the many options available in this program. With the Main Menu screen shown, press the arrow key to highlight option "I. Options." Then press Enter, and the overlay screen will appear as shown.

```
A.   Control Charts
B.   Distribution Graphs
C.   PIE/BAR/PARETO/TABLE
D.   Scatter Diagrams
E.   Process Specifications
F.   Data File Formats
G.   Fonts & Font Sizes
H.   Titles/ Stats/ etc.
I.   Saving/Recalling Options
J.   Display Current Options
Return to MAIN MENU
```

Press the down arrow to highlight option "C. PIE/BAR/PARETO/TABLE." Then press Enter and the overlay shown will appear.

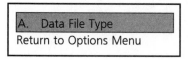

The option highlighted "A. Data Label Type" is what we want, so press Enter and the overlay shown will appear.

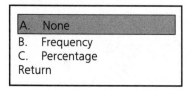

Press the down arrow to select "C. Percentage" and press Enter. Esc back to the Main Menu. Then select option "C. View Graphic" to see the pie chart in a percentage format.

Now It's Your Turn

Follow the general instructions previously given, select and display a bar graph contained in the BARCHART data file. Please do this before reading further.

Selecting and Displaying a Bar Graph

By now you should understand how to work your way through the SPC EXpert Software, so the instructions will not be as detailed as before. To display the BARCHART data file, begin with the main menu screen and highlight the option "A. Select Data File." Press Enter once for the overlay and once more for a file listing. Highlight the file "BARCHART" and press Enter.

Then highlight option "B. Select Graphic Type" and press Enter. This time option is: "B. Diagrams and Graphs," which should be highlighted. Then press Enter. Finally option "A. Bar Graph" will be highlighted by default, so just press Enter to activate it. Esc back to the main menu and highlight option "C. View Graphic." Press Enter and the bar chart will appear as shown.

If percentages are shown (because the previous selections are active), select the "I. Option" from the main menu. Then change the "Data Label Type" from percentages back to frequencies.

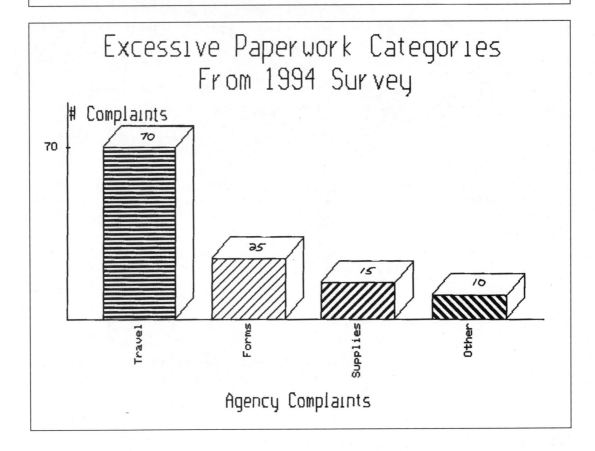

Excessive Paperwork Categories From 1994 Survey

Complaints

70

70

25

15

10

Travel

Forms

Supplies

Other

Agency Complaints

This SPC program can display some data files in different formats. For example, the BARCHART file can be be displayed in pie, bar, Pareto and table format. Try it and select the format that is best for your application.

Now It's Your Turn

Select and display the PARETO data file. The Pareto chart will appear as shown.

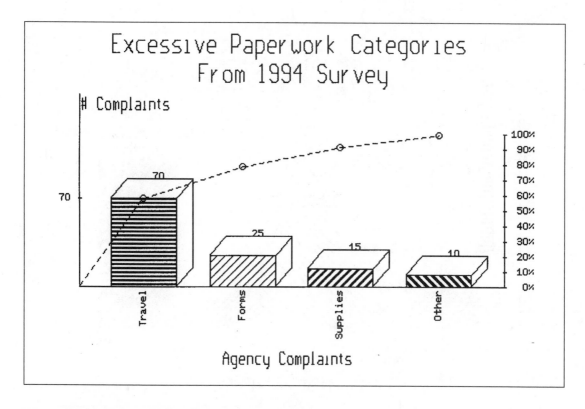

Creating Your Own Files

The PARETO data file which produced the Pareto chart is identical to the BAR-CHART and PIECHART data files and is shown below. Lines 1 through 4 of each data file is from 0 to 70 characters. These lines are required, but may be blank if desired (i.e., simply press Enter when creating the file for a blank line).

Excessive Paperwork Categories	<- Line #1: Title
From 1994 Survey	<- Line #2: Subtitle
Agency Complaints	<- Line #3: X Axis Label
# Complaints	<- Line #4: Y Axis Label
70 Travel	
25 Forms	
15 Supplies	
10 Other	

You can either edit these files as previously explained or create your own data files.

Displaying and Creating Histograms

Select and display the HISTO_1 data file. The Histogram will appear as shown.

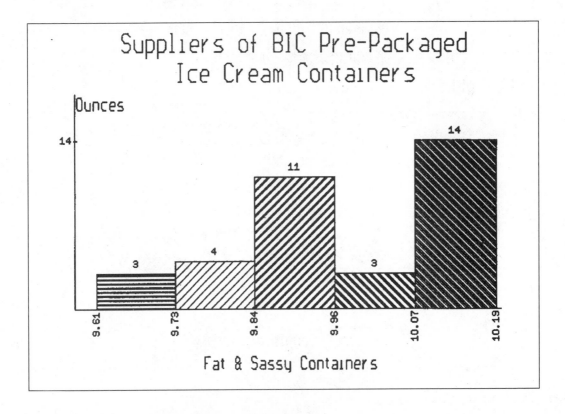

The first eight lines of the HISTOGRM data file are shown. Again, lines 1 through 4 are from 0 to 70 characters in length. Type the data and press Enter at the end of the data line (this program will handle up to 16,000 data lines). Then save the file.

Suppliers of BIC Prepackaged	<- Line #1: Title
Ice Cream Containers	<- Line #2: Subtitle
Fat & Sassy Containers	<- Line #3: X Axis Label
Ounces	<- Line #4; Y Axis Label
9.83	
10.17	
9.86	
10.14	

Technical note: The manual method explained in construction of a histogram is the technically correct, statistical method. Although the number of categories varies due to rounding, the SPC EXpert program is far quicker and produces the same end results without making clerical errors.

Any of the graphics displayed can be printed by selecting option "H. Print/Export" from the main menu. Prior to actually printing the graph, go to option "C. Printer Type" on the overlay and select the appropriate printer. Then print the graph.

Displaying and Creating Scatter Diagrams

Select and display the SCATTER (Scatter Diagram) data file. The scatter diagram will appear as shown.

The first eight lines of the SCATTER data file are shown. Again, lines 1

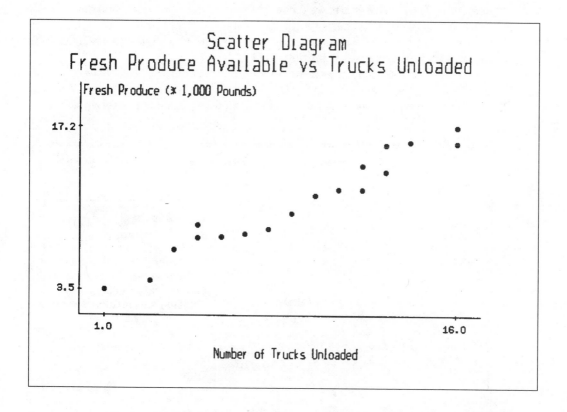

through 4 are from 0 to 70 characters in length. Type the data pairs to be plotted, separated by a space, and press Enter at the end of the data line (this program will handle up to 16,000 data lines). Then save the file.

```
Scatter Diagram                                 <- Line #1: Title
Fresh Produce Available vs Trucks Unloaded      <- Line #2: Subtitle
Number of Trucks Unloaded                       <- Line #3: X Axis Label
Fresh produce (* 1000 pounds)                   <- Line #4: Y Axis Label
   16   17.2
   16   15.9
    1    3.5
    3    4.3
         .
         .
         .
```

Displaying and Creating $\bar{x}$ and R Control Charts

Remember the control charts we created? Frankly, it was a tedious process. XBAR charts ($\bar{x}$) and range (R) charts with UCL (Upper Control Limits) and LCL (Lower Control Limit) values are difficult to calculate and plot by hand. However, the SPC EXpert program will greatly simplify the task.

With the Main Menu screen shown, highlight option "A. Select Data File" and press Enter. Press Enter again, press the down arrow to highlight the XBAR data file. Then press Enter and the Main Menu screen will appear as shown.

```
                    SPC EXpert  : MAIN MENU


              CURRENT STATUS
              - - - - - - - - - - - - - -      ┌─────────────────────────────┐
                                               │ A.  Select Data File        │
Raw Data File :                                │ B.  Select Graphic Type     │
                 C:\SPC\XBARCHART              │    □ View Graphic           │
Chart Type :                                   │    □ Control Chart Analysis │
                 <Not Selected>                │    □ View Chart Patterns    │
                                               │    □ Expert Consultation    │
                 INVALID!                       │ G.  On-Line Documentation  │
                 No Type                        │ H.  Print/Export           │
                                               │ I.  Options                 │
Analysis         N/A                           │ J.  Editor & File Manager   │
# Patterns       N/A                           │ K.  Shell to Dos            │
                                               │ Quit                        │
                                               └─────────────────────────────┘

  □ Prev (Esc)   □ Save To File (F3)   □ Exit (F2)   □ Help (F1)
```

Press the down arrow to highlight "B. Select Graphic Type." Press Enter and the overlay will appear as shown.

```
A.   Control Charts
B.   Diagrams and Graphs
Return to SPC MAIN MENU
```

Press Enter to select option "A. Control Chart" and the overlay will appear as shown.

```
A.   Automatic chart selection
B.   X (Run) Chart
C.   Xbar Chart
D.   R Chart
E.   S Chart
F.   Moving Range chart
G.   Xbar-R control chart
H.   Xbar-S control chart
I.   X Moving Range control chart
J.   pn control chart
K.   p control chart
L.   c control chart
M.   u control chart
Return to Previous Menu
```

Press Enter on the highlighted option "A. Automatic chart selection" and the overlay will appear as shown.

```
What type of process data          A.   Measurement
are you measuring?                 B.   Attribute
```

Press Enter to select the "A. Measurement" option and the overlay will appear as shown.

```
In what range is your              A.   1
logical group (sample)             B.   2 to 10
size?                              C.   Larger Than 10
```

Press the down arrow to highlight the "B. 2 to 10" option (remember the sample size in our first control chart problem was 3). Press Enter and another overlay screen will appear as shown.

Do you want to show process values, variability, or both?

A. Values
B. Variability
C. Both

Press the down arrow, highlight option "C. Both," press Enter and Esc back to the Main Menu. With the Main Menu screen shown, highlight option "C. View Graphic," and press Enter to produce the *XBAR* and *R* (Range) chart shown.

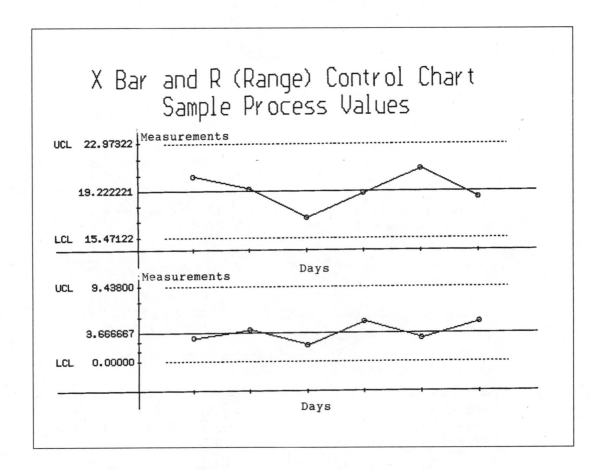

You will get "the hang" of this software quickly, and soon be able to move around the various overlays. The contents of the XBAR data file and the format of the file is:

X Bar and R (Range) Control Chart	<- Line #1: Title
Sample Process Values	<- Line #2: Subtitle
Days	<- Line #3: X Axis
Measurements	<- Line #4: Y Axis
3	<- Sample Size
22 19 20	
21 20 17	
16 17 18	<- Process measurements;
20 16 21	See control chart
23 20 20	problem in book.
19 16 21	

Displaying and Creating *p* Charts

As you remember from reading about *p* charts in the book, a *p* chart is used for attribute inspection, such as percent defective. In the problem previously discussed, we sampled 100 medical forms for 20 days and recorded the errors found in each sample. This data is contained in the *p* chart data file.

With the Main Menu screen shown, follow the procedure previously explained to select the P_CHART data file. Then with the Main Menu screen shown, select option "B. Select Graphic Type." Press Enter when the overlay appears to select "A. Control Charts" and the overlay shown will appear.

```
A.    Automatic chart selection
B.    X (Run) Chart
C.    Xbar Chart
D.    R Chart
E.    S Chart
F.    Moving Range chart
G.    Xbar-R control chart
H.    Xbar-S control chart
I.    X Moving Range control chart
J.    pn control chart
K.    p control chart
L.    c control chart
M.    u control chart
      Return to Previous Menu
```

Press the down arrow to highlight option "K. p control chart" and press Enter. Then Esc back to the Main Menu, and select option "C. View Graphic." The *p* chart will appear as shown. The accuracy of this *p* chart is superior to the manual computations undertaken in the book.

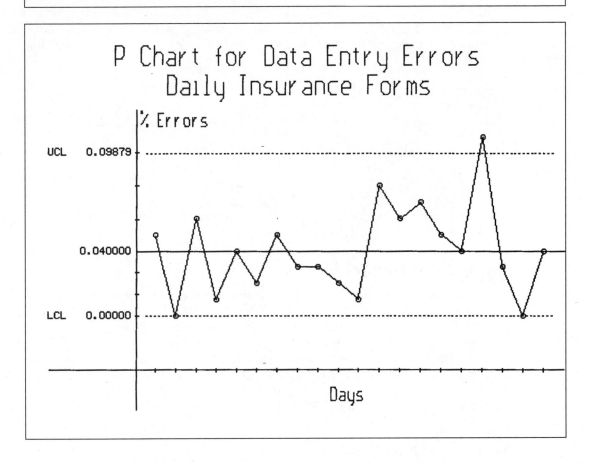

The contents of the first eight lines of the *p* chart data file is:

P Chart for Data Entry Errors	<- Line #1: Title
Daily Insurance Forms	<- Line #2: Subtitle
Days	<- Line #3: X Axis
% Errors	<- Line #4: Y Axis
100 5	
100 0	
100 6	<- Process measurements;
.	Sample size, Errors
.	See control chart
.	problem in book.

Answers to Selected Problems

CQI Story

Some of the many possible answers are shown.

1. *"Our commmercial suppliers have returned about 15 percent. . . . "*

   Fifteen percent of our order forms are being returned due to errors.

2. *"We need to improve sales by 20 percent."*

   Current sales are 20 percent below the target level.

3. *"We are not meeting our second-day delivery...."*

   Second-day delivery promises are not being met for our in-town customers.

4. *"It takes us five days longer to produce...."*

   Other departments are being adversely affected by our quarterly inventories taking five days longer than a year ago.

5. *"We need to reduce customer returns by 10 percent."*

   Customer returns are 10 percent above company goals.

6. *Big City Electronics CQI Story theme:*

   We are misrepresenting sale items in local newspaper ads.

7. *Big City Electronics problem statement:*

   For the fourth time this year, sale prices were quoted below actual sales price in the local newspaper.

8. *How the analysis might proceed:*

   A flow chart of the transfer of information between the advertising and sales department is needed.

Basic QI Tools

1. *A trend chart could be used to show the reduction after a speed limit was reduced.*

2. *A pie chart would be useful in displaying the major budget categories.*

3. *A Pareto chart would be useful in identifying major complaints. In addition, a bar chart could be used.*

4. *A trend chart could be used to show decreased customer returns.*

5. *A flow chart is recommended to show steps in restocking an item.*

Check Sheet

1. *Data collection form for furniture ordering/delivery time:*

Number of days from ordering date

1	2	3	4	5	6	7	8	9	10	11	12	13	14	15	16	17	18	19	20	21	22	23
													X									
												X	X									
												X	X	X								
											X	X	X	X								
											X	X	X	X								
											X	X	X	X	X							
									X	X	X	X	X	X	X	X						
						X	X	X	X	X	X	X	X	X	X	X	X	X				

Enter an X in the lowest unoccupied box under the number of working days from the customer's order date, until the delivery was made.

Driver: _____

2. *Data collection form for office temperature (after recording the temperature by a dot on the form, the dots were connected by a line.)*

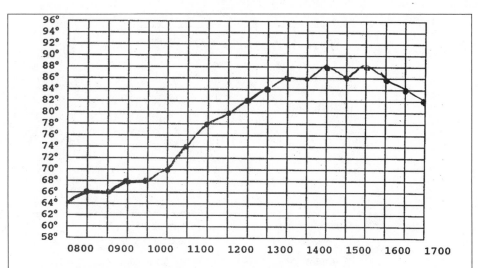

- **Read the temperature of the office to nearest degree (°F) from thermostat #21.**
- **Plot the temperature on the grid using a dot (.).**
- **Connect the dots with a line.**
- **Use the note section to record anything unusual.**
- **Readings must be taken on the half-hour, ±3 minutes.**
- **Begin at 0800 (8:00am) take next reading at 0830, again at 0900, etc.**

Fact versus Inference: Thompson Engineering

All the statements are inferences for the reasons stated.

1. Pat Johnson works for the Engineering Department. Perhaps Johnson works for Manufacturing, Quality, Inside Transportation, or any other department.
2. Mr. Pat Johnson is employed by Thompson Engineering. Who said Pat is a man?
3. Pat Johnson has left the Thompson Engineering building. Perhaps Johnson is in another department in the building.
4. Engineering drawings for Ajax Builders have again been changed. This could simply be an "early" revision, and no changes have been made.
5. No one in the Engineering Department knew about the 11:00 A.M. meeting. Only the secretary and who he/she checked with didn't know about the meeting.
6. Pat Johnson has a mobile phone. Perhaps the notification was over a loud speaker and Johnson was still inside the building.
7. Ajax Building's construction is at a site remote from Thompson Engineering. Perhaps Thompson Engineering facilities are at the building site.

Pareto Diagram

1. *Claim payment delays.*

Claim payment delay categories	Number of occurrences
Automobile	70
Homeowner	25
Apartment	15
Other	10
Totals	120

Claim payment delay categories	Number of occurrences	%	Cumulative %
Automobile	70	58.3	58.3
Homeowner	25	20.8	79.1
Apartment	15	12.5	91.6
Other	10	8.3	100.0[1]
Totals	120	100.0	

[1]Rounded.

2.

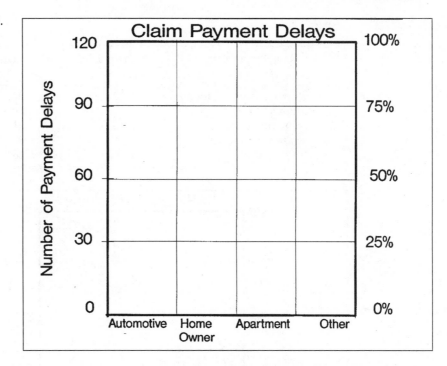

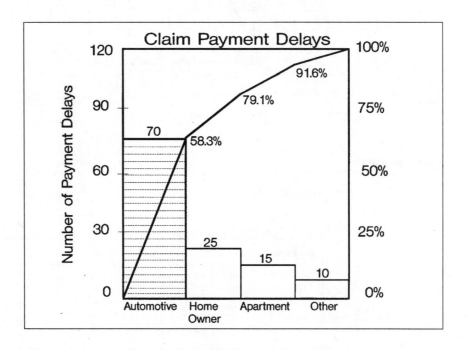

3. *Shipping.*

Shipping problem categories	Number of occurrences	Cumulative occurrences	Cumulative %
Incorrect documentation	22	22	32.4
Address label wrong	16	38	55.9
Wrong container	13	51	75.0
Incorrect packing	11	62	91.2
Other	6	68	100.0

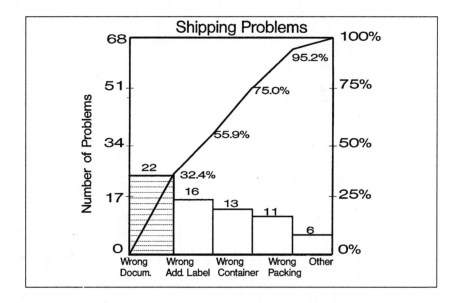

Histograms

1. *Travel reimbursements.*

Days to Process Travel Reimbursements				
30	40	102	45	44
109	80	95	84	108
107	76	64	104	78
44	60	47	35	59
94	70	41	32	60

Range: $\qquad$ $R = X_{Max} - X_{Min} = 109 - 30 = 79$

Number of classes: $\qquad$ $k = \sqrt{n} = \sqrt{25} = 5$

Class width: $\qquad$ $h = R/k = 79/5 = 15.8$

Unit of measurement: $\quad$ $m = 1.00$

Final class width: $\qquad$ $h = 16.00$

Lower boundary: $\qquad$ $(L_1) = X_{Min} - (m/2) = 30 - (1/2) = 29.5$

$L_2 = L_1 + h = 29.5 + 16 = 45.5$

$L_3 = 45.5 + 16 = 61.5$

$L_4 = 61.5 + 16 = 77.5$

$L_5 = 77.5 + 16 = 93.5$

$L_6 = 93.5 + 16 = 109.5$

Frequency Table
Travel Reimbursements

Class intervals	Tally	Frequency
29.5–45.5	||||| |||	8
45.5–61.5	|||||	4
61.5–77.5	|||	3
77.5–93.5	|||	3
93.5–109.5	||||| ||	7
Total		25

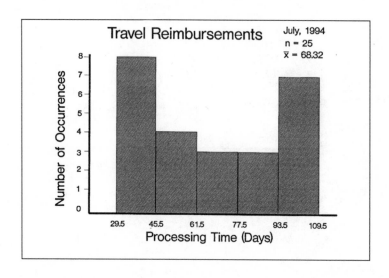

Interpreting Distributions

1. *Better Ice Cream.*

BIC Ice Cream Company: Vendor Ounces per Container

Class intervals	Tally: Fat & Sassy	Frequency
9.605–9.705	||	2
9.705–9.805	||	2
9.805–9.905	||||| ||||| |	11
9.905–10.005	|||	3
10.005–10.105	|||||	5
10.105–10.205	||||| ||||| ||	12
Total		35

Class intervals	Tally: Chubby & Chunky	Frequency
9.605–9.705		
9.705–9.805		
9.805–9.905		
9.905–10.005	|||	3
10.005–10.105	||||| ||||| ||||	
10.105–10.205	||||| ||||| |||||	14
	|||	18
Total		35

Class intervals	Tally: Butter Cup Co.	Frequency
9.605–9.705		
9.705–9.805		
9.805–9.905	||||| ||||| ||||	14
9.905–10.005	||||| ||||| |||||	19
	||||	
10.005–10.105	||	2
10.105–10.205		
Total		35

Suppliers of BIC Prepackaged Ice Cream Containers

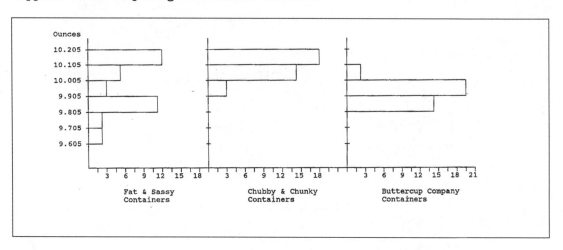

Suppliers of BIC Prepackaged Ice Cream Containers Specification Limits?

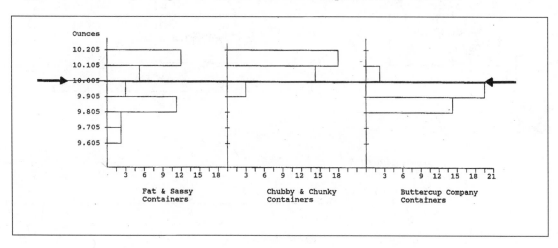

2. *Histogram gap. This is a "classic" problem. What is happening is that the inspectors are "ignoring" products that are close to specifications. That is, if the product is between −.01 and −.02 (or between +.01 and +.02), the inspectors are "passing" the product. Which is only natural as we want products (as well as people) to pass and be successful.*

Fishbone Diagram

1.

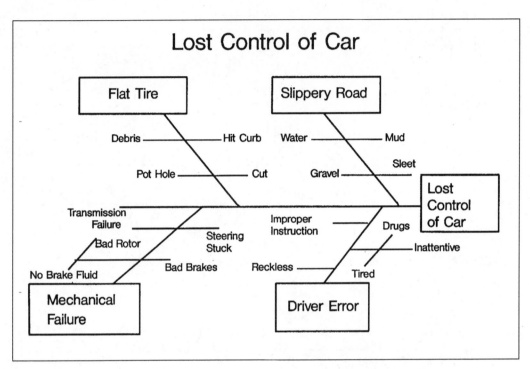

Control Charts

1. *Instructor's grades.*

Control Chart: Instructor's Grades

Month	Grades	R	$\Sigma\Xi$	$\bar{x}$
November	4, 4, 4, 4, 4	0	20/5 =	4.0
December	3, 4, 3, 4, 4	1	18/5 =	3.6
January	3, 0, 4, 4, 4	4	15/5 =	3.0
February	4, 4, 4, 4, 4	0	20/5 =	4.0
March	4, 4, 4, 4, 4	0	20/5 =	4.0
April	3, 4, 3, 4, 3	1	17/5 =	3.4
Total		6/6		22/6
		1		3.67

$$\text{LCL}_{\overline{R}} = D_3 * \overline{R}; 0 * (1) = 0$$

$$\text{UCL}_{\overline{R}} = D_4 * \overline{R}; 2.114 * (1) = 2.11$$

$$\text{LCL}_x = \overline{\overline{X}} + A_2 * \overline{R} = 3.67 - .577 * (1) = 3.09$$

$$\text{UCL}_x = \overline{\overline{X}} - A_2 * \overline{R} = 3.67 + 5.77 * (1) = 4.25$$

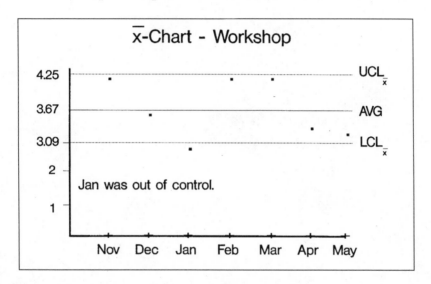

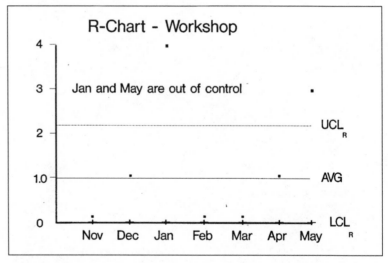

January is out of control on both $\overline{x}$ and R chart. The calculated $\overline{x}$ for May is 3.2 which is in control. The calculated R value for May is 3. May is out of control because the range is outside the upper control limit.

Control Chart: Instructor's Grades

Day	Scores	R	Σx	$\bar{x}$
Sunday	18,19,20,20	2	77/4 =	19.25
Monday	21,20,20,20	1	81/4 =	20.25
Tuesday	19,19,19,19	0	76/4 =	19.00
Wednesday	23,17,20,20	6	80/4 =	20.00
Thursday	20,20,20,21	1	81/4 =	20.25
Friday	19,20,21,20	2	80/4 =	20.00
Total		12/6		118.75/6=
		2		19.79

$$LCL_R = D_3 * R;\ 0 * (2) = 0$$
$$UCL_R = D_4 * R;\ 2.28 * (2) = 4.56$$

$$LCL_x = \bar{x} + A_2 * R = 19.79 - .729 * (2) = 18.33$$
$$UCL_x = \bar{x} - A_2 * R = 19.79 + 7.29 * (2) = 21.20$$

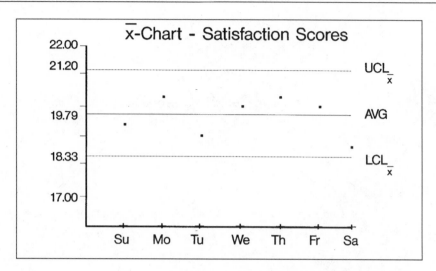

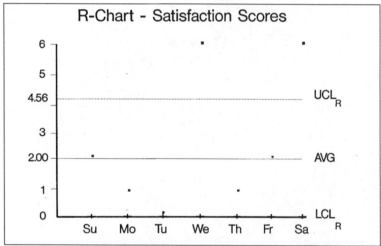

The x̄ for Saturday is 18.5. Thus all days are within x̄ chart UCL and LCL. However R for Saturday is 6 which is above the UCL. Both Wednesday (see chart) and Saturday are out of control.

Process Capabilities

1. *Fishing for fun.*

$$C_p = \frac{USL - LSL}{6\sigma} = \frac{12.1 - 11.9}{6(.11)} = \frac{.2}{.66} = .30$$

The process is not capable of meeting specification.

2. *Burpie.*

$$C_p = \frac{USL - LSL}{6\sigma} = \frac{16.3 - 15.7}{6(.1)} = \frac{.6}{.6} = 1.0$$

The process appears capable of meeting specifications, but .27 percent rejects will be produced. Next, check to determine if the lower specification limits can be met.

$$C_{pl} = \frac{\overline{X} - LSL}{3\sigma} = \frac{15.9 - 15.7}{3(.1)} = \frac{.2}{.3} = .67$$

Lower specification limits will not be met. Next, although the process is not under statistical control, double check that the upper specification limits can be met.

$$C_{pu} = \frac{USL - \overline{X}}{3\sigma} = \frac{16.3 \quad 15.9}{3(.1)} = \frac{.4}{.3} = 1.33$$

Upper specification limits are fine.

3. *Delphi Foods. The government would be concerned that there might not be enough product (i.e., their concern is on the Lower Specification Limit). LSL for peas would be 2.0 − .1 or, 1.9 oz.*

$$C_{pl} = \frac{\overline{x} - LSL}{3\sigma}$$

Peas $$= \frac{2.1 - 1.9}{3(.1)} = \frac{.2}{.3} = .67$$

Cannot meet lower specifications.

Carrots $$= \frac{3.1 - 2.8}{3(.1)} = \frac{.3}{.3} = 1.0$$

Can meet lower specifications, but defects will be produced.

Potatoes $$= \frac{3.0 - 2.9}{3(.02)} = \frac{.1}{.06} = 1.67$$

Hamburger $$= \frac{6.0 - 5.6}{3(.1)} = \frac{.4}{.3} = 1.33$$

Both potatoes and hamburger can meet lower specification limits without difficulty.

Eat Well will encounter problems on the peas and should not use them. Some problems may be encountered meeting specification limits with carrots, but the process should be acceptable. No problems are anticipated with potatoes and hamburger portions.

p Chart

1. *Pretty Lady.*

Pretty Lady: Hosiery		
S number	Defects	%
1	1	.01
2	0	.00
3	1	.01
4	1	.01
5	1	.01
6	5	.04
7	0	.00
8	1	.01
9	1	.01
Defects = 11		

$$\bar{p} = \frac{\text{Total number of errors}}{\text{Total number of records examined}} = \frac{11}{120 * 9}$$

$$= \frac{11}{1080} = .0102$$

$$\sigma_p = \sqrt{\frac{p(1-p)}{n}}$$

$$\sigma_p = \sqrt{\frac{(.0102)(1-.012)}{120}} = \sqrt{\frac{(.0102)(.9898)}{120}}$$

$$\sigma_p = \sqrt{\frac{(.010096)}{120}} = .0092$$

$$UCL_p = \bar{p} + 3\sigma = .0102 + 3(.0092) = .0102 + .0276 = .0378$$

$$LCL_p = \bar{p} - 3\sigma = .0102 - 3(.0092) = .0102 \quad .0276 = 0.00$$

Day 6 was out of control.

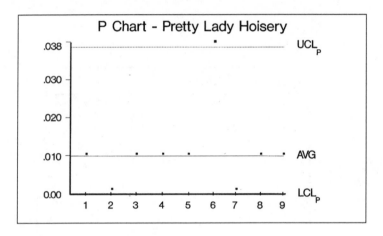

2. *Packaging Errors.*

Packaging Errors

S number	Errors	%	S number	Errors	%
1	0	.00	16	0	.00
2	1	.01	17	0	.00
3	1	.01	18	1	.01
4	0	.00	19	0	.00
5	1	.01	20	1	.01
6	1	.01	21	0	.00
7	0	.00	22	0	.00
8	1	.01	23	0	.00
9	1	.01	24	0	.00
10	0	.00	25	4	.03
11	1	.01	26	1	.01
12	3	.02	27	0	.00
13	0	.00	28	0	.00
14	0	.00	29	0	.00
15	0	.00	30	1	.01

Total Defects 18

[a] Day 31: 2 packaging errors
[b] Day 40: 4 packaging errors

$$\bar{p} = \frac{\text{Total number of errors}}{\text{Total number of records examined}} = \frac{18}{144 * 30}$$

$$= \frac{18}{4320} = .0042$$

$$\sigma_p = \sqrt{\frac{p\,(1-p)}{n}}$$

$$\sigma_p = \sqrt{\frac{(.0042)(1-.0042)}{144}} = \sqrt{\frac{(.0042)(.9958)}{144}}$$

$$\sigma_p = \sqrt{\frac{.00418}{144}} = .0054$$

$\text{UCL}_p = \bar{p} + 3\sigma = .0042 + 3(.0054) = .0042 + .0162 = .0204$

$\text{LCL}_p = \bar{p} - 3\sigma = .0042 - 3(.0054) = .0042 - .0162 = 0.00$

Day 25 (at .030) was out of control. Day 31 with 2 package errors out of 1 gross sample (144) had an error rate of .014. This day was in control. Day 40 with 4 package errors out of 1 gross sample (144) had an error rate of .0278, which is out of control.

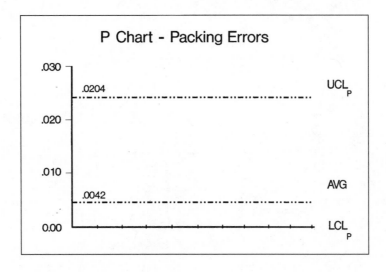

Horizontal Bar Chart

> **1.** *RoadMaster Carburetor.*

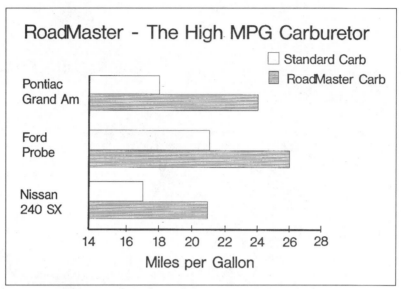

> **2.** *Cigarettes. The base (filter) is so large that it hides meaningful data movements. Besides, a decline from 1012 to 1010 is not significant. Thus no conclusions should be drawn from the change.*

Frequency Chart

> **1.** *Adjustor tickets.*

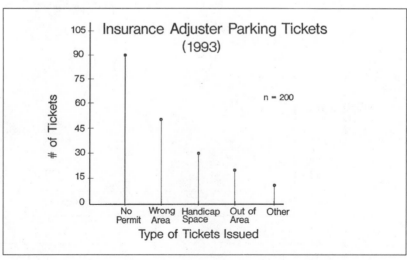

Stratification

1. *Builder's theme. Defects have increased 20 percent in the past year. Builder's problem statement: Defects are delaying final house payment. Builder's analysis: Stratify the type of defects to determine their root cause.*

2. *Banker's theme. There are numerous errors in banking deposits. Banker's problem statement: Sixty percent of all deposit errors were at the window teller using generic forms.*
   Bank Deposits:

Stratification of Bank Deposits

General breakdown	Number of of errors	Window— generic	Window— printed
Window	14	12	2
Night	2	—	2[a]
Mail	4[b]	4[b]	—
Totals:	20	16	4

Note:
[a]Night, preprinted forms
[b]Mail, generic forms

Bar graph of bank deposit errors.

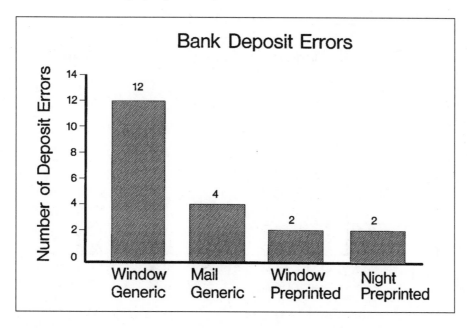

3. *Coffee machines. thirty-three percent of all defects are from factory C, operator 2, supplier Y.*

Stratification of Defective Coffee Machines

Factory totals		Operator[a] 1	Operator 2	Supplier		
				X	Y	Z
A	5	4	1	0	1	4
B	4	2	2	3	0	1
C	6	1	4	1[b]	5	0
Totals	15					

Notes:
[a]Each factory has two operators, for a total of six operators.
[b]Factory C, operator 2 created error.

For an innovative solution to this problem, notice the factories that had no problems with suppliers. That is, factory A experienced no problems with supplier X. Factory B had no problem with supplier Y, and factory C had no problem with supplier Z.

Carefully study the bar chart shown. Perhaps each factory should simply buy from the supplier that created no problems.

Defective coffee machines bar graph.

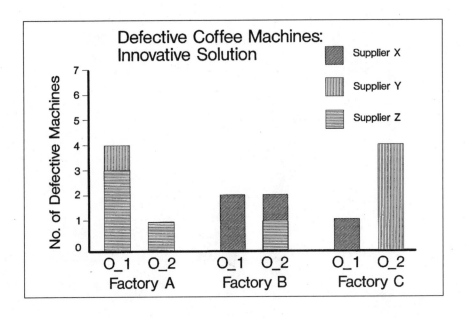

4. *Friendly hotel.*

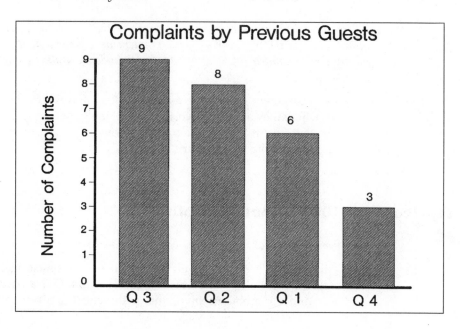

Radar Chart

1. *Clothing store.*

Vision and Mission Statements

1. *AT&T. The vision must be bold, such as: To be the dominant supplier of communications in the world. The mission statement is somewhat more complex, mostly due to limited information. This will undoubtedly vary depending on your opinion.*

   Our customers are anyone using data for information, no matter where they are in the world. We will make whatever investments to assure we are the premier provider of information in all forms in the next century.

The Problem with 100 Percent Inspection

1. *How many times does the letter "a" occur? 19 times.*

   All the king's men, and all the awful people assisting king Author, couldn't put him back together again. Our answer to any and all problems involving arithmetical analysis: about face!

Quality Functional Deployment

Reasons for Use		Time saving
		Wrinkle free clothes
		Quick touch up
		Smooth appearance
		Force of habit
Problems	User	Drugery
		Burned fabric
		Difficult to use
		Backward image
	Instrument	Storing hot iron
		Correct temperature
		Out of water
		Dirty plate
		Moisture control

1. First, concentrate on developing the left-hand side of the QFD diagram. The consumer probably views household irons as a "necessary evil," and there are problems associated with using an iron, but there are reasons for using an iron. Study this diagram, and complete the top portion containing the product features. Check your approach against the complete QFD diagram in step 2.

2. *Household iron.*

			Teflon coated	Safety features	Cord storage	Self-cleaning	See-thru reservoir	Spray features	Instant on/off	Light weight	Steam knob
Reasons for Use		Time saving									
		Wrinkle free clothes									
		Quick touch up									
		Smooth appearance									
		Force of habit									
Problems	User	Drugery									
		Burned fabric									
		Difficult to use									
		Backward image									
	Instrument	Storing hot iron									
		Correct temperature									
		Out of water									
		Dirty plate									
		Moisture control									

Gap Analysis

1. *Sample questionnaire for convention room "buyers."*

This questionnaire asks your opinion about services you expect at hotels hosting conventions. Please choose the one number that best matches how you feel about the statement. The further away from the middle (4), the stronger is your feeling about the statement.

For example, if you felt that hotels should have a concierge, but that it isn't absolutely vital, you might cross through the number "6" as shown.

Convention hotels should have a concierge.	Strongly Disagree 1	2	3	4	5	6	Strongly Agree 7	Unknown 0

In My Opinion:	Strongly Disagree						Strongly Agree	Unknown
1. Hotels should provide airport transportation.	1	2	3	4	5	6	7	0
2. Hotels should have express. check-in.	1	2	3	4	5	6	7	0
3. Hotels should offer nonsmoking floors.	1	2	3	4	5	6	7	0
4. Hotels should have health facilities	1	2	3	4	5	6	7	0
5. Hotel rooms should be clean.	1	2	3	4	5	6	7	0
6. Hotel rooms should be newly decorated.	1	2	3	4	5	6	7	0
7. Hotels should provide excellent food.	1	2	3	4	5	6	7	0
8. Hotels should be able to provide room listings of people attending convention.	1	2	3	4	5	6	7	0
9. There should be a special registration area for conventions.	1	2	3	4	5	6	7	0
10. Meeting rooms should have no columns.	1	2	3	4	5	6	7	0
11. Meeting rooms should have solid walls.	1	2	3	4	5	6	7	0
12. Meeting rooms should have built-in speakers.	1	2	3	4	5	6	7	0

2. *Sample questionnaire for people who were at a Friendly Hotel convention.*

This questionnaire asks your opinion about services you received while at a convention at Friendly Hotel. Please choose the one number that best matches how you feel about the statement. The further away from the middle (4), the stronger is your feeling about the statement.

For example, if you felt that Friendly Hotel's parking facilities were adequate, but that parking could have been better, you might cross through the number "6" as shown.

Friendly Hotel had adequate parking.	Strongly Disagree 1	2	3	4	5	~~6~~	Strongly Agree 7	Unknown 0
In My Opinion:	Strongly Disagree						Strongly Agree	Unknown
1. Friendly Hotel provided airport transportation.	1	2	3	4	5	6	7	0
2. Friendly provided express check-in.	1	2	3	4	5	6	7	0
3. Friendly provided nonsmoking floors.	1	2	3	4	5	6	7	0
4. Friendly provided health facilities	1	2	3	4	5	6	7	0
5. The rooms at Friendly were clean.	1	2	3	4	5	6	7	0
6. The rooms at Friendly were newly decorated.	1	2	3	4	5	6	7	0
7. Friendly Hotel's food was excellent.	1	2	3	4	5	6	7	0
8. Friendly provided room listings of people attending our convention.	1	2	3	4	5	6	7	0
9. There was a special registration area for our conventions.	1	2	3	4	5	6	7	0
10. Our meeting rooms had no columns.	1	2	3	4	5	6	7	0
11. Our meeting rooms had solid walls.	1	2	3	4	5	6	7	0
12. Meeting rooms had built-in speakers.	1	2	3	4	5	6	7	0

Note: An optional "0" response could be provided for "Unknown."

3. *The gap analysis questionnaires would be administered to both groups, and the results tabulated in the format shown.*

Friendly Hotel: Room "Buyers"—Users Gap Analysis Summary			
Question	Buyers' scores	Users' scores	Difference in scores
1. Airport transportation			
2. Express check-in			
3. No smoking floors			
4. Health facilities			
5. Clean rooms			
6. Newly decorated rooms			
7. Excellent food			
8. Convention listing			
9. Registration area			
10. Columns			
11. Solid walls			
12. Speakers			

Appendix **C**
Quality Improvement Forms

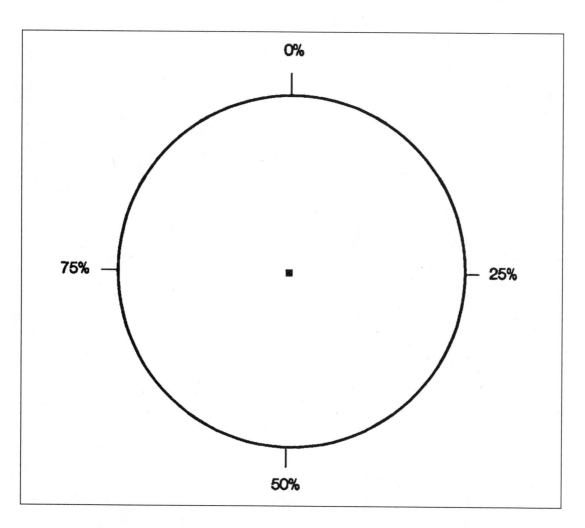

Quality Improvement Forms

Pareto Template: Five Categories

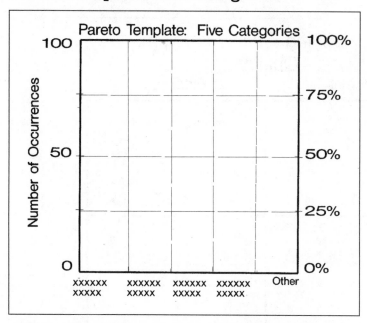

Pareto Template: Seven Categories

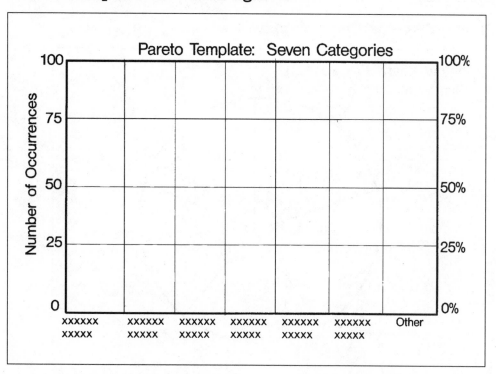

Classifying Quality Problems

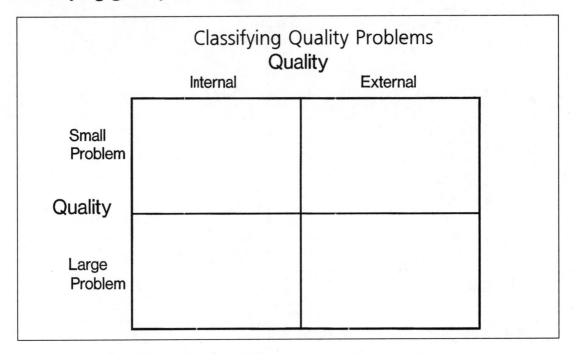

Radar Chart—Five-Position Template

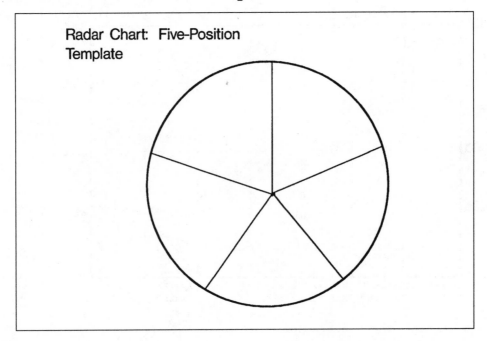

Radar Chart—Six-Position Template

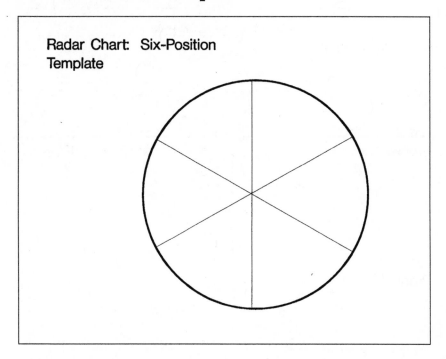

Radar Chart: Six-Position
Template

Personal Quality Checklist: Pocket Form

Personal Quality Checklist	
Week of	
Category	Total

Personal Quality Checklist	
Week of	
Category	Total

Force Field Analysis

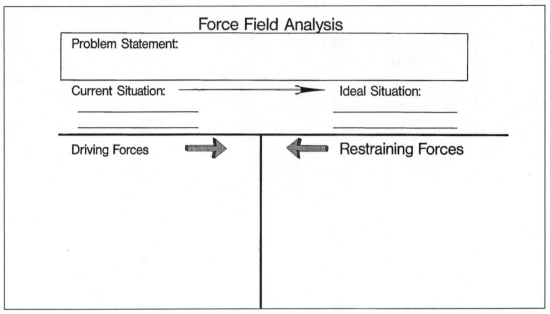

Customer Needs Map

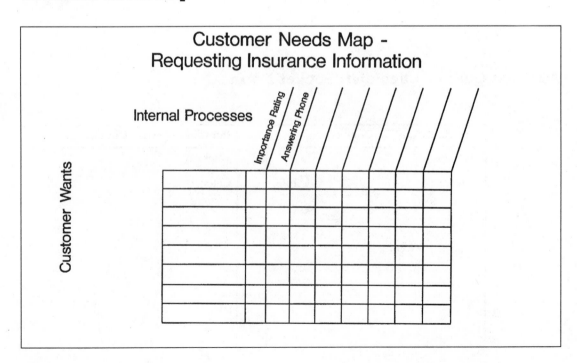

Average

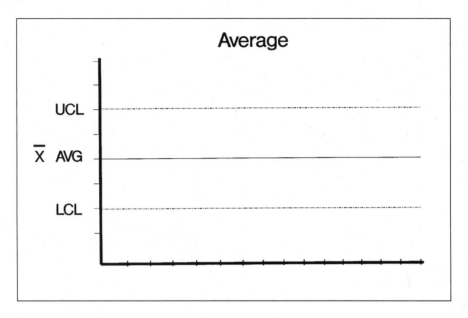

Range

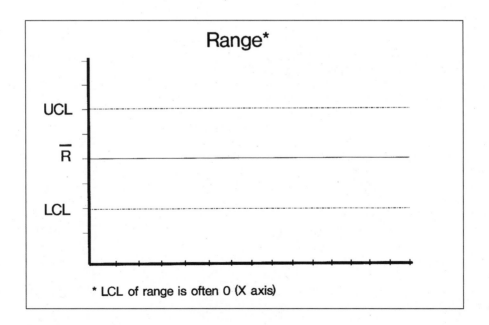

Index

Index

About the Author

Peter Mears is a professor of management at the College of Business Administration, University of Louisville. Trained as an industrial engineer, he has extensive experience in the private sector with such companies as Goodyear and Martin Marietta. A 1993 Malcolm Baldrige Award examiner, he is currently involved with installing a quality management program at the University of Louisville, where he has also created courses and curricula for teaching quality on both the undergraduate and graduate levels.

The *SPC EXpert* Order Form

Use this form to order your copy of *SPC EXpert*. This valuable disk, explained in Appendix A, helps you get the most out of the tools and techniques covered in this book. It's easy to install and use, will save you time, and will improve the appearance of your outputs.

Please send me _____ copies of *SPC EXpert* (ISBN 0-07-852726-0) for $19.95 each, plus $4.50 each for local tax, postage, and handling.

Name _____

Firm/Organization _____

Daytime Phone _____ (for verifying orders _____

Address _____

City _____ State _____ ZIP _____

You may also call 1-800-722-4726 24 hours a day to order, or fax this order form to 1-614-755-5645.

(Cut this form out, fold on dotted lines, tape, and mail. The postage is paid.)

Method of payment

❏   Check enclosed (Payable to McGraw-Hill, please)

❏   Visa

❏   American Express

❏   Mastercard

Account No. _____

Expiration date _____

▼ Tape Here

▼ Fold on Line

No Postage
Necessary
If Mailed
in the
United States

BUSINESS REPLY MAIL
FIRST CLASS MAIL PERMIT NO. 60 BLACKLICK, OH

POSTAGE WILL BE PAID BY ADDRESSEE

MCGRAW-HILL PUBLISHING
PO BOX 545
BLACKLICK OH 43004-9907

▼ Fold on Line